Tax Guide 402

TAX-DEFERRED EXCHANGES

by

Holmes F. Crouch
Tax Specialist

Published by

Allyear Tax Guides
20484 Glen Brae Drive
Saratoga, CA 95070

ISBN 0-944817-67-X

LCCN 2003108854

Printed in U.S.A.

Series 400
Owners & Sellers

Tax Guide 402

TAX-DEFERRED EXCHANGES

For other titles in print, see page 224.

The author: **Holmes F. Crouch**
For more about the author, see page 221.

PREFACE

If you are a knowledge-seeking **taxpayer** looking for information, this book can be helpful to you. It is designed to be read — from cover to cover — in about eight hours. Or, it can be "skim-read" in about 30 minutes.

Either way, you are treated to **tax knowledge** . . . ***beyond the ordinary***. The "beyond" is that which cannot be found in IRS publications, FedWorld on-line services, tax software programs, Internet chatrooms, or e-mail bulletins.

Taxpayers have different levels of interest in a selected subject. For this reason, this book starts with introductory fundamentals and progresses onward. You can verify the progression by chapter and section in the table of contents. In the text, "applicable law" is quoted in pertinent part. Key phrases and key tax forms are emphasized. Real-life examples are given . . . in down-to-earth style.

This book has 12 chapters. This number provides depth without cross-subject rambling. Each chapter starts with a head summary of meaningful information.

To aid in your skim-reading, informative diagrams and tables are placed strategically throughout the text. By leafing through page by page, reading the summaries and section headings, and glancing at the diagrams and tables, you can get a good handle on the matters covered.

Effort has been made to update and incorporate all of the latest tax law changes that are *significant* to the title subject. However, "beyond the ordinary" does not encompass every conceivable variant of fact and law that might give rise to protracted dispute and litigation. Consequently, if a particular statement or paragraph is crucial to your own specific case, you are urged to seek professional counseling. Otherwise, the information presented is general and is designed for a broad range of reader interests.

The Author

INTRODUCTION

An "exchange" is a tax-recognized form of barter. It is the swapping of property items or property interests between owners and others where very little money, relatively speaking, changes hands. Any money involved is for the sole purpose of equalizing the market valuations and transactional expenses associated with the property or properties being exchanged.

Where property has increased significantly in value while being held, used, or improved, and is sold outright, there is tax to pay on any net capital gain realized. Many property owners prefer to defer said tax whenever they can.

Suppose, for example, you paid $10,000 for an exchangeable item, which currently is worth $100,000. If you have not yet sold the property, you have what is called an "unrealized" $90,000 of taxable capital gain. But if you were to trade your property item for one or more exchangeable items worth, say, $115,000, you would have no immediate tax to pay. Yes, there are certain computations to make, basis adjustment rules to follow, and certain tax forms to complete. Nevertheless, when properly executed, your exchange would be TAX FREE . . . at that moment only.

Theoretically, as the holder of any marketable asset, you can exchange, and exchange, and exchange . . . ad infinitum. At some point downstream, however, either you, your estate, or your heirs will pay tax on the capital gains that you did not pay when you made your first — and subsequent — nontaxable transfers. No exchange is tax free forever.

The U.S. Tax Code lists 14 specific laws which it characterizes as: ***Common Nontaxable Exchanges***. The section numbers extend from 1031 through 1045. Not all of these will interest everyone. For example, Section 1043 is titled: *Sale of Property to Comply with Conflict-of-Interest Requirements*. It applies only to officers and employees of the Executive Branch of Government. As such, it is quite limited in the number of taxpayers likely to be involved. We'll skip over this section and a few others which address special or limited applications.

In contrast, there is Section 1041. It is titled: ***Transfers of Property between Spouses or Incident to Divorce***. This section affects nearly 50% of all married couples in the United States. Obviously, we'll address this section in quite some detail.

The great grandfather of all tax-deferred exchanges is Section 1031. It is titled: ***Exchange of Property Held for Productive Use or Investment***. It comprises about 2,000 words of statutory text and nearly 50,000 words of regulations, rulings, and interpretations. It is a very popular exchange law for real estate entrepreneurs, farmers, mining companies, businesses, and other property interests such as in livestock, equipment, franchises, and leases. We devote four chapters to this one section alone. It is basic and fundamental to all asset exchanging.

Another extremely important — and compassionate — exchange law is Section 1033. It is titled: ***Involuntary Conversions***. It covers such events as—

(a) property seized or condemned for public projects (airports, schools, dams, highways);
(b) property sold pursuant to reclamation laws (conservation, environmental, contamination);
(c) property damaged in Presidentially declared disasters (floods, hurricanes, fire storms, earthquakes, tornadoes, terrorism); and
(d) livestock sold on account of disease, drought, or other weather-related conditions.

All exchanges are tricky, some more so than others. Much documentation and much computation are required. Starkly put, the IRS is not going to let you enjoy a substantial tax-free/tax-deferred bonanza, and permit you to walk away cavalierly. You are expected to do some serious homework on your own, and understand what you are doing. In this respect, this book will definitely be of instructional help even if you engage a professional to do the "finalizing" for you.

CONTENTS

Chapter		Page

1

THE 14 EXCHANGE RULES

Whereas A "Sale" Is The Transfer Of Property For Money, An "Exchange" Is The Transfer Of Property For Other Property, Where Little Or No Money Is Involved. The Attraction Of An Exchange Is That No Immediate Tax Is Imposed On The Capital Gain Derived. Thus, At The Time Of The Exchange, The Event Is TAX FREE. All Total, There Are 14 Tax Qualified Exchange Processes. Of This Number, The Most Common Are: [1] Like-Kind Exchanges, [2] Involuntary Conversions, [3] Marital Dissolutions, And [4] Venture Capitalism. No Exchange Is Tax Free Forever. There Comes A Time (During Life, Upon Death, Or After) When The "Tax Ax" Must Fall.

We have already tipped you off that an "exchange" is the swapping of property (or property interests) between one or more owners/investors where little or no money changes hands. To accomplish this, the property item (or items) must have determinable market value at the time of the exchange. Included in its market valuations the implication that the property carries with it a determinable amount of potential gain. The idea is that, if the property were not exchanged, its transfer of ownership would constitute a fully taxable event.

The term "property" here is used in the generic sense. It applies to any form of property — real, tangible, intangible, or personal — that is comparable in nature and quality to that being exchanged. The term does not include money or its equivalents. Nor does it include "boot" which is property not similar in kind to the properties being exchanged. Money and boot do not enjoy any tax-free/tax-deferred benefits whatsoever.

The comparability of properties being exchanged is a fundamental qualification of all exchange rules. For example, the exchange of a male breeding animal for a female breeding animal does not constitute comparable properties for tax-deferred purposes. However, exchange a male breeding animal of one species for a male breeding animal of another species (say, a horse for an elephant) would be comparable properties. Similarly, exchanging an airplane for a heavy-duty truck would not be comparable, whereas exchanging a computer for a printer would be comparable.

Accordingly, in this introductory chapter, we want to whisk you through the various Tax Code sections that legitimize the nontaxability of exchanges. We want to do this in a way that you become aware that there are other exchange rules than the one or two with which you may already be familiar. It is possible that you may have missed some exchange opportunities in the past. All exchange rules are premised on the concept that, were it not for there being a qualified exchange, the transaction would be a sale. As a sale, any gain realized would be tax recognized. Should there be any loss realized in an exchange transaction, no tax deferment benefits accrue. Consequently, there is no point in exchanging loss property. Do your exchanging with gain property only.

Foundation in Tax Code

The "Tax Code" to which we refer is the ***Internal Revenue Code***. This embodiment of federal tax laws consists of 100 chapters, approximately 1,800 sections, and spans approximately 4,000 pages of statutory text. The text is "statutory" because the U.S. Congress promulgated all laws therein, which were approved by the President of the United States. This text contains no regulations, court rulings, or administrative interpretations. The Code text, however, does include amendments to various sections therein, and notations concerning any former sections that have been repealed.

Chapter 1 of the Tax Code is titled: ***Normal Taxes and Surtaxes***. Within Chapter 1, there are 24 subchapters: A through

X. The exchange rules for tax deferment purposes are found in Subchapter O titled: ***Gain or Loss on Disposition of Property***. This subchapter heading implies clearly two prerequisites to an exchange. The first prerequisite is that a property owner/investor must relinquish — dispose of — his entire interest in the property he is offering for exchange. The second prerequisite is that the property offered for exchange must be a type where gain or loss can be determined. There may be capital gain or ordinary gain; or there may be capital loss or ordinary loss. At this point, though, we are not concerned with the extent of gain or loss.

We are concerned only with the functional substance of the exchange rules. These rules are all grouped together in Part III of Subchapter O which is titled: ***Common Nontaxable Exchanges***. We take issue with the term "nontaxable," because it is misleading. Without further reading of the exchange rules themselves, "nontaxable" implies a forever tax-free bonanza. As we stressed in our Introduction, such foreverness is definitely not the case. For income tax purposes, any gain on property exchanged is tax postponed until the property received in the exchange is disposed of in a transaction other than an exchange. We would have preferred that Part III be titled: "Common *Tax-Deferred* Exchanges."

Nevertheless, Part III (of Subchapter O of Chapter 1) consists of Sections 1031 through 1045. Sequentially, the count is 14 sections. But, as you will come to realize below, there are less than this number that are significant to most taxpayers.

We list in Figure 1.1 all 14 of the year 2003 exchange rules. We list the titles exactly as they appear in the Tax Code. We have done no editing or abbreviating. You might want to take a moment now to read through the entire list. Surely, some of these you've not heard of before. As an index of the relative complexity of each rule, we have added its statutory word count.

Note the Anomalies

As you read down the section numbers sequentially in the left-hand column in Figure 1.1, what is the first odd thing you note? Do you see a Section 1034? There's a Section 1033 and a Section 1035; but no Section 1034. How did this happen?

INTERNAL REVENUE CODE		
Subchapter O: Gain or Loss on Disposition of Property		
X X X X	Part III - Common Nontaxable Exchanges	X X X X
Section No.	Title	Word Count *
1031	Exchange of property held for productive use or investment.	2,000
1032	Exchange of stock for property.	80
1033	Involuntary conversions.	3,400
1035	Certain exchanges of insurance policies.	560
1036	Stock for stock of same corporation.	110
1037	Certain exchanges of U.S. obligations.	530
1038	Certain reacquisitions of real property.	1,100
1040	Transfer of certain farm, etc., real property **[Before 2010]** .	170
1040	Use of appreciated carryover basis property to satisfy pecuniary bequest **[After 2009]** .	220
1041	Transfer of property between spouses or incident to divorce.	430
1042	Sales of stock to employee stock ownership plans or certain cooperatives.	3,200
1043	Sale of property to comply with conflict-of-interest requirements.	780
1044	Rollover of publicly traded securities gain into specialized small business investment companies.	1,030
1045	Rollover of gain from qualified small business stock to another qualified small business stock.	460
* *Approximate statutory text; excludes legislative annotations.*		

Fig. 1.1 - The 14 Tax-Code-Authorized Exchange Rules

There was previously a Section 1034. It was titled: ***Rollover of Gain on Sale of Principal Residence***. It was repealed. Before so, it was the most popular — and most recordkeeping burdensome —

exchange rule of all. The idea of being able to roll over the gain on the sale of one's primary residence, and paying no immediate tax on the gain, sale after sale over the course of 35 to 50 years of home ownership, was indeed salivating. The problem was that most homeowners never properly kept track of their cumulative gain rollovers. And they seldom paid the proper tax when they claimed their one-time (limited) exclusion of gain in their retirement years. As a consequence of this inattention to cumulative gain tracking, the former Section 1034 was repealed in 1997. It was replaced by Section 121: ***Exclusion of Gain on Sale of Principal Residence*** (up to $250,000 per person). Unlike an exchange, an "exclusion" is forever nontaxable.

There is also another missing section in the listing sequence in Figure 1.1. Can you spot it? It is Section 1039. Note its absence between Section 1038 and Section 1040. There was previously a Section 1039 titled: ***Certain Sales of Low-Income Housing Projects***. This former rule suspended any gain from such sales where the proceeds were reinvested (within a limited period of time) in new or rehabilitated low-income housing. Because the suspended gain benefits focused solely on "projects" of multiple housing units, large capital investments were required. This led to Section 1039 becoming a popular tax sheltering activity. Tax writeoff abuses became rampant to the point where the section was repealed in 1990. It was replaced by Section 42 titled: ***Low-Income Housing Credit***. Instead of gain rollovers and reinvestment discounts, a liberal credit is allowed. Unlike an exchange, a "credit" is a dollar-for-dollar offset against the tax due each year for which the property is held for low-income occupants.

What other anomaly do you note in the sequential section numbering in Figure 1.1? Have you noticed that there are **two** Sections 1040? No; the listing is **not** a duplication of the section numbers. There are actually two separately time-framed sections. The first listed Section 1040 is applicable only to years *before* 2010; the second section 1040 is applicable to years *after* 2009. Why this time-frame change? Because a new carryover basis rule on the receipt of property after death goes into effect on January 1, 2010. We are queasy about far-out rules that address special situations, particularly when property is transferred at time of death.

Sections We Eliminate

Of the 14 Tax Code sections listed in Figure 1.1, we can eliminate five of them right off. As a group, they do not affect many taxpayers at a given tax-accounting time. More importantly, pure voluntary exchanging between two or more independent and willing taxpayers is not an option. Special circumstances must prevail before each eliminated exchange rule is applicable. The five rules we eliminate are:

Sec. 1035 — Certain exchanges of insurance policies,
Sec. 1037 — Certain exchanges of United States obligations,
Sec. 1040 — Transfer of certain farm, etc., real property [*before* year 2010],
Sec. 1040 — Use of appreciated carryover basis property to satisfy pecuniary bequest [*after* year 2009], and
Sec. 1043 — Sale of property to comply with conflict-of-interest requirements.

Our reasons for eliminating these sections follow.

Section 1035 addresses the exchangeability of life insurance, endowment, and annuity policies. A life insurance contract may be exchanged for an endowment contract, or for an annuity contract . . . or vice versa. But who does the exchanging? It is the issuing entity only: an insurance company. Each insurance company (a big corporation) sets its own terms for exchanging the contracts that it alone issues. Taxpayer A cannot exchange his life insurance policy with Taxpayer B for B's annuity contract. Taxpayer A has to contact his own insurance company and abide by whatever exchange terms his company offers. If he goes to another insurance company, any exchange made would be treated as a sale and repurchase.

Section 1037 addresses the exchangeability of "old" U.S. Treasury bonds for "new" similar bonds. The old bonds (paying $1^1/2$ to $3^1/2$ percent interest)were those issued under the Second Liberty Bond Act of 1959. The exchangeability of such bonds with newer later-issued bonds (paying $3^1/2$ to $4^1/2$ percent interest) are set forth in more than 100 different Treasury Department Circulars and Announcements. Bondholders seeking to make such exchanges must deal with either: (1) a Federal Reserve Bank or Branch; (2) the Bureau of Public Debt, Division of Loans and Currency; (3) the U.S. Treasury Department; or (4) a duly licensed bond broker who has entered into qualified exchange agreements with government. We categorize this as a controlled (rather than a free) exchange.

Section 1040 *before* year 2010 and Section 1040 *after* year 2009 are not tax-deferred exchanges in the customary sense. The co-designated sections deal with the carryover basis of appreciated property inventoried in the estates of decedents. The benefits apply only to qualified heirs. These are decedent-related persons who elect under Section 2032A (***Valuation of Certain Farm, etc., Real Property***) "special use" valuation for basis step-up purposes. The amount of gain taxable to an estate or trust is limited to the post-death appreciation of the property. Post-death appreciation is the difference between the property's fair market value on the date that a bequest to heirs is satisfied with estate or trust assets, and its estate tax value on date of death (determined *without regard* to Code Sec. 2032A). More appropriately therefore, the co-sections 1040 "before" and 1040 "after" should be addressed under carryover basis rules rather than under the exchange rules.

Section 1043 — transfers of "conflict-of-interest" property — addresses the sale of property by an officer or employee of the executive branch of the U.S. government. The property is sold pursuant to a "certificate of divestiture" issued by the Office of Government Ethics. When so sold, and followed within 60 days by the acquisition of U.S. obligation or ethics-approved diversified investment funds, no gain or loss is tax recognized. Such transactions constitute an exchange in that they are necessary to comply with federal conflict-of-interest statutes, executive orders, and congressional committee requests as a condition of confirmation. As we pointed out in our Introduction, only a relatively few taxpayers are affected by Section 1043.

The Ongoing Sections

After eliminating the above five sections (1035, 1037, 1040-before, 1040-after, and 1043), we are left with nine exchange sections to address. Captioning each with a short title, we list the nine said sections in Figure 1.2. The "short titles" are those commonly used in tax literature and referencing by tax professionals.

Section No.	SHORT TITLE	Professional Text	
		Pages	Words
1031	Like-Kind Exchanges	118	82,000
1032	Exchange - Stock for Property	10	7,000
1033	Involuntary Conversions	72	50,000
1036	Stock for Stock	4	3,000
1038	Reacquisitions - Real Property	24	16,000
1041	Property Transfers - Divorce	15	10,000
1042	Stock Sales to Plans or Co-Ops	16	10,000
1044	Publicly Traded Securities Gain	4	3,000
1045	Rollover from Small Business Stock	4	3,000

Fig. 1.2 - Our 9 Selected Exchange Rules for Close Attention

Short titles are simply that. They shorten the verbal time for describing the essence of a particular rule when using its section number. For example, Section 1045 carries the longest word count of all exchange-law titles. It has 14 words (count them), namely: ***Rollover of Gain from Qualified Small Business Stock to Another Qualified Small Business Stock.*** We can shorten this to: *Rollover from Small Business Stock*, without losing the gist of what Section 1045 is about.

In Figure 1.2, we list all of the short titles for you. Compare them if you wish to the official titles in Figure 1.1. Figure 1.2 also gives the number of pages of "professional text" that are devoted to each of our nine ongoing exchange rules. We also show the approximate word count of our reference professional text. Said reference is Standard Federal Tax Reporter, Vol. 12 (2002), published by CCH Incorporated of Chicago. CCH (Commerce Clearing House) is a venerable tax-reporting establishment dating back to 1913 when the U.S. income tax was first constitutionalized.

We show in Figure 1.2 the page and word count as an index of the relative importance of each exchange rule. Both counts include the following types of information:

(1) Complete statutory text of the code section.
(2) Congressional committee commentary for adoption, amendment, or revision of law.
(3) All relevant regulations, including those which are temporary and proposed.
(4) Narrative commentary by the Editorial Staff of CCH, Inc.
(5) Pertinent Revenue Procedures and Rulings by the IRS.
(6) Digests of published court rulings on interpretation of the law, under taxpayer-contested situations.

Tax laws which are popular and beneficial to a broad range of taxpayers are usually accompanied by various regulations. Tax laws which are unpopular and contentious cause much legal challenging in the courts. Court rulings take precedence over IRS rulings.

With the above points in mind, what section stands out most when you glance at the word-count column in Figure 1.2? It is — obviously — Section 1031: some 82,000 words. It dominates all other exchange rules in terms of importance and applicability to a wide range of owners of (or investors in) businesses and real estate. So widespread is the use of this exchange rule that mere mention of Section 1031 automatically translates into: ***Like-Kind Exchanges***. Its official title: ***Exchange of Property Held for Productive Use or Investment***, is almost entirely disregarded in the popular excitement over the tax savings via exchanges. So much so that we are going to devote four separate chapters to this one section alone. When you get through absorbing the like-kind exchange concept and its computational procedures, you'll have a strong handle on what is expected of you in other exchanges.

Section 1033: Involuntary Conversions

The second most dominant exchange rule in Figure 1.2 is Section 1033. In this case, the short title and official title are one and the same: ***Involuntary Conversions***. Of its 50,000-word professional text, its statutory text is about 3,500 words. Section 1033 is a very complicated exchange rule: difficult to explain and interpret. This is because of the *involuntary* nature of the "exchange" and the diversity of taxpayer situations addressed.

Complications are based, in part, on determining when property is *compulsorily and involuntarily converted*, **and**, in part, on the requirement that replacement property be *similar or related in service* to that which was converted. Whereas Section 1031 deals with "like-kind" properties exchanged voluntarily, Section 1033 deals with "similar or related in service" properties exchanged involuntarily. As a consequence, Section 1033 exchanges are not as common and not as well known as Section 1031 exchanges. But when conversion by compulsion occurs, there is no other tax-deferment rule that can adequately address the situation. Section 1033-affected taxpayers must be careful not to translate replacement property into "like-kind" rather than "similar or related."

Another complication in Section 1033 exchanges is the replacement *time* requirement. Whereas a Section 1031 exchange must be completed within 180 days of the exchange event, a Section 1033 exchange must be completed within—

> *2 years after the close of the first taxable year in which any part of the gain upon the conversion is realized.*

The statutory marker point (when replacement time begins) is when the cumulative reimbursements received exceed one's cost basis in the property converted. Reaching the "marker point" itself often takes several years. The delay is caused by litigation, insurance processing, and government agency procedures.

Section 1033 consists of 10 subsections whose captions alone are instructive at this time. These subsection captions are—

(a) General rule: (1) Conversion into similar property; (2) Conversion into money.

(b) Basis of property acquired through involuntary conversion.

(c) Property sold pursuant to reclamation laws.

(d) Livestock destroyed by disease.

(e) Livestock sold on account of drought.

(f) Replacement of livestock with other farm property where there has been environmental contamination.

(g) Condemnation of real property held for productive use in trade or business or for investment.

(h) Special rules for property damaged in Presidentially declared disasters.

(i) Replacement property must be acquired from unrelated person in certain cases.

(j) Sales or exchanges to implement microwave relocation policy.

Are you getting the idea that Section 1033 is a very comprehensive tax law? It attempts to address real life problems of property ownership, when conversion is caused by events which are beyond the property owner's/investor's control. Its focus, however, is strictly on conversion *gain*: not on conversion loss. Surprisingly, conversion gain results more often than does a conversion loss. If there is a conversion loss, said loss is addressed separately in Section 165 (Casualty Losses) and/or Section 1231 (Special Rules for Trade or Business Losses).

Section 1038: Certain Reacquisitions

Next in line of professional text importance (in Figure 1.2 — 16,000 words) is Section 1038: ***Reacquisitions of Real Property.*** The official title to this section is: ***Certain Reacquisitions of Real Property.*** Here, the term "certain" has special meaning of its own. This term would have been more self-explanatory had the official title been: *Reacquisition of Real Property by Seller-Mortgager.* A "seller-mortgager" is one who sells a parcel of real estate and, as part of the sales agreement, accepts a mortgage note (installment loan) which is secured by the property itself. The mortgage note is not one which is arranged through a commercial lending institution. It is arranged solely between the seller and buyer themselves. This form of transaction is referred to as a "seller-financed sale."

Should the buyer default on the mortgage arrangement, the seller reacquires the property and recomputes his tax basis and realized gain therewith. This can be thought of as an exchange in reverse. The seller conveys conditional title to the property, in exchange for a lien against it as security for the payoff of the mortgage. If full payoff is not completed as agreed, the property-for-mortgage exchange is reversed. The mortgage is rescinded and the property is conveyed back to the seller.

The tax deferment of gain on a seller-financed sale is prescribed by Section 453: ***Installment Method.*** This is a method by which gain is taxed only proportionately to the payments received on principal each year. If the payments on principal stop prematurely, so does taxation of any gain on the installments received. For the reacquisition process only, whether by agreement (via voluntary conveyance from the purchaser) or by process of law (such as foreclosure by judicial sale), the rules of Section 1038 apply. In all other respects, the prorata tax-on-gain rules of Section 453 apply. We'll tell you more about Section 453 when we explain Section 1038 more fully in a separate chapter.

Seller-financing, by spreading out (deferring) of its taxable gain is highly attractive for owners of rental real estate, commercial buildings, farm land and forests, mineral (oil, gas, geothermal) property, and primary residences. Installment selling is also a great retirement planning tool.

Section 1041: Divorce Transfers

Dissolution of marriage (divorce) is a common occurrence in the U.S. In many cases, the process is contentious, emotional, and time consuming. Tax matters are given the "back burner" treatment, until all dust clears. The clearing occurs when all of the marital property is redesignated into "his" and "her" components. At this point, the provisions of Section 1041 come into focus.

Section 1041, recall from Figure 1.2, is short titled: ***Property Transfers—Divorce.*** The full official title is: ***Transfers of Property Between Spouses or Incident to Divorce.*** The use of the term "or" in this title has special significance. It means — and is intended to mean — that there can be an exchange of marital properties prior to divorce, or prior to any proceedings therewith. The nontaxability of marital property exchanges is not contingent upon divorce becoming final or even being imminent. In other words, Section 1041 enables the spouses to work out their property rearrangements among themselves, if they so choose. There are no immediate tax consequences to either party . . . IF proper cost records are kept. The property separation — as portrayed in Figure 1.3 — does not have to be 50/50.

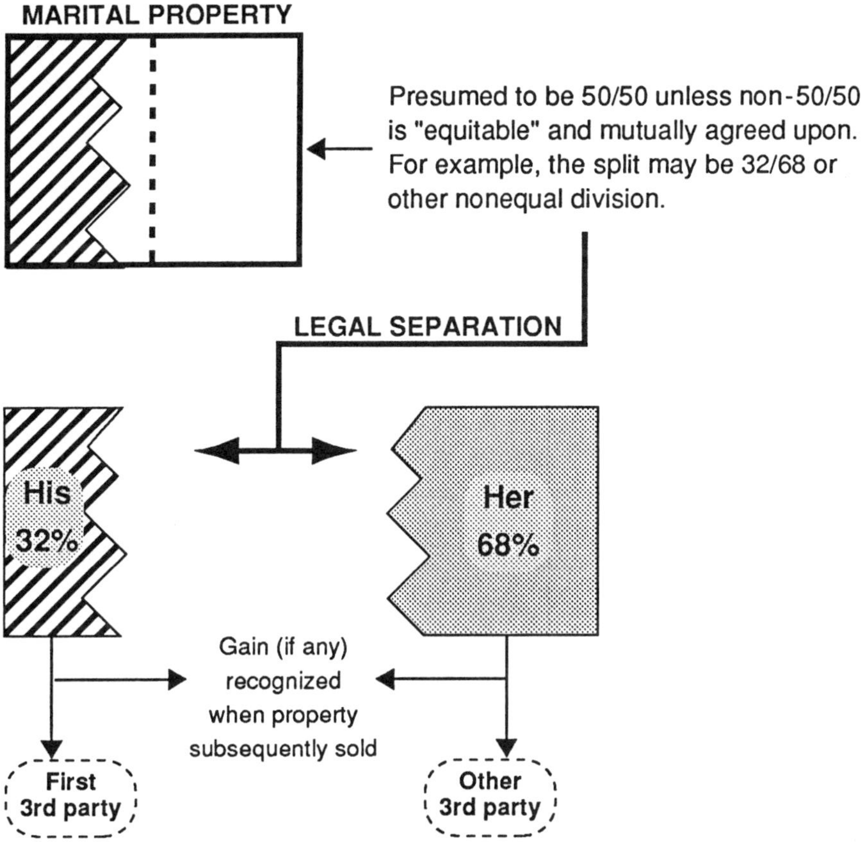

Fig. 1.3 - No Tax Consequences When Marital Property Separated

What kind of spousal transfers are covered by Section 1041? Only transfers of *property* are covered: **not** services. What kind of property? All kinds: real, personal, tangible, and intangible. It can be real estate, personal-use autos and household furniture, business-use equipment, mutual funds, pension plans, insurance policies, and bank accounts. Anything that has a determinable fair market value when offered to the general public qualifies as "property" for Section 1041 purposes.

The gist of Section 1041 is that: *No gain or loss shall be recognized on the transfer of property* . . . between spouses or former spouses. The rationale for this tax position is that the properties are co-owned by both spouses, from date of marriage to date of separation. When co-owned marital property is redesignated as his and her "separate" property, there is no tax consequence at that time. When an item of separate property is subsequently sold to an unrelated third party, full tax accounting is then required. This is the bottom line gist of Figure 1.3.

For the rationale of Section 1041 to hold, it does not matter that each item of marital property is "split" equally or unequally, or that each gets some part of all property items. What matters is that the spouses agree voluntarily that the property separation is fair and equitable to each. Otherwise, a court order (judicial mandate) on the fairness of the property separation must be sought.

So much for the general rationale behind Section 1041. In a separate chapter, we'll expose you to its statutory and regulatory specifics. There is much flexibility and wisdom in Section 1041. And — yes — there are many ambiguities also. Although there is not an abundance of case law (court rulings) on Section 1041, that which does exist is highly instructive.

Section 1042: Employee Stock Plans

Next, continuing down our Figure 1.2 count list of professional text is Section 1042. Its full title is: ***Sales of Stock to Employee Stock Ownership Plans or Certain Cooperatives.*** For this Tax Code section, the professional-text count is approximately 10,000 words. Included in this word count are approximately 2,800 words of statutory text. Why so many statutory words, relatively speaking?

Answer: Because the exchanging involves corporate stock — an intangible item. Corporate stock is a "piece of paper" (or multiple pieces of paper) which has no physically inherent value in and of its own. Presumably, such stock is supported by underlying physical assets which can be tangibly valued. Because of its intangibility, corporate stock is often a tool for victimizing frugal employees . . . and their retirement savings. Section 1042 offers some protection to such employees.

In generalized form, Section 1042 povides for nonrecognition of gain from the sale of "qualified securities" to (1) an employee stock ownership plan [ESOP] or to an eligible worker-owned cooperative, and (2) within a qualified period, the seller acquires replacement securities of another corporation beyond the ESOP plan. The idea is to give workers the opportunity to own part of the company for which they are working, while simultaneously providing for employee retirement. The term "qualified securities" means common stock issued by the employer (as sponsor of the retirement plan) which is readily tradable on an established securities market.

A key requirement of Section 1042 is that the employer establish a *defined contribution retirement plan* which is either a stock bonus plan or a combination stock bonus and money purchase plan. The "plan" must be organized for the exclusive benefit of the plan sponsor's employees. Furthermore, the plan must hold at least 30 percent of each class of stock (other than preferred stock) issued by the qualifying employer. When an employee retires, he can sell his share of ESOP stock in any manner that he chooses. At that time, of course, he pays tax on any cumulative gain derived. Meanwhile, he pays no income tax on the appreciation of his ESOP share while in an ESOP trust which is tax exempt.

Section 1032 & 1036 Exchanges

Sections 1032 and 1036 are similar in many respects. Both address tax-deferred exchanges of corporate stock that is tradable in established securities markets. This means that market values are readily determinable on any regular business day. The key difference between these two exchanges is reflected in each section's official title. Whereas section 1032 is titled: ***Exchange of Stock for***

Property, Section 1036 is titled: ***Stock for Stock of Same Corporation.***

Section 1032 is one of the shortest of all exchange laws. It consists of only about 66 words. The essence of these words is that: *No gain or loss shall be recognized . . . on the receipt of money or other property in exchange for stock . . . of* [the offering] *corporation.*

This is the premise on which all corporations rely for gathering money and property from owners, investors, and employees. The money and property are used to conduct an ongoing business for which the corporation was organized. The presumption is that the corporation was legitimized under State law, and upon so being, was authorized to offer a designated number of stock shares to the general public. Otherwise, without Section 1032 as tax protection, very few ordinary corporations would ever get going.

Section 1036 is also a short-word-count tax law. It consists of about 96 words. Its "no gain or loss" thrust is the same as that in Section 1032. The exchange process under Section 1036 is limited to those shareholders who have already acquired stock in a given corporation. Thus, within the **same corporation**, common stock can be exchanged for common stock, **or** preferred stock can be exchanged for preferred stock. The nonrecognition rule does **not** apply when exchanging common for preferred stock (or vice versa) in the same corporation. Section 1036 is useful in corporate reorganizations, recapitalizations, and certain (qualified) mergers and acquisitions. The idea is to preserve the capital on hand while rearranging the voting and dividend rights among diverse shareholders.

Section 1044 & 1045 Rollovers

The last two exchange rules that we intend to address are Sections 1044 and 1045. Both deal with small business entities in corporate and partnership form. A "small business" is one whose gross receipts for a given year do not exceed $100,000,000 (100 million). This is the threshold for the issuance of restricted stock in anticipation of "going public" should the business flourish into an ongoing, expanding enterprise.

The idea behind these two sections is to encourage investment in certain small businesses by using the *nonrecognition of gain* feature (which is characteristic of all exchange rules) to maximize one's available capital for new undertakings. These two sections are particularly attractive to venture capitalists who seek to pay no tax during multiple rollovers (of the deferred gain) over a 5-year-or-so period. We depict in Figure 1.4 the kind of intrigue involved.

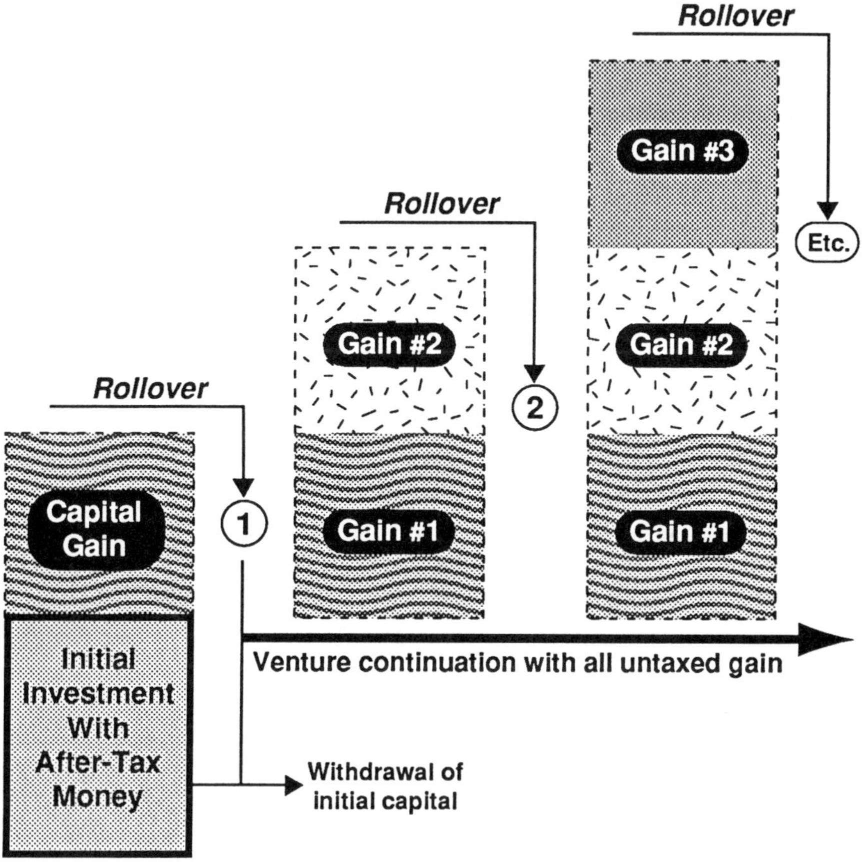

Fig. 1.4 - The Intrigue of Venture Capital With Gain Rollovers

There are two types of special activities targeted by Sections 1044 and 1045. You can glean what these activities are from the official section titles themselves. Said titles read:

Sec. 1044 — *Rollover of Publicly Traded Securities **Gain** into Specialized Small Business Investment Companies*: SSBICs (szz-bics) as they are called.

Sec. 1045 — *Rollover of **Gain** from Qualified Small Business Stock to Another Qualified Small Business Stock*: QSBS or QSB stock as it is called.

In both cases, the tax-free rollover-of-gain period is limited to 60 days after the sale of qualified stock. In both cases, there are annual limits and cumulative limits on the amount of gain that is not taxed. For individuals, the amount of gain that can be deferred in any one taxable year is $50,000 or $500,000 over any cumulative period of time. For C corporations, the annual limit is $250,000, where the cumulative limit is $1,000,000 (of deferred gain). To enjoy these benefits, the replacement stock must be held at least six months before being again rolled over.

The above rather large cumulative tax-free gains clearly imply a special modus operandi. That is, it is O.K. for a venture capitalist to get his initial (after tax) money back, then play the field with only his tax-deferred gain. This is a powerful incentive for putting pre-tax money into risky start-up ventures. Should the new venture flounder, an investor will not have lost his own money. He will only have lost money on which he paid no tax. This is a win-win situation both for the investor and for public policy. We'll discuss Sections 1044 and 1045 together more fully in a separate chapter herein.

2

IMPORTANCE OF "TAX BASIS"

One's Basis In Property Is AFTER-TAX Money Invested In That Property. The Amount Of Said Money (Or Money Equivalent) Usually Varies Over Time, Such That ADJUSTMENTS To Basis Must Be Made. Section 1016 Lists Some 30 Types Of Potential Adjustments. Different Initial Basis Rules Apply Depending On How Property Is Acquired: Purchase, Gift, Inheritance, Foreclosure, Exchange, Etc. In A Qualified Exchange, "Adjusted Basis" Is The Reference Benchmark For Establishing The Amount Of Capital Gain That Can Be Deferred. BOTH The Adjusted Basis AND The Deferred Gain Are Transferred To The Replacement Property.

All tax-free/tax-deferred exchanges relate to specific property items called: *capital assets*. A capital asset is real property (land, buildings, structures, natural resources, fruit and nut trees, timber, boat docks), tangible property (vehicles, machinery, equipment, livestock, hardware, software), and certain intangible property (corporate stock, partnerships/LLC interests, franchises, patents, covenants, mortgages). When any of these items are sold outright, there may be capital gain or there may be capital loss. The gain or loss is tax recognized immediately. This means that the transaction is fully taxable (or fully tax accountable) at time of sale.

Instead of selling a capital asset outright, suppose it is exchanged for another equivalent property item or items. If there is a gain, and the applicable rules are followed, the gain can be carried over tax free to the exchange-acquired property. Doing so legitimately and nonabusively is what the exchange rules in Chapter 1 are all about.

Should there be a capital loss on the exchange (instead of a gain), there is no carryover of that loss to the replacement property. As a consequence, it is better to sell loss property outright. Then follow the regular capital loss rules to claim any tax offsetting advantage that might be applicable.

Another point to note is that the exchange rules do not apply to ordinary income processes. Such processes include earnings and profits of a business, wages and salaries, interest, dividends, royalties, rental income . . . and so forth. Only capital gain property qualifies as a candidate for exchanging.

Even so, the extent to which the exchange rules apply depends on your **tax basis** in the property exchange. This is the amount of after-tax money or money-equivalent that you have at risk. Your at-risk tax basis is the fundamental reference for establishing gain or loss in any capital transaction.

Accordingly, in this chapter we want to review with you the many variations in tax basis accounting. Whether you exchange a $10,000 property item or a $10,000,000 ($10 million) property item, all exchange rules are premised on the concept of transferring your current basis in property directly to the exchange-acquired property. Your transferred basis becomes the starting point for establishing your ongoing basis in the replacement property. Unless you can account properly for this basis transfer, the tax-free portion of the gain may be curtailed considerably, or it may be disallowed altogether.

Reference Benchmark: Adjusted Basis

Your tax basis in a capital asset is the amount of after-tax money (capital) that you have invested in that asset. Said amount is seldom static. It usually changes from time of acquisition to time of disposition. It may change up, such as with additions and improvements; it may change down, such as with depreciation allowances and capital withdrawals. No matter which way the basis change may go, at the time of an exchange you have what is called:

an *adjusted basis.* This is the reference figure you use for computing the amount of capital gain that can be exchange deferred.

Your adjusted basis represents your cumulative capital investment in property over the period of time that you have held it. The longer you hold, the more difficult it is to trace the cumulative changes — additions and subtractions — that you have incurred. This is because most persons remember what they paid when they first acquired the item, but tend to get careless as they put additional capital in or take capital out.

Let us illustrate with a simple example of the need for attention to basis accounting. Suppose you bought 100 shares of stock in a mutual fund. You paid $15 per share at the time (total investment $1,500). You hold the shares for five years, after which you sell them. During the 5-year holding period, you were paid taxable dividends, nontaxable dividends, stock dividends, and stock splits. You let all the dividends and distributions, including capital gain distributions, roll over. You now have 135 shares of stock. What is your basis, as adjusted, in each of your shares?

You have a problem with this, don't you? Most everyone does. This is because only a few persons keep a running account of their basis adjustments as they occur.

The rollover of taxable dividends and taxable capital gain distributions is a plus adjustment to basis. You have added capital to your investment because, separately, you'll be paying tax on these items. The assignment of nontaxable dividends and other property distributions is a minus adjustment to basis. Nontaxable dividends and property distributions constitute the return of some of your own money. If you allow these to roll over, there is no change in your basis. A stock dividend increases the number of shares you hold, with no outlay of money on your part. This dilutes the basis in each of your initially acquired shares. A stock split also increases your number of shares without your contributing any additional money.

Are you beginning to see what we mean about basis adjustments?

Unless you have a static asset (no gain or loss potential) or a sterile asset (no current income generated), adjusting your tax basis requires vigilance at all times. Unless you adjust as you go along, should push come to shove, the IRS can assert it to be "zero." This forces you to pay higher taxes than you need to, and deprives you of loss benefits should you experience capital loss instead of capital gain. The obvious antidote to a zero basis assertion is to cumulatively track all basis adjustments as you go along.

Applicable Law: Section 1011

The "adjusted basis" concept — generally shortened to just the term "basis" — is fundamental to ALL capital asset transactions. Whether the transaction is a sale, an exchange, a gift, an inheritance, an abandonment, a discovery, or any other form of property transfer from one person or entity to another person or entity, the basis concept must be adhered to. This is the gist of what is mandated by Section 1011 of the Tax Code. The title of this section is: ***Adjusted Basis for Determining Gain or Loss***. This title alone clearly implies that one's adjusted basis in property is THE BENCHMARK OF REFERENCE when disposing/conveying legal title in any property transaction.

The general rule on this point is subsection 1011(a). This rule reads in full as—

> *The adjusted basis for determining the gain or loss from the sale or* ***other disposition of property****, whenever acquired, shall be the basis (determined under* ***section 1012*** *or other applicable sections of this subchapter and subchapters C (relating to corporate distributions and adjustments), K (relating to partners and partnerships), and P (relating to capital gains and losses)), adjusted as provided in* ***section 1016***. [Emphasis added.]

Note the cross references to Sections 1012 and 1016. Section 1012 is titled: ***Basis of Property—Cost***; Section 1016 is titled ***Adjustments to Basis***. Section 1012 addresses the basis of property when it is purchased. Most property items are acquired by purchase, rather than by exchange, gift, inheritance, etc. Section 1016 enumerates approximately **30** different kinds of adjustments to basis, regardless of how the property is acquired. We'll come back to Sections 1012 and 1016 shortly.

What If No Gain?

A general depiction of the adjusted basis concept is presented in Figure 2.1. For identifying convenience, we have captioned various items that we will address either now or later in this chapter. At the moment, though, we call your attention to the item in Figure 2.1 marked: *Transaction Event.* In general terms, such event is that point in ownership time when Owner A transfers legal title of the property to Owner B. It is also that point in time where gain or loss has to be determined relative to Owner A's adjusted basis in the property transferred. We now raise the question: What happens when there is no gain? That is, What happens when the fair market value (FMV) of the property transferred is equal to, or less than, the adjusted basis of the item involved?

There are two distinct answers. In both cases, the consequences are tax free. Let us explain.

When the FMV at time of the transaction event equals the adjusted basis, there is no gain and there is no loss. This situation is referred to as: *Return of capital,* or recovery of investment. This means that the amount of capital invested in the property at the time of the transaction is returned to the owner when legal title is conveyed to the new owner. The return of this capital is tax free. This is because, presumably, all tax has been paid on the money used to invest in the property. Thus, there is no second tax on the return of capital that already has been taxed.

Now, what happens in the case where the FMV is less than the adjusted basis in the property? This is a *capital loss* situation. In and of itself, there is no income tax on a capital loss. Would you not consider such as being tax free?

You could. But, actually, the loss can be used to offset other capital gains in the year of the Figure 2.1 event. If there are no concurrent capital gains for offsetting purposes, up to $3,000 capital loss per year can be written off against other sources of ordinary income [IRC Sec. 1211: ***Limitation on Capital Loss***].

At this point in our discussion, there is no difference whatsoever between a sale, an exchange, or other form of property disposition. If there is no gain, there is no tax. If there is a loss, there is no tax. In effect, then, when there is no gain or when there is a loss, there

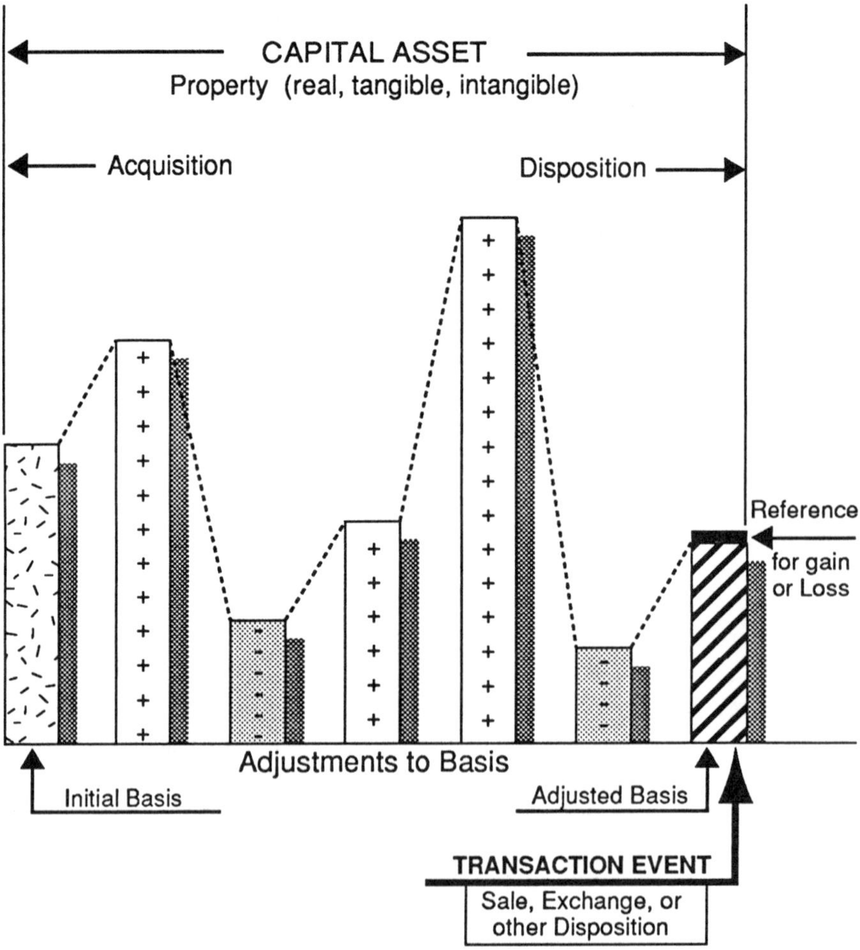

Fig. 2.1 - Conceptual Changes in Tax Basis Over Time

are tax-free components of the property transfer. Therefore, in these two tax-free situations, why make an exchange when there is no tax to be deferred by doing so?

How an Exchange Works

As pointed out previously, an exchange makes sense only when there is likelihood of capital gain. This being the case, what are some of the elements of a successful exchange?

Answer: An exchange involves the express intent and plan to replace the property conveyed with comparable property acquired by exchange. In principle, an exchange is the simultaneous giving up of legal title to one property (or group of properties) for legal title in another comparable property (or group of properties). Thus, you should think of an exchange as a **continuation** of property holdings. The "continuation rules" differ depending on the type of property or properties being exchanged, and on the specific tax law that is applicable.

In other words, if the property conditions are right, and the rules are followed, an exchange involving capital gain can be tax free. Anything that is tax free, even if only for a short period of time, is a genuine tax saving. This tax savings feature, however, is contingent upon the following accounting processes:

1. That the adjusted basis in the property conveyed in the exchange is transferred (carried over) directly to the replacement property acquired.

2. That the untaxed capital gain is also transferred directly to the replacement property as part of the built-in excess of FMV over the transferred adjusted basis.

3. That the transferred adjusted basis becomes the starting point for the continuation of adjustments to basis, after ownership of the replacement property is settled.

4. That the exchange of properties takes place within statutorily prescribed time limits.

Strictly for the instructional convenience of those readers who are not experienced property exchangers, we present in Figure 2.2 the basic elements of an exchange. We do so to provide every reader with a "level field" starting point. Yes, we have overly simplified the elements. But, as you'll see in subsequent chapters, real life exchange computations can get rather complex. Still, the continuation of basis adjustments and the rolling over of capital gain is fundamental to all types of exchanges.

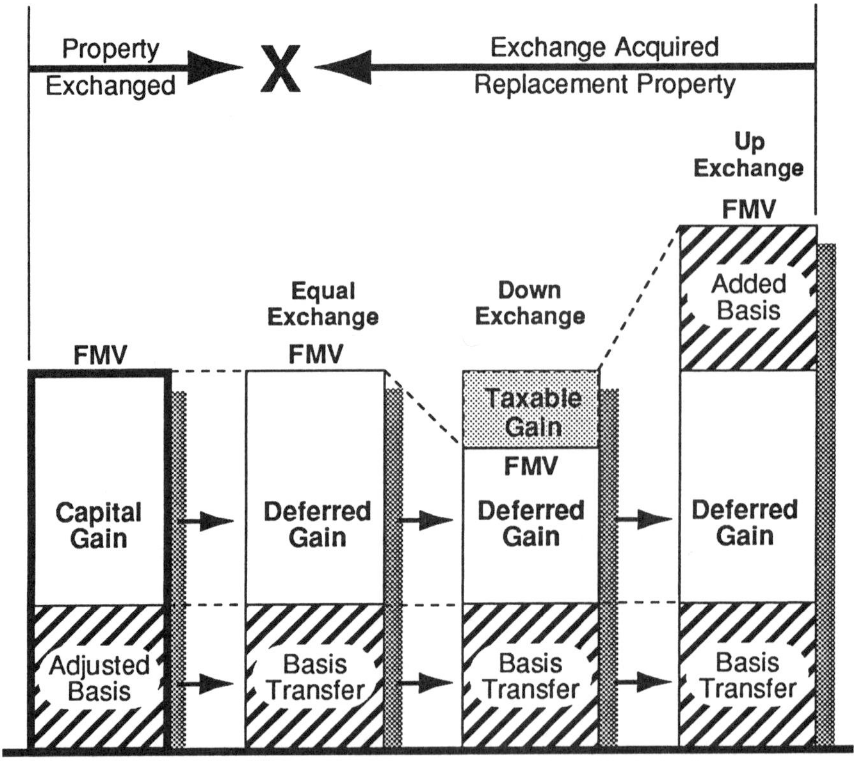

Fig. 2.2 - Fundamental Features of Any Qualified Exchange

If you get nothing else out of Figure 2.2, it is that the tax-free feature of an exchange is temporary only. The required continuation of accounting automatically defers any capital gains tax to the next transactional event downstream. As illustrated, you can exchange more than once and still get tax-free benefits each time.

Eventually, someday, the property will be sold. When it is, the cumulative untaxed gain will literally "pop out" of the transactional computations. The capital gains tax rules and tax rates applicable at that time will apply.

Primary Basis is Cost

For an item of property to qualify for an exchange, it must have a marketable value in excess of its adjusted basis. This raises the question: What is the primary starting point from which the adjusted basis is derived?

Property of value does not appear out of thin air. At some point in past time, the original form of the property item had to be created, produced, and maintained. This effort required expenditures in the form of materials, supplies, and services. Expenditures of money imply cost or cost equivalents in prior time. This prior time aspect is stated in the above-cited Section 1011 as follows:

> *The adjusted basis . . . shall be the basis determined in* ***section 1012 and other applicable sections*** *. . . as provided in section 1016.* [Emphasis added.]

Now, we have to switch to Section 1012. What does it say? Its title is: ***Basis of Property — Cost.*** It reads in part—

> *The basis of property shall be the cost of such property, except as otherwise provided . . .*

In general terms, cost is the amount paid in cash, plus debt obligations assumed, plus other property conveyed (which has a cash equivalent in market value), plus expense of acquisition. Variations apply when the elements of direct cost have faded into the various transitions of the property over time. When property is acquired by gift, inheritance, distribution from an entity (partnership, trust, corporation), foreclosure, or exchange, nonpurchase basis rules apply.

The components of cost consist of every expenditure necessary to acquire legal title to the property item sought. This includes all directly associated expenditures such as sales taxes, shipping charges, purchase commissions, installation and testing charges, revenue stamps, recording fees, legal and accounting fees, assumption of existing debt on the property, the borrowing of money to complete the purchase, loan "points," settlement costs . . . and so on. It is immaterial whether the transaction is a good bargain or a bad bargain, so long as there is no silent gift or barter involved. If personal services are performed by the purchaser for which a property item is received, and if the purchaser reports the FMV of the item as income on his tax return, the amount so reported becomes the (or part of the) cost basis in the item purchased. Every property owner has the burden of proving his cost basis in those items that he acquired by purchase.

When Inherited or Gifted

Common forms of acquisitions of property by nonpurchase involve inheritances and gifts. At the time of the transfer of ownership, the acquirer pays no money out of his own pocket. When property is acquired by inheritance, the recipient takes on a fair market value (FMV) basis. When property is acquired by gift, the recipient takes on as his basis the basis of the donor plus a tax credit adjustment. The specific basis rules are set forth in Sections 1014 and 1015 respectively.

Section 1014 is titled: ***Basis of Property Acquired from a Decedent.*** This section consists of approximately 1250 words. The essence and general rule are that—

> *The basis of property in the hands of a person acquiring the property from a decedent or to whom the property passed from a decedent shall, if not sold, exchanged, or otherwise disposed of before the decedent's death by such person, shall be—*
>
> *(1)* *the fair market value of the property at the date of the decedent's death,*
>
> *(2)* *. . . at the* [alternate] *applicable valuation date prescribed . . ., or*
>
> *(3)* *its value determined under* [special use] *elections prescribed.*

The underlying point is that each item of property of a decedent must be expressly valued at time of death. The value determined becomes the tax basis for the recipient, regardless of the basis of the property in the hands of the decedent before his death. The theory behind Section 1014 is that a death tax credit and death tax apply before legal title to the property can be passed on to the recipient.

Section 1015 is titled: ***Basis of Property Acquired by Gifts and Transfers in Trust.*** This section consists of about 1,000 words. The essence of the basis transfer concept lies in subsections (a) and (d). Subsection (a), general rule, reads in part—

> *If the property was acquired by gift . . . the basis shall be the same as it would be in the hands of the donor . . ., except that if such basis . . . is greater than the fair market value of the property at the time of the gift, then for the purpose of determining loss the basis shall be such fair market value.*

Subsection (d), increase in basis, goes on to say, in part—

> *The basis shall be the basis determined under subsection (a), increased (but not above the fair market value of the property at the time of the gift) by the amount of gift tax paid with respect to such gift.*

Donors and donees often fail to realize that any transfer of property by gift in excess of $10,000 is subject to gift tax accounting (Form 709: ***U.S. Gift Tax Return***). The accounting requires that the gifted property be fair market valued, deduct $10,000, then use the gift tax rate schedules to establish the amount of gift tax. In most cases, the gift is structured so that the amount of gift tax is within the gift tax credit range. The gift tax credit, when proportionalized to the appreciation in value of the property, is added to the donor's basis in the property. The donor's initial basis plus the gift tax proportional amount becomes the donee's basis when the property is accepted by the donee.

When Exchange Acquired

Another common form of nonpurchase pertains to exchanged-acquired property. Technically, said property is called: *Exchanged basis property.* Such property is defined in Section 7701(a)(44):

> *The term "exchanged basis property" means property having a basis under* ***any provision*** *of subtitle A* [Income Taxes] . . .

> *providing that the basis shall be determined in whole or part* ***by reference to other property held*** *at any time by the person for whom the basis is to be determined.* [Emphasis added.]

From this citation alone, it is not evident that there are three components to establishing the basis in exchanged-acquired property. The basis components are:

1. Reference to other property held by the exchanger (which is the subject of exchange);
2. Those basis rules found in any provision of the tax code relating to nonrecognition of gain transactions; and
3. Cost add-ons necessitated by the financial, legal, and accounting rules applicable at time of the exchange.

In other words, no one basis rule applies universally to all forms of exchanges. This is why we devote separate chapters subsequent hereto to various forms of nontaxable exchanges. Nevertheless, we depict in Figure 2.3 the essence of what is involved in the basis of exchanged-acquired property.

Particularly note in Figure 2.3 that deferred gain is NOT part of the new start basis. Deferred gain is never part of basis inasmuch as no tax has been paid on it. It merely "floats along" until the property is disposed of in a taxable transaction.

No matter how nontaxable an exchange may be, there is no relief from the cost aspects thereof. There are always expenses to be paid, commissions to pay, conveyance of "boot" (noncash, nonlike items), debt relief (basis reduction), debt assumption (basis increase), and other FMV equalizing arrangements. No owner is going to exchange property worth $100,000 for another property worth $85,000 without some FMV equalizing arrangement.

Adjustments to Basis

No matter how property is acquired, whether by purchase or nonpurchase, there are subsequent adjustments to its acquisition basis. We mentioned this earlier with respect to the term "adjusted basis" of property. Further, recall that in the citation of Section

1011, reference was made to Section 1016. The Section 1016 is titled: ***Adjustments to Basis.***

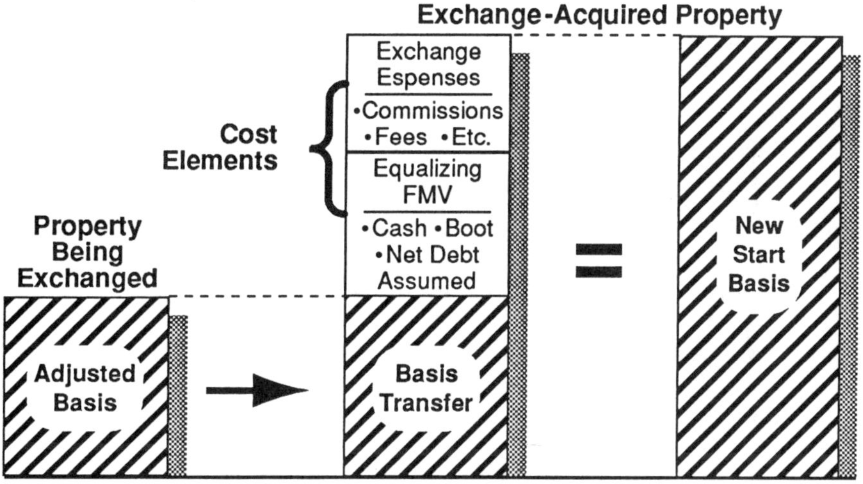

Fig. 2.3 - The "Cost" Elements in Basis of Exchange-Acquired Property

Section 1016 comprises about 2,200 statutory words. Within this body of text, there are about 30 paragraphs of specific adjustments to be made. Obviously, we'll cite only the more general portions. These will give you the essence of what is expected of you, both before and after a nontaxable exchange event.

Accordingly, subsection 1016(a): General Rule, reads in part—

Proper adjustments in respect of the property shall in all cases be made—

(1) *for expenditures, receipts, losses, or other items, properly chargeable to capital account, but no such adjustment shall be made . . . for which deductions have been taken by the taxpayer in determining taxable income for the taxable year or prior taxable years;*

(2) *for exhaustion, wear and tear, obsolescence, amortization, to the extent of the amount* ***allowed*** *as deductions in computing taxable income . . . but not*

> *less than the amount **allowable** under* [applicable] *income tax laws; . . .* [Emphasis added.]

These two introductory paragraphs are followed by 26 other adjustment paragraphs under subsection (a).

Subsection 1016(b): ***Substituted Basis***, reads—

> *Whenever it appears that the basis of property in the hands of the taxpayer is a substituted basis, then the adjustments provided in subsection (a) shall be made **after first making** . . . proper adjustments of a similar nature in respect of the period during which the property was held by the transferor, donor, or grantor, or during which the other property was held by the person for whom the basis is to be determined.*

The message in subsection (b) is that, for any nonpurchase situation, adjustments to basis must be made both before and after the transfer of property. The purpose in doing so is to provide an accurate capital reference for computing gain or loss when the property is ultimately sold. It is also necessary to assure that no double benefits have been taken. For example if a capital improvement was made to property and it was expensed off as a deduction (to reduce income tax), it cannot be added to basis for a second tax-free return.

Apportionment of Basis

When a bundle of property is acquired as a whole and subsequently disposed of a portion at a time, there must be an allocation of the "cost or other basis" (as adjusted) over the several units involved. This is the essence of Regulation § 1.61-6(a): ***Gains derived from dealings in property***. Of the part relevant here, this regulation reads—

> *When a part of a larger property is sold* [or exchanged], *the cost or other basis of the entire property shall be equitably apportioned among the several parts. . . . The sale* [or exchange] *of each part is treated as a separate transaction and*

the gain or loss shall be computed separately on each part [by reference to its apportioned basis]. *Thus, gain or loss shall be determined at the time of sale* [or exchange] *of each part, and not deferred until the entire property is disposed of.*

For example, suppose you acquired in one lump sum transaction three items of property. You intend to renovate and recondition the three items and sell/exchange them one at a time. How do you apportion your total acquisition basis to each of three acquired items which you intend to sell separately?

Answer: The apportionment is done by the ratio of each item's FMV to the total FMV of all properties, times the acquisition basis. This requires a conscientious effort to determine the FMV of each item in the bulk acquisition.

Let us assume that the bulk acquisition basis is \$100,000. Let us also assume the respective FMVs are: item A \$35,000; item B \$26,000; and item C \$54,000. That is, the total FMV of the three property items combined is \$115,000 (Disregard any difference between the acquisition basis and the separately determined FMVs when totaled.) The respective apportioned basis of each item then becomes—

Item A: $\frac{35{,}000}{115{,}000} \times \$100{,}000 =$ \$30,430 basis in A.

Item B: $\frac{26{,}000}{115{,}000} \times \$100{,}000 =$ \$22,610 basis in B.

Item C: $\frac{54{,}000}{115{,}000} \times \$100{,}000 =$ 46,960 basis in C.
\$100,000

The apportionment rationale is that, if an item of property (when acquired in bulk with other items) can be sold or exchanged separately, it is more likely than not to be disposed of separately. This is particularly likely in a nontaxable exchange. Rarely is just one item of property exchanged solely for one other item of property. At least one of the two or three exchange participants will wind up with two or more items of property.

Errors in Prior Years

Every owner of a property item has the tax burden of establishing his cost or other basis, as adjusted, at the time of disposition of that item. This is because gain or loss is determined at time of disposition: not at time of acquisition. The longer the holding period between acquisition and disposition, the greater the likelihood of errors creeping into the adjustment processes. Some errors are made in the plus adjustments, such as expensing improvements while simultaneously adding them to basis. Most errors, however, are made in the minus adjustments, such as for depreciation (Sec. 167), amortization (Sec. 197), and depletion (Sec. 611). Depreciation, amortization, and depletion are statutorily allowable current-year deductions for those property items regularly used in an operating trade or business.

What often happens is that business property owners seek to accelerate current-year writeoffs. Doing so, reduces their otherwise taxable income for that year. Then, when the property is disposed of, they are taken aback by the "allowed or allowable" rule affecting adjustments to basis. (Recall the emphasized wording in Section 1016(a)(2) . . . starting at the bottom of page 2-13.)

The allowed-or-allowable rule says that if you take more depreciation, amortization, or depletion than statutorily allowed, your adjusted basis in that item is reduced below that which it would be otherwise. If you take less than the statutorily allowed amount, your adjusted basis in that item is penalized by an additional subtraction for the amount allowed which you did not take. In other words, without realizing it, you could have permitted errors to creep into your adjusted basis computations. All such errors have to be corrected at time of disposition of each property item.

The IRS (and the courts) take the position that the correction of basis errors extends all the way back to acquisition of the property by the current owner-disposer. Hence, the general rule applicable is: ***Allowed or allowable since acquisition.*** This is your cue that proving your adjusted basis at time of disposition should not be taken lightly.

3

SECTION 1031 OVERVIEW

The Grand Model Of Tax-Free Exchanging Is Section 1031. It Addresses LIKE-KIND Capital Assets Which Are Reciprocally Exchanged For Continued Use In A Trade, Business, Or Investment. The Term "Like Kind" Refers To CHARACTER Or CLASS, And Not To Grade Or Quality. Candidate Assets Are [1] Real Estate (Land, Farms, Mines, Buildings), [2] Depreciable Tangibles (Vehicles, Machinery, Equipment), And [3] Other Property. There Is A 45/180-Day TIME CONSTRAINT. ... No Exceptions. Basis Transfers, Market Valuations, Deferred Gain, Debt Encumbrances, And Commissions And Costs Are Computational Challenges.

The concepts behind a tax-free exchange go back as far as 1927. That year was the first recorded court ruling on point. The case was that of *K.A. Spalding*, 7 BTA 588, Dec. 2601 (Acq.). [***Ed. Note***: The "BTA" is Board of Tax Appeals; the "Dec." is Decision number; the "Acq." means Acquiesced (agreed to) by the IRS.] The BTA (predecessor of the present-day U.S. Tax Court) ruled in part as follows:

> *To constitute an exchange, there must be a* ***reciprocal transfer of properties*** *as distinguished from the transfer of property for money. In an exchange, neither principal would pay a commission to the other, although if a broker negotiated the exchange for either principal, the fact that he was paid a*

> *commission for his services would not of itself classify the transaction as other than an exchange.* [Emphasis added.]

In 1939, the IRS incorporated the reciprocal transfer concept into its now Regulation § 1.1002-1: ***Sales or Exchanges***. This regulation stresses that, unless the property transaction meets the strict conditions of a qualified exchange, it would be regarded as a sale: not as an exchange. In addition, the regulation espouses that:

> *The underlying purpose of an exchange must be germane to, and a necessary incident of, the investment or enterprise in hand. The assumption is that the new property is* ***substantially a continuation*** *of the old investment still unliquidated . . . or of the old enterprise still unliquidated.* [Emphasis added.]

One of the first sections of the current Tax Code to embrace the reciprocity and continuity concepts of an exchange is Section 1031. Its title is: ***Exchange of Property Held for Productive Use or Investment***. As we pointed out in Figure 1.2, its short title is: ***Like-Kind Exchanges***. Accordingly, in this chapter we want to overview Section 1031 with you, and select from it those highlights which best represent the underlying features of a qualified exchange. As we point out the highlights to you, you'll conclude on your own that Section 1031 is indeed the genesis for all other exchange laws. If you grasp the significant characteristics of Section 1031, you'll have a good handle on the features involved in Sections 1032 through 1045.

Prelude to Section 1031

The general rule pertaining to gain or loss on the disposition of property is Section 1001. That section is titled: ***Determination of Amount of and Recognition of Gain or Loss***. The portion of this rule that is pertinent here is its subsection (c): ***Recognition of Gain or Loss***. This 30-word subsection reads in full:

> ***Except as otherwise provided*** *in this subtitle* [Subtitle A — Income Taxes], *the entire amount of the gain or loss,*

determined under this section, on the sale or exchange of property ***shall be recognized.*** [Emphasis added.]

The point in Section 1001(c) is that unless some other specific section of the tax code applies to the contrary, gain or loss shall be recognized on any disposition of property. This is the fallback position the IRS and the courts take, when the validity of a tax-free exchange is questioned. Furthermore, both the IRS and the courts have taken the position that, unless a sale or exchange involves a capital asset, the entire gain will be treated as *ordinary income*: not as capital gain. So be forewarned.

The first exception to Section 1001(c) is Section 1031. This section relates to the **nonrecognition** of gain when like-kind business/investment properties are exchanged. Section 1031 consists of just over 2,000 statutory words. These 2,000 words are backed up by 115 pages (approximately 8,000 words) of regulations and rulings. This amount of interpretive backup is necessary to assure that those property dispositions which purport to be an exchange are indeed compliant with the provisions of Section 1031. It is because of these supportive rulings that Section 1031 is now regarded as a model of what any tax-qualified exchange should be.

Section 1031 is embodied in the Internal Revenue Code (1986 version) under Subchapter 0: ***Gain or Loss on Disposition of Property***, Part III thereof: *Common Nontaxable Exchanges.* It consists of eight subsections — (a) through (h). For overview purposes, we list in Figure 3.1 the captions of these eight subsections and their numbered paragraphs. We urge that you take a moment now to read through the list of captions. It will give you an overall sense of what is involved in a Section 1031 exchange. The theme that seems to come through is that there are three kinds of 1031 exchanges. These are: (1) like-kind exchanges, (2) nonlike-kind exchanges, and (3) exchanges between related persons.

Particularly note in Figure 3.1 paragraph (2) of subsection (a): ***Exceptions.*** The gist here is that certain property items (mostly intangibles) are expressly excluded from Section 1031. The inference is that other exchange sections of the tax code may apply, but not Section 1031. We'll address the more common of these "other exchange sections" in subsequent chapters.

Section 1031		EXCHANGE OF PROPERTY HELD FOR PRODUCTIVE USE OR INVESTMENT
Subsec.	Para.	Caption
(a)		Nonrecognition of Gain or Loss From EXCHANGES SOLELY IN KIND
	(1)	In General
	(2)	Exceptions
	(3)	Requirement Property be Identified, etc.
(b)		Gain from Exchanges **NOT SOLELY IN KIND**
(c)		Loss from Exchanges **NOT SOLELY IN KIND**
(d)		**BASIS OF PROPERTY ACQUIRED ON EXCHANGE**
(e)		Exchanges of Livestock of Different Sexes
(f)		Special Rules for Exchanges **BETWEEN RELATED PARTIES**
	(1)	In General
	(2)	Certain Dispositions Not Taken Into Account
	(3)	Related Person
	(4)	Treatment of Certain Transactions
(g)		Special Rules Where **SUBSTANTIAL DIMINUTION OF RISK**
	(1)	In General
	(2)	Property to Which Subsection Applies
(h)		Special Rules for **FOREIGN REAL AND PERSONAL PROPERTY**
	(1)	Real Property
	(2)	Personal Property

Fig. 3.1 - Overview Contents of IRC Section 1031

The First 50 Words

As already mentioned, Section 1031 consists of about 2,000 words. We definitely are not going to cite all of the 2,000 tax-legal words. We'll cite only those which are meaningful, informative, and comprehensible. In this regard, our first citation is subsection (a), Paragraph (1). We'll cite its 50 words in full. Then, we'll dissect it in a way that brings out the wisdom of why tax-freeness makes economic sense.

Subsection 1031(a) is captioned: ***Nonrecognition of Gain or Loss from Exchanges Solely in Kind.*** Its paragraph (1), general rule, reads—

> *No gain or loss shall be recognized on the exchange of property held for productive use in a trade or business or for investment if such property is exchanged solely for property of like kind which is to be held* ***either*** *for productive use in a trade or business or for investment.*

From your reading of these 50 words, what appears to be the qualifying essence for nonrecognition of capital gain?

Answer: There are three fundamental requirements, namely—

1. A reciprocal transfer of business or investment properties;
2. The properties must be "solely of like kind"; and
3. Either a business or an investment must continue after the exchange.

If these and other conditions are met, and a capital gain is realized, the tax on the gain is deferred until some later transaction not involving a qualified exchange. How does this arrangement make economic sense, when we all know that the preeminent role of the IRS is to assess tax and collect revenue at every opportunity it can? "Every opportunity" does not mean: right now.

Section 1031 makes sense because, sooner or later, tax on the deferred capital gain will be assessed . . . and collected. The tax-freeness is temporary only. It is not forever. We have pointed out this fact several times previously.

Section 1031 makes economic sense in another more practical way. The function of the IRS is not to put ethical entrepreneurs out of business. As long as some form of productive business or investment continues after the exchange, the IRS still collects other forms of tax from those who participate in the ongoing business or investment. Were the capital gain fully taxed at the time of an exchange, the business or investment would either discontinue, or, if continued, would do so in substantially reduced form. Any reduction in business activity automatically reduces other forms of taxes that the IRS can collect. Hence, both the property exchanger and the IRS mutually benefit.

Meaning of "Like Kind"

Section 1031(a)(1) applies to exchanges of properties which are *solely . . . of like kind.* Nowhere in Section 1031 itself is the term "like kind" specifically defined. Hence, there is a need for some regulation or ruling. Fortunately, the term is defined in Regulation § 1.1031(a)–1(b): ***Definition of "like kind"***.

This pertinent regulation reads—

> *As used in section 1031(a), the words "like kind" have reference to the* ***nature or character*** *of the property and not to its grade or quality. One kind or class of property may not be exchanged for property of a different kind or class. The fact that any real estate involved is improved or unimproved is not material.* [Such] *fact relates only to the grade or quality of the property and not to its kind or class.*

For the purpose of like-kind exchanges, property is divided into three broad classes. There are—

Class I — Real property (land and its improvements)

Class II — Depreciable tangible personal property, and

Class III — Other personal property (intangible, non-depreciable, etc.)

Shortly below, we'll expand on the kinds of property considered like-kind within each of these three classes. Needless to say, there are subclasses within each class.

Meanwhile, subsection (e): ***Exchanges of Livestock of Different Sexes***, says—

> *For purposes of this section* [Section 1031], *livestock of different sexes are not property of a like kind.*

And subsection (h): ***Special Rules for Foreign Real and Personal Property***, says—

(1) Real property located in the U.S. and real property located outside of the U.S. are not property of a like kind.

(2) Personal property used predominantly within the U.S. and personal property used predominantly outside the U.S. are not property of a like kind.

Furthermore, as per paragraph (2) of subsection (a), the like-kind exchange rules do **not** apply to—

(1) stock in trade [such as inventory] or other property held primarily for sale to customers;
(2) stocks, bonds, or notes of indebtedness;
(3) other securities, or evidences of indebtedness or interest;
(4) [ownership] interests in a partnership;
(5) certificates of trust, or beneficial interests; and
(6) choses in action [contracts, covenants, and promises].

In other words, the primary focus of Section 1031 is on the exchanging of real and tangible property as opposed to intangible items. Both before and after an exchange, the property must be held either for productive use or for active investment.

Like-Kind Real Estate

It is not necessary that property held for productive use in a trade or business be exchanged solely for property held for productive use in continuing the former trade or business. Property held for productive use may be exchanged for investment property, OR investment property may be exchanged for productive use in a trade or business. Property recently acquired or constructed merely for the purpose of effecting a like-kind exchange is not treated as having been "held" for productive use. We try to clarify these options and nonoptions for you in Figure 3.2.

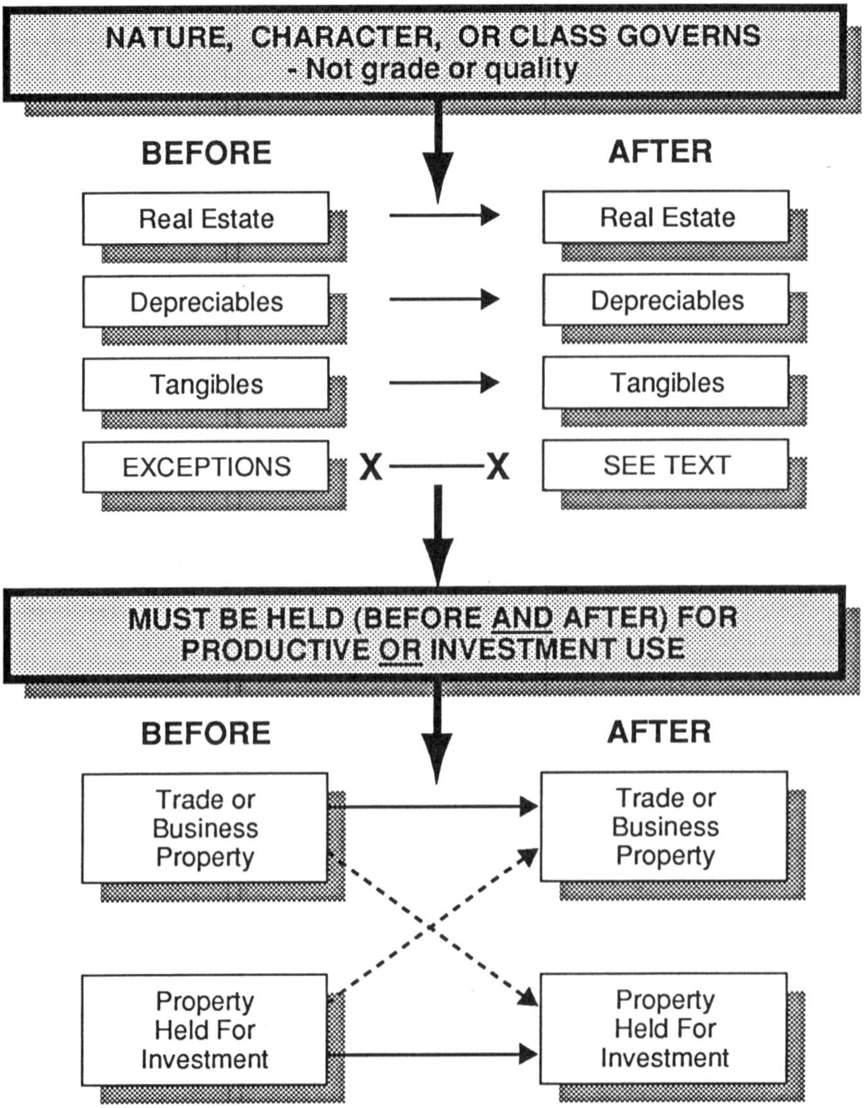

Fig. 3.2 - Qualifying Features for Like-Kind Property Exchanges

While not expressly stated in Section 1031, exchanges of real estate are more favored than other forms of property transfers. The rationale is that any parcel of real property is like kind with any other parcel of real property. This rationale holds irrespective of how dissimilar the properties may be in location (within the U.S.), in attributes (resources and improvements), or in capabilities for profitable use.

The only stickler in real estate exchanging is the form of legal title (ownership and use) of the properties. Whatever the titular form is before the exchange must continue after the exchange for the same owner(s) or user(s). The cleanest of titular forms is *fee simple.* Said title means indefinite ownership duration with absolute right of inheritance under state law where the realty is located. If a property owner (or owners) owns the real estate in fee simple before the exchange, he (or they) must own the exchange-acquired realty also in fee simple after the exchange. That is, the **rights** in the properties, and not just the properties themselves, must be similar and like kind.

In fee simple title transactions, the following types of real estate exchanges have qualified as like kind:

(1) Timberland containing some virgin timber and substantial stands of second growth timber for timberland containing only virgin timber.
(2) Timberland for bare land.
(3) Real estate in a city for a farm or ranch.
(4) Undeveloped ranch land for a commercial building.
(5) A commercial building for commercial condominium offices.
(6) An apartment building for vacant land plus golf course improvements.
(7) A deep-water terminal facility for inland terminal sites along a pipeline.

[Ref: CCH Standard Federal Tax Reporter 2002, Vol. 12, pp. 54,636-65,639]

A leasehold interest with 30 years or more to run is of like kind to a fee simple interest in real property. Two leases of less than 30 years would also be like-kind property. A life estate in realty would qualify as like kind, if the exchange-acquired property were subject to a life estate interest or to a remainder (of life) interest. Like-kind treatment is also applicable to an exchange of one remainder interest for another remainder interest. In the case of natural resources, mineral rights, and gas and oil access, the question of whether the rights in the exchanged properties are similar, generally turns on whether the access and removal rights have the same (or approximately the same) duration. In all nonfee realty ownership forms, the treatment-equivalency under state law governs.

Like-Kind Tangible Property

Tangible property consists of vehicles, equipment, furnishings, and fixtures. There are two general types of such property: depreciable and nondepreciable. Depreciable property is that which is used in a trade or business. For such productive use, a current expense deduction for depreciation is allowed. In contrast, nondepreciable tangible property is that which is not used in a trade or business. Consequently, depreciable and nondepreciable tangible property items are nonexchangeable under the like-kind precepts of Section 1031. Depreciable property requires a negative adjustment to basis over time. Not so for nondepreciable items.

Depreciable tangible property items are exchangeable only if exchanged within the same asset or product class. That is, farm equipment for farm equipment: not for office equipment; heavy duty trucks for heavy duty trucks: not for passenger autos, etc. The IRS has gone to great lengths to categorize depreciable items into specific like-kind classes. The most common of these general asset classes are—

00.11	—	office furniture, fixtures, and equipment;
00.12	—	information systems (computers and peripheral equipment);
00.13	—	data handling equipment, except computers;
00.21	—	airplanes and helicopters (including airframes and engines), except those used in commercial or contract carrying of passengers or freight;
00.22	—	automobiles and taxis;
00.23	—	buses (passenger carrying);
00.241	—	light general purpose trucks;
00.242	—	heavy general purpose trucks;

00.25 — railroad cars and locomotives, except those owned by railroad transportation companies;
00.26 — tractor units for use over-the-road;
00.27 — trailers and trailer-mounted containers; and
00.28 — vessels, barges, tugs, and similar water transportation equipment, except those used in marine construction.

A depreciable property item that is not identified in an IRS asset class may, nevertheless, qualify as like kind in an exchange. For example, a sanding machine for a wood lathe; an old printing press for a new printing press; or an off-road tractor of one manufacturer for an off-road tractor of another manufacturer. Some common sense and practical business judgment has to be used.

The general rule for the like-kind attributes of nonclassified assets looks to the trade-in practices of dealers in such properties. Would a dealer in new and used heavy duty trucks accept a small private aircraft as a trade-in? Not likely. But a dealer in logging trucks and equipment might accept a helicopter as a trade-in, if the helicopter could be used for timber logging in inaccessible terrain. To determine whether depreciable tangible property is like kind, all pertinent facts and circumstances must be considered.

Like-Kind Other Property

Property which is not real estate in nature and that which is not depreciable in business use is categorized as "other personal property." This category includes all property items (tangible, intangible, and nondepreciable) *held for investment*. Such items include patents, copyrights, player contracts, antiques, coin collections, works of art, etc. Because of the diversity of these items, no specific like-kind classes have been designated. The general rule thereon is that the like-kindness feature must be "quite like" . . . in a self-evident way.

Patents, copyrights, player contracts, etc. are tax-recognized forms of intangible personal property held for investment. The determination of like-kindness depends entirely on the underlying physical assets to which the intangibles relate. For example, a patent relates to the creation of a physical item which has mechanical, electrical, chemical, and other hardware-type properties. A copyright relates to the creation of a magazine article, a book, an artistic painting, or composition of music. A player contract is a binding arrangement between players and club owners participating in professional sports (football, ice hockey, basketball, etc.) For any of these intangibles to be tax free, the exchange must relate to the type of underlying assets represented by each intangible.

For example, a patent would not be tax-free exchangeable for a copyright, nor a copyright for a player contract. A patent on an airplane part could be exchanged for a patent on a different airplane part, but not for a patent on an automobile part. A copyright on a book novel could be exchanged for a copyright on a different book novel, but not for a copyright on a song or piece of music. A football payer contract could be exchanged for a different football club, but not for an ice hockey player contract. Do you see the "quite-like" point?

Nondepreciable personal property items include antiques, works of art, coin collections, stamp collections, gun collections, etc. If the physical nature of the items intended for exchange is quite similar, the arrangement may qualify under Section 1031. The premise would be that the items are being held solely as an investment. But subtle differences can arise to make the exchange taxable instead of nontaxable.

Consider the matter of bullion-type gold coins and numismatic-type gold coins. They are both gold coins. Are they tax-free exchangeable? No; they are not of like kind. Why not?

The value of numismatic-type coins is determined by age, mint, history, art, aesthetics, condition, and metal content. In contrast, the value of bullion-type coins is determined solely on the basis of metal content. For example, a U.S. $20 gold coin has numismatic value. In contrast, a South African Krugerrand and a Canadian Maple Leaf gold coin are valued for their gold content alone. Krugerrands and Maple Leafs can be exchanged tax free, but not with U.S. $20 gold pieces. Similarly, gold coins and silver coins are not like kind. Silver is primarily an industrial commodity, whereas gold, while used in jewelry and dentistry, is held primarily for investment.

In way of summarizing the above, we present in Figure 3.3 the key tests for assessing the like-kindness of real estate, tangible, property, and other property items.

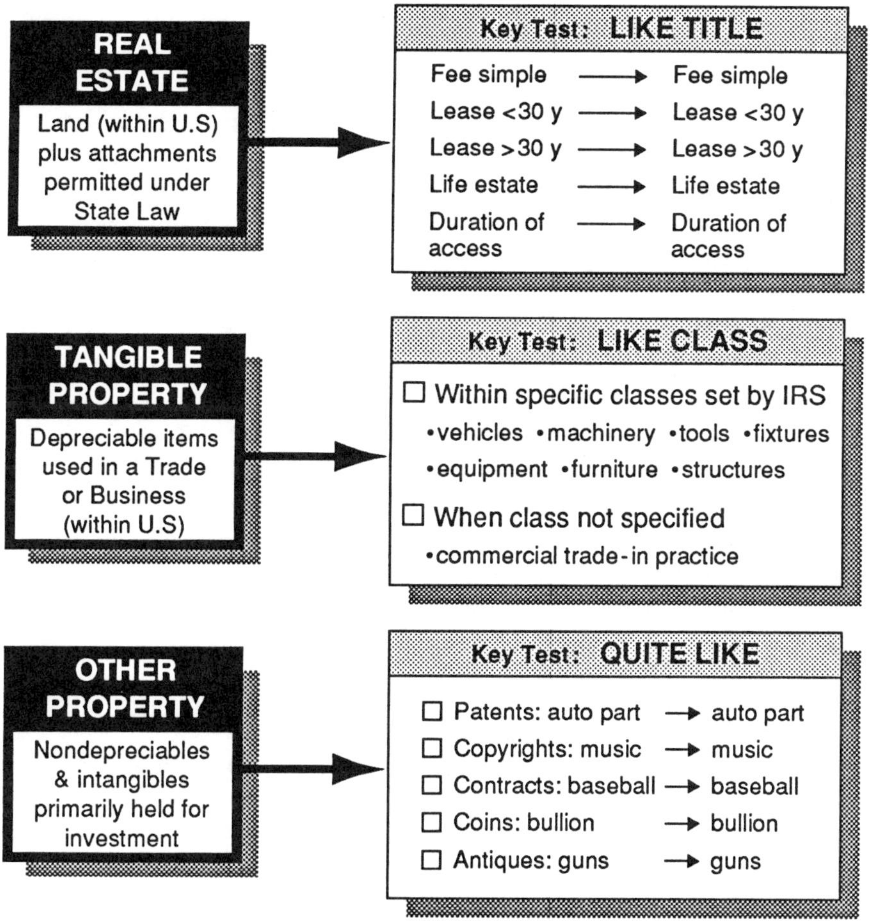

Fig. 3.3 - Key Tests for Determining the Like-Kindness of Properties

Exchange of Similar Businesses

Glancing again at Figure 3.3, other than the like-kind aspects, what other common features are present? They are implied from our discussion above, but they are not self-evident.

There are two common features in a "pure" like-kind exchange. First of all, a pure exchange deals with a *single* asset or single class of assets. And, secondly, such an exchange addresses *capital* assets. Only a capital asset experiences capital gain or capital loss upon its disposition. This is the basic premise upon which Section 1031 relies. Noncapital assets do not participate in the 1031 benefits. Other tax rules apply to such assets.

Suppose, now, you exchange two small businesses which are very similar in nature. For example, a hardware store for a hardware store, or a TV station for a TV station. The exchange-acquired property is in a different location from the exchange-conveyed property. Otherwise, the operation and customers of each business exchange are similar. Would such a transaction constitute a pure exchange?

Answer: No, it would not. It might not even qualify as a partial exchange. Here's why.

A business is treated as a basket of multiple assets. Some of the assets may be of like kind with those exchanged; some may not be like kind at all. In either case, some will be capital assets and some will be noncapital assets. Almost any ongoing business will have between five and ten separate categories of assets.

For example, a small business could consist of—

1. Land or leasehold thereon,
2. Building and structures or a lease thereof,
3. Furniture and fixtures,
4. Vehicular equipment,
5. Nonvehicular equipment,
6. Accounts receivable,
7. Customer lists,
8. Systems in place (computers, personnel, supplies),
9. Covenant not to compete, and
10. Goodwill and going concern value.

While all of these assets count in the valuation process for achieving FMV equality of the exchange, they are not all of like kind. Accounts receivable, for example, is an ordinary income asset; it is not subject to Section 1031 rules. Where similar businesses are in two different geographic locations, the customer lists and goodwill (both of which are capital assets) are not of like kind. There are other nonlike aspects also.

In an exchange of similar businesses, the IRS has ruled (Rev. Rul. 89-121) that the two businesses must be examined and compared on an *asset-by-asset* basis. Under Section 1031, it is not enough that the businesses be similar in nature. This asset-by-asset analysis requires compliance with Section 1060.

Section 1060 is titled: ***Special Allocation Rules for Certain Asset Acquisitions***. Its general rule, subsection (a) encourages allocation by agreement between the parties. It reads—

> *In the case of any applicable asset acquisition, for purposes of determining both—*
>
> *(1) The transferee's basis in such assets, and*
> *(2) the gain or loss of the transferor with respect to such acquisition,*
>
> *the consideration received for such assets shall be allocated among such assets* . . . [in accordance with what] *the transferee and transferor agree in writing as to the allocation of any consideration* . . .

Here, the term "consideration" includes money, property other than money (preferably of like kind), swapping of debt liabilities, and nonlike property items which are readily marketable.

The premise on which Section 1060 rests is the involvement of multiple assets in any sale or exchange of a business operation. Matters can get very complicated indeed. We'll expose you to the complications in chapters which follow.

Exchange Time Constraints

Section 1031(a)(1) uses the term . . . ***on** the exchange of property* . . . etc. For years, the IRS has interpreted this term to mean an "immediate exchange." The term "immediate" was meant to be that period of time comparable to the ordinary time for closing a sale. Without the tax-free rules to follow, most property sales are concluded within 30, 60, or 90 days, and, occasionally, 120 days. If an exchange required more time than this, the IRS held that the nonrecognition provisions of Section 1031 did not apply.

As the tax-free benefits of property exchanges became more widespread, and as multi-party and multi-asset exchanges became more common, the IRS's position was court tested many times. The most famous of such test cases was that of *B. Starker* (CA-9, 79-2 USTC ¶ 9541). In this landmark case, the Ninth Circuit Court of Appeals ruled that Starker's 5-year replacement of property contract qualified under Section 1031. The court reasoned that where there are bona fide difficulties in finding like-kind replacement properties, the IRS's insistence on an immediate exchange was unreasonable. Needless to say, the Starker case encouraged the testing of other time periods less than five years, but of more than 120 days.

Finally, in 1984, Congress and the IRS got their heads together to amend Section 1031. They did so by adding a new paragraph (3). The new paragraph is titled: ***Requirement that property be identified and that exchange be completed not more than 180 days after transfer of exchanged property*** [Sec. 1031(a)(3)].

The substance of Section 1031(a)(3) is that: (A) the property to be received must be identified within 45 days after the property conveyed is transferred, and (B) the property to be received is indeed received within the *earlier* of (i) 180 days, or (ii) the due date (including extensions) of the tax return reporting the exchange. For visualization purposes, a synopsis of these time constraints is presented in Figure 3.4.

If the Figure 3.4 time constraints are not met,

> *. . . any property received by the taxpayer* ***shall be treated*** *as property which is* ***not*** *like-kind property.* [Emphasis added.]

There are no exceptions. So do not waste your money going into court seeking a way around the 45/180-day replacement rule. If no suitable replacement property can be acquired within the 45/180-day period, the transaction will be treated as a sale . . . and taxed accordingly.

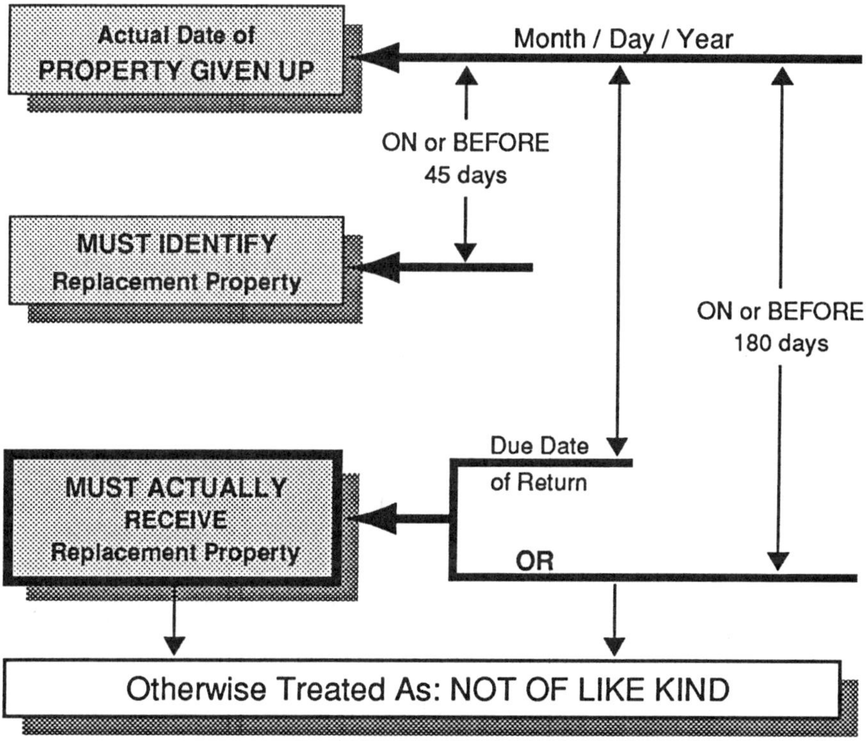

Fig. 3.4 - Visual Depiction of Time Constraints for a 1031 Exchange

Basis in Property Received

In Chapter 2: Importance of "Tax Basis," we tried to prepare you for the adjustments to make to the like-kind property that you acquire in a 1031 exchange. We synopsized this for you in Figure 2.3. You may want to take a moment and glance back at Figure 2.3: it is on page 2-13. We just want you to get the sense of what is expected of you, after the exchange is financially complete. Again, we remind you that our focus in this chapter is on like-kind or "pure" (solely in kind) exchanges.

The particular portion of Section 1031 that addresses basis matters is subsection (d): ***Basis***. It consists of about 200 words. The first 65 of these words (one sentence) addresses pure exchanges; the remaining 135 words address partial exchanges. We'll cover partial 1031 exchanges in our next chapter.

The bulk of the first sentence in subsection 1031(d) reads—

> *If property was acquired on an exchange described in this section, . . . then the basis* ***shall be the same*** *as that of the property exchanged,* ***decreased*** *in the amount of any money received by the taxpayer and* ***increased*** *in the amount of gain that was recognized on such exchange.* [Emphasis added.]

The "shall be the same" clause means that the adjusted basis-old is transferred directly to the property acquired, to become its starting basis. From this point on, the basis in the exchange-acquired property is adjusted up or down depending on the tax and financial considerations involved. If you receive money in the exchange, the new-start basis is decreased. This generally happens when you exchange down. If you pay money in the exchange, the new-start basis is increased. This generally happens when you exchange up.

In virtually every 1031 exchange, money or other consideration changes hands. Other consideration may consist of (i) property not of like kind; (ii) the effect of debt, mortgages, and liens; and (iii) the effect of commissions and expenses. Rarely is an exchange so pure that no "other consideration" is involved.

Effect of Debts & Liens

Most property worthy of 1031 exchange effort involves real estate or natural resources. These capital assets tend to be debt encumbered with personal loans, mortgages, and liens. If the property of both exchangers is similarly debt encumbered, the usual practice is to "swap the debt" reciprocally. In such case, one of the exchangers winds up with net debt relief; the other winds up with new debt assumption. Where there is net debt relief, the arrangement is treated as money received (basis reduction). Where there is new debt assumption, the arrangement is treated as money paid (basis increase). For the unwary, debt swapping can sometimes lead to being a victim of money laundering.

The concept of debt exchange in Section 1031(d) is addressed in Regulation § 1.1031(d)-2: ***Treatment of assumption of liabilities.*** The substance of this regulation is that—

> *The amount of any liabilities of the taxpayer assumed by the other party to the exchange . . . is to be treated as money received by the taxpayer upon the exchange.* [This holds] *whether or not the assumption resulted in a recognition of gain or loss to the taxpayer.*

Let us exemplify the net effect of the swapping of debt. Suppose that Owner A had a total encumbrance on his property of $535,000 [$35,000 secured personal loan; $450,000 mortgage; and a $50,000 federal tax lien]. In the like-kind exchange, Owner A acquired Owner B's property which had a total encumbrance on it of $465,000. The net result of this debt swapping is that Owner A received debt relief to the extent of $70,000 [535,000 – 465,000]. This net debt relief *reduces* Owner A's basis in Property B by $70,000.

Owner B, on the other hand, has assumed $70,000 of additional debt on Property A. This *increases* his capital basis in Property A. That is, whatever was his adjusted basis in Property B, his basis in the exchange-acquired Property A is his basis in Property B . . . PLUS $70,000 (of new debt assumed).

In Figure 3.5, we illustrate the reciprocal effects of basis transferring and debt swapping. Of course, we have oversimplified the schematic aspects of an exchange. But wait until we get to Chapter 6: A True-Life 1031 Example. There, you'll see how simple concepts can become computationally complex.

Effect of Commissions, Etc.

Even though like-kind exchanges of property may be tax free, they are never commission free or expense free. In every like-kind exchange, there are two sellers . . . and two commissions. There is Exchanger A who becomes Seller A when he relinquishes Property A and acquires Property B. Similarly, there is Exchanger B who becomes Seller B when he relinquishes Property B to acquire Property A. For tax, legal, and contractual reasons, all Section 1031 exchanges are transacted through a licensed broker, an established title company, or some attorney overseeing the settlement process. These intermediaries are third parties (persons or entities) who

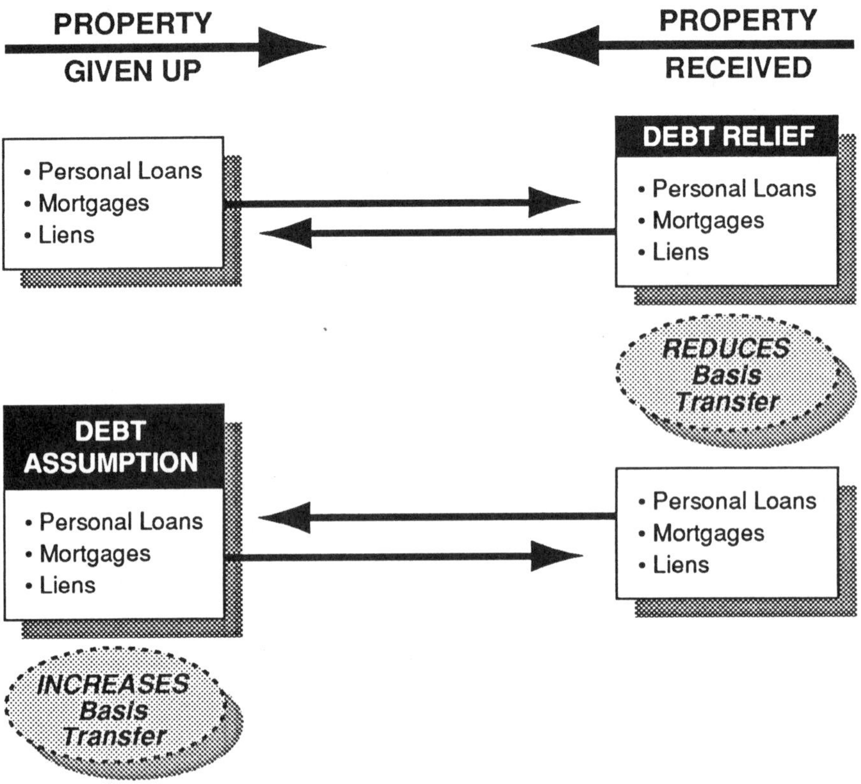

Fig. 3.5 - The "Basis Effect" of Reciprocal Exchange of Debt

facilitate the exchange and to whom commissions, fees, and other costs are paid. He who pays the commissions, etc. includes them in his exchange computations.

A "commission" is an agreed percentage of the FMV (Fair Market Value) of the property being sold/exchanged. A "fee" is a stated amount for the rendering of professional services, such as appraisals, inspections, geological surveys, tax advice, and accounting. A "cost" is any other expenditure (title search, credit report, loan fee, secretarial effort, recording fees, photocopying, mailing, etc.) necessary for closing the deal. How these items play out in the exchange computations depends on who pays them. There is no swapping of these commissions and costs as in the case of debt assumptions.

In every 1031 exchange where a commission, fee, or cost is paid by a party to the exchange, the aggregate amount affects the computation of:

(1) the amount realized in the exchange;
(2) the amount of gains tax recognized (if any) by the exchange; and
(3) the basis of the property acquired as a result of the exchange.

An Illustrative Example

As an illustration of what we are getting at, consider that you own 10 acres of prime agricultural land (FMV'd at $350,000) which you exchange for two acres of residentially-zoned land (FMV'd at $285,000). You receive $65,000 cash out of the deal (to equalize the two FMVs). Simultaneously, you pay out $25,000 in commission, fees, and costs. Your adjusted basis in the 10 acres of agricultural land is $250,000. How does all this play out in computations (1), (2), and (3) above?

Computation (1) is the amount you realize in the transaction. The commission, etc. paid show up as follows:

	FMV of land received	$285,000
	Cash received	65,000
		350,000
	LESS	
	Commission, etc. paid	<25,000>
(1)	Amount realized	$325,000

Computation (2) is the amount of gain realized that is tax recognized. This happens most often when you exchange down (as in our example). The amount of gain recognized is the **lesser** of gain realized or net cash received. The computations proceed as follows:

Amount realized	$325,000
LESS	

	Basis in land conveyed	<250,000>
	Gain realized	75,000
		- - - - - - -
	Net cash received ($65,000 received – $25,000 commission paid)	40,000
(2)	Gain recognized . . . the LESSER OF	$ 40,000

Computation (3) relates to the new-start basis of the property acquired. The computation goes like this—

	Basis in land conveyed	$250,000
	LESS	
	Cash received	<65,000>
		185,000
	PLUS	
	Gain recognized in (2) above	40,000
	PLUS	
	Commission, etc. paid	25,000
(3)	Basis in land acquired	$250,000

Instead of an exchange down as illustrated above (350,000 FMV ⟶ 285,000 FMV), suppose you had exchanged up (350,000 FMV ⟶ 415,000 FMV). In this case, instead of receiving $65,000 in cash, you would have *paid* $65,000 in cash (415,000 – 350,000). No part of the gain realized would be tax recognized: the "lesser of" result. Therefore, your basis in the land acquired would be: $250,000 (basis in land conveyed), **plus** $65,000 (cash paid), **plus** $25,000 (commission paid), for a new basis start of $340,000.

4

PARTIAL 1031 EXCHANGES

The First Effort In A 1031 Transaction Is To "Balance The Equities" (Investments At Risk) Between Like-Kind Properties. This Necessitates The Use Of CASH And BOOT. "Boot" Consists Of Promises To Pay Money Plus Nonlike Property Fair Market Valued. Often A Portion Of The Cash And Boot PLUS Net Debt Relief Is Taxed As RECOGNIZED GAIN. The Recognized Gain Is Subtracted From REALIZED GAIN To Become DEFERRED GAIN Which "Floats In The Air." When The Process Is Finalized, Basis In The New Property Has To Be Established. All Tax Accounting Is Reported To The IRS On Form 8824: LIKE-KIND EXCHANGES.

Not all Section 1031 exchanges involve pure like-kind properties. It would be rare indeed for the exchange of property A to be an equal-value match with property B, or that the debt encumbrances on properties A and B would be equal, or that the commissions and exchange costs would be shared equally between the exchangers. In real life situations, nonlike property and money are required to make the exchange "go." There has to be some equalizing facilitation (money and/or other property) to make the exchange mathematically fair and balanced. In those situations, the 1031 process is called: *Exchanges not solely in kind.* They are also called: *Partial 1031 exchanges.*

In other words, a partial 1031 exchange consists of two distinct property classes: like-kind and nonlike-kind. The like-kind exchange arrangement is tax free, whereas the nonlike arrangement is not tax free. If any gain results from the nonlike activities, it is taxed. The overall effect is that of **two** separate, commingled, property exchanges taking place concurrently.

Subsections (b) and (c) of Section 1031 come into play at this point. Subsection 1031(b) is captioned: ***Gain from Exchanges not Solely in Kind***, whereas subsection 1031(c) is captioned: ***Loss from Exchanges not Solely in Kind***. There are extensive and illustrative regulations covering both of these subsections. We are not going to cite any of these regulations for you. Instead, in this chapter we want to acquaint you with the computational fine points of partial exchanges, present some illustrations, and discuss how to report the results on Form 8824, Part III: ***Realized Gain or (Loss), Recognized Gain, and Basis of Like-Kind Property Received***.

Role & Definition of "Boot"

To truly grasp the computational aspects of a 1031 exchange, you must understand the role and definition of "boot." The term is often used loosely to mean anything and everything required to close the exchange transaction, other than the like-kind properties themselves. The narrower view treats boot as nonlike property (other than cash). Cash stands alone, as either party may give cash or receive cash. Cash is a fixed-value item for which, in and of itself, there is no capital gain or capital loss potential. In contrast, nonlike property (including promises to pay money) may be subject to capital gain (which **is** taxed) or it may be subject to capital loss (which *may be* tax recognized). Boot and cash, in essence, are the equalizers of equities between the like-kind properties being exchanged.

Boot (as well as cash) can be given, and boot (as well as cash) can be received. Therefore, it is important to distinguish between the transferor of boot and the recipient of boot. Usually, the transferor of boot is the party who is acquiring like-kind property greater in value than the like-kind property he is conveying. But this generality falls apart when basis matters and debt encumbrances on either or both of the like-kind properties are involved.

Perhaps a simple illustration will clarify the true role of boot. As a transferor of boot, you offer a parcel of land worth $100,000 and shares of stock worth $60,000 for a parcel of land worth $160,000. Neither parcel of land is encumbered with debt. Your basis in the $100,000 parcel is $100,000. Your realized gain (before tax) in this situation is $60,000 [$160,000 of acquired property minus $100,000 basis in conveyed property]. This $60,000 gain, being from nonlike property (the shares of stock), is fully taxable. Once the tax on the $60,000 is separately reported and paid, your basis in the acquired property is increased to $160,000 (from $100,000 originally).

Instead of offering stock as boot, you offered another parcel of land (probably smaller than your $100,000 parcel) worth $60,000 (which is also your basis therein). Since the second parcel of land is like-kind with the acquired parcel of land (worth $160,000), no gain is tax recognized in the exchange. There is no boot involved.

Now back to the $60,000 shares of stock as boot. Suppose your basis in the stock is $80,000. As a separate capital asset of its own (totally aside from the exchange transaction), you have a capital loss of $20,000 [$60,000 "sale" proceeds minus $80,000 basis]. Is this loss tax recognized?

Answer: Yes . . . as an investment capital asset. But suppose, instead of stock, the $60,000 boot was a luxury motor home personally used by you and your family. You paid $80,000 for it. Would the $20,000 capital loss be tax recognized?

Answer: No . . . a capital loss on personally used property is never tax recognized. Yet, such property is perfectly qualifiable as boot, provided it is acceptable to the recipient of the boot.

In short, boot is *nonlike property other than cash.* It may consist of a tangible item (vehicle, equipment, or set of golf clubs) or an intangible item (promissory note, service contract, or franchise right), or a combination of both. Whether tangible or intangible, the boot must be capable of being fair market valued. The recipient may want to convert the boot into money, immediately after the exchange.

In every qualified 1031 transaction, certain common terms are used for computational purposes. So that all readers have a common reference, we present in Figure 4.1 some of the basic terms used in this chapter. A quick glance at them now may be helpful, if you are not already familiar with 1031 tax jargon.

TERM	DESCRIPTION
Property	Strictly like-kind only. May be real estate, structures, machinery, equipment, vehicles.
FMV	Fair Market Value. The equivalent in money when offered to the general public.
Debt	Existing on the like-kind properties: Mortgages, liens, trust deeds (unpaid balances).
Equity	FMV minus debt existing on like properties. Fundamental to exchange process.
Cash	Deposit towards principal only. Not to be confused with commissions, fees, costs, etc.
Promise(s)	To pay money towards principal only. Loan(s) acquired external to the properties exchanged.
Nonlike/Unlike	Other property items not solely in kind. Accepted by mutual agreement as to FMV.
Boot	Promise(s) of money & nonlike items which, together with cash, balance the like-kind property equities.
Exchange Expenses	Commissions, fees, costs, & other expenses for closing the exchange & quieting the titles.
Escrow	Documents held in trust by neutral agent until all financial and legal aspects of exchange are settled.
Gain Realized	True amount of economic gain that would have resulted, had the transaction been a sale.
Gain Recognized	The taxable portion of realized gain. May consist of ordinary gain & capital gain.
Gain Deferred	Capital gain portion only. Ordinary gain (if any) is immediately taxed (not deferred).

Fig. 4.1 - Basic Terms Associated With 1031 Exchanges

Balancing the Equities

In our comments above, we omitted any discussion about the effect of debt encumbrances on the determination of boot. The "debt" to which we are referring, of course, is that which is intrinsic (or existing on) the like-kind properties being exchanged. The real goal of boot is to balance the **equities** of the properties being exchanged: NOT their FMVs. The term "equity," as you know, is the FMV of each like-kind property being exchanged minus its corresponding debt encumbrance (mortgages, liens, deeds of trust). One's equity in property is the true sign of its worth.

Suppose that two candidate 1031 properties have equal FMVs — say, $100,000 each. Property A has a debt burden of $70,000 while property B has debt of only $20,000. Such being the case, the owners' equities in these properties would be widely unequal: $30,000 in property A versus $80,000 in property B. Would owner B who has $80,000 of investment at risk be satisfied with replacing this amount with a $30,000 at-risk property? Doesn't make economic sense, does it? Owner B wants a more level economic package than this. Here's where boot and cash come into their own.

In Figure 4.2, we present in step-wise fashion the computational aspects for the balancing of equities between two like-kind properties, A and B. Note that there are seven steps required. We suggest that you read down these steps, one at a time. Particularly note the nomenclature at steps 2 and 5: *Intrinsic* debt and *Extrinsic* debt. Intrinsic debt is that which already exists on the properties at the time of the exchange. Verification of the exact dollar balances owing on these debts (if any) is essential. So, too, is verification — by professional appraisers — of the FMVs of the candidate properties. Only after the true FMV and intrinsic debt of each property is known can the exact amount of equalizing boot be established.

Extrinsic debt is money borrowed, or a promise to pay money, without encumbering the like-kind property itself. It is distinguished from cash in that cash is an immediate payment of money from one or more after-tax financial accounts of the property exchanger. Note in Figure 4.2 that steps 4, 5, and 6 comprise (respectively) cash, extrinsic debt, and nonlike property. We treat all three of these items as boot (for the time being). Subsequently, we'll use the term "cash and boot" to more narrowly imply that cash and boot are two different things. Step 4 is only that amount of cash necessary for fine-tune balancing the equities between the properties being exchanged. It is the amount of cash deposited towards principal. Step 4 has nothing to do with broker commissions, miscellaneous exchange expenses, and title closing costs. These items come later.

With Figure 4.2 as our outline, let us provide simple numbers to illustrate how the equity balancing process works. We present two cases: "X" for equal FMVs and "Y" for unequal FMVs. We

EQUITY COMPARISON: PROPERTY BY PROPERTY OF LIKE-KIND			
	Item	Amount	
		Property A	Property B
1.	FMV of Property Exchanged		
2.	Existing Debt [Intrinsic]	< >	< >
3.	Existing Equity (subtract 2 from 1)		
	AMOUNT OF BOOT NEEDED		
4.	Cash deposit		
5.	Promises of money [Extrinsic]		
6.	Nonlike property (FMV)		
7.	EQUITIES AS BALANCED		

Fig. 4.2 - Steps for Balancing Equities Between Exchanged Properties

display in Figure 4.3 the computations of boot that result. You can use other numbers of your choice. You need to establish the amount of cash and boot required — by both parties to the exchange — before going forward computationally. In this chapter, we focus on single-property exchange only. In Chapter 5, we'll address multiple-property and multi-party exchanges.

Basis of Property Conveyed

In a 1031 two-party exchange, owner A conveys his property to owner B. In return, owner A receives replacement property from owner B. For obvious reasons, the exchange transaction does not actually occur until all the financials are worked out (cash and boot, FMVs, verification of debt, exchange expenses) and all title procedures under state law have been fulfilled. Once the exchange transaction is legally closed, owners A and B need share no further information with each other. Each is thereafter on his own, insofar as tax accounting and reporting to the IRS are concerned.

Tax accounting on the exchange event starts with the basis of the property conveyed. Basis, as we explained in Chapter 2, is the benchmark of reference for establishing the amount of capital gain

	Item	CASE "X" Equal FMVs		CASE "Y" Unequal FMVs	
		Prop. A	Prop. B	Prop. A	Prop. B
1.	Like-kind FMVs	100,000	100,000	140,000	100,000
2.	Existing Debt	<60,000>	<20,000>	<100,000>	<40,000>
3.	Existing Equities	40,000	80,000	40,000	60,000
4.	Cash Down	3,000			10,000
5.	Promise of Money	20,000		60,000	
6.	Other Nonlike	17,000			30,000
7.	Equities in Balance	80,000	80,000	100,000	100,000

Fig. 4.3 - Numerical Illustration of the Equity Balancing Process

that resulted from the exchange. Owner A has no interest in, nor responsibility for, owner B's basis in property B, which is now in the possession of owner A. Owner A, however, is responsible for establishing (to the satisfaction of the IRS) his basis in property A that was conveyed to owner B. This is where all of the tax accounting begins (for owner A).

In Chapter 2, we stressed the importance of cumulatively trading all adjustments to basis, "allowed or allowable," over time. This tracking starts with the acquisition of property A: often called "cost or other basis" or, simply, initial basis. Adjustments for capital improvements, depreciation, depletion (of natural resources), withdrawal of capital, etc., are conscientiously made. For this purpose, adequate backup worksheets and records should be gathered up and organized.

Your basis data should then be summarized. Do so as follows:

1. Description of property conveyed
2. Acquisition date ____________
3. How acquired (by purchase, gift, inheritance, prior exchange, foreclosure, or other)
4. Exchange date ____________
5. Initial basis $______________
6. Cumulative adjustments allowed or allowable $____________

7. Adjusted basis of property conveyed $__________
   [combine steps 5 and 6]

Overall Gain Realized

The computational aspects outlined in Figure 4.3 and above constitute the foundational phases for your post-exchange accounting. The real work starts when establishing the true amount of overall gain realized on the transaction. If your tax basis in the property conveyed is greater than the FMV of property received (both like kind and nonlike), you should realize actual gain. Part of the realized gain will be tax deferred and part may be tax recognized. It all depends on how the numbers fall out. Some of the gain may be ordinary income (we'll explain later) and some may be capital gain. Only when there is a net realized gain — capital gain, that is — does a Section 1031 exchange offer any benefits. We covered this point previously in Chapter 3.

The amount of gain realized is NOT the amount that necessarily will be taxed at the time of the exchange. It is the amount that would be taxed, if the transaction were an outright sale instead of an exchange. The term "net gain realized" is—

Total consideration received	$__________
LESS	
Total consideration given	< __________ >

Total consideration consists of [1] cash (paid or received), [2] boot (money equivalents, promises to pay or receive money, nonlike property), [3] FMV of like-kind property received, and [4] exchange expenses (paid by the conveyor of property). At this point, we must distinguish between the term "cash" and "exchange expenses." Cash is that amount necessary to equalize the equities between the property owners. Once the agreement of exchange (contract) is placed in escrow, the sum total of all commissions, fees, costs, and expenses comprises a separate accounting item of its own. Exchange expenses are also paid in cash. And herein lies some computational confusion. Escrow agents generally designate equity cash as a **deposit** towards principal (either given or received).

It is a one item entry. Thereafter, all relevant exchange expenses are itemized in detail: one set for exchanger A and a separate set for exchanger B. As you'll see in Figure 4.4, the exchange expenses have a bottom line effect on net gain realized.

DATA NEEDED FOR COMPUTING OVERALL REALIZED GAIN				
Step	Description	Amount		
1.	FMV of property received			
2.	Cash received (to balance equities)			
3.	FMV of boot received			
4.	Debt balance on property conveyed (assumed by other party)			
5.	**TOTAL CONSIDERATION RECEIVED** (Add steps 1 thru 4)			
	LESS			
6.	Adjusted basis of property conveyed			
7.	Cash given (to balance equities)			
8.	Adjusted basis of boot given			
9.	Debt assumed on property received			
10.	Exchange expenses you paid			
11.	**TOTAL CONSIDERATION GIVEN** (Add steps 6 thru 10)			
12.	**GAIN REALIZED** - had there been a sale instead of exchange (Subtract step 11 from step 5)			

Fig. 4.4 - Steps for Determining Gain Realized (Before Tax)

With the above comments as background, we present in Figure 4.4 the required computational steps for establishing the net gain realized in a Section 1031 exchange. Note that there are **twelve** distinct steps. There is no magic way of shortcutting this number. Consequently, we urge that you take a moment now to read down (and digest) every one of the indicated steps. Although 1031 exchanges are dominated by real estate transactions, we've tried to generalize the wording at each step so that the sequence presented is also applicable to like-kind exchanges other than real estate.

Analysis of the Gain

The bottom line in Figure 4.4 is the *Net Gain Realized* on your exchange. Next, you have to determine what portion of this realized gain, if any, is tax recognized immediately. To do this, more computations are required (of course). At least **eight** steps are required. Several are combinations of prior steps and prior data generated. We present the required steps to you in Figure 4.5.

There is a key to understanding what is taking place in Figure 4.5. A quick perusal thereof reveals that FMV and basis matters are not mentioned whatsoever. The challenge there is to compare cash and boot and debt relief, compare them, then compare the result with the gain realized in the overall transaction.

Note in Figure 4.5 that there are three distinct analysis phases: (1) cash and boot, (2) debt relief, and (3) comparison with gain realized. The goal in analysis (1) is to establish the net cash and boot *received.* The term "boot," recall, is noncash and nonlike property. These two items are presumed to be immediately convertible to cash, should the recipient exchanger choose to do so. Cash and boot, therefore, constitute monetary consideration received, which is totally independent of the 1031 property itself.

The goal in analysis (2) is to establish the net debt relief to party A in the exchange. The presumption here is that there is a swapping of debt between parties A and B. This is a very common practice in real estate deals. Rarely is a piece of real estate offered in an exchange, totally debt free. After the swapping by assumption of each party's debt (mortgages, liens, trust deeds, promissory notes, etc.), party A may — or may not — have net debt relief. If party A has assumed more debt than the amount of which he has been relieved, the net debt relief is zero (obviously). This is the significance of step 7 in Figure 4.5.

The goal in analysis (3) is to establish the amount of gain that is immediately tax recognized. At the same time, the goal is to clarify what portion of the gain is tax deferred. The amount of gain deferred is simply the amount realized less the amount recognized.

FACTORS FOR DETERMINING AMOUNT OF GAIN RECOGNIZED				
Step	**Description**	**Amount**		
	Cash and Boot			
1.	Cash & FMV of boot received			
2.	Cash & Adjusted Basis of boot given			
3.	Exchange expenses you paid			
4.	Net cash & boot received [Step 1 less steps 2 + 3]			
	Debt Relief			
5.	Debt on property conveyed			
6.	Debt assumed on property received			
7.	Net debt relief [Step 5 less step 6, but NOT below zero]			
	Gain Recognized			
8.	**TOTAL TAXABLE GAIN** [Add steps 4 and 7. Cannot exceed GAIN REALIZED: Step 12 in Fig. 4.4]			
9.	**Ordinary Income Recapture** (See text re line 10 in Fig. 4.6)			
10.	**Taxable Capital Gain** [Subtract step 9 from step 8]			

Fig. 4.5 - Analysis of Total Gain "Tax Recognized" on 1031 Exchange

As you'll see shortly, the deferred amount is automatically taken care of when transferring your basis in the property conveyed to your replacement property.

Meanwhile, we want to summarize how the amount of gain recognized is determined, and what it consists of. As shown in Figure 4.5, the total taxable gain is the sum of steps 4 (*net cash and boot received*) and 7 (*net debt relief*). This becomes step 8: *total taxable gain.* The rules tell you that step 8 cannot exceed the gain realized (step 12 in Figure 4.4). The rules also tell you that step 8 may consist of two types of gain: ordinary gain (called: recapture income) and capital gain. This is the significance of steps 9 and 10 in Figure 4.5.

Reporting of Gain Recognized

Where there is a significant amount of cash and boot and debt relief involved, almost invariably some portion of the gain will be tax recognized. This is the presumption behind every partial 1031 exchange. How, where, and on what tax form do you report to the IRS the amount of gain recognized?

Answer: On IRS **Form 8824** titled: ***Like-Kind Exchanges.*** Whether wholly of like kind or partially of like kind, all Section 1031 exchanges are reported on Form 8824. The purpose of this form is to—

(a) separate the like-kind property from the nonlike property;
(b) tax the nonlike property (whether gain or loss);
(c) determine the amount of recognized gain (if any) on the like-kind property conveyed; and
(d) establish the basis of the like-kind property received.

Form 8824 consists of three applicable parts, namely:

Part I — Information on the Like-Kind Exchange.
Part II — Related Party Exchange Information.
Part III — Realized Gain or Loss, Recognized Gain, and Basis of Like-Kind Property Received.

We'll skip Part II because it addresses non-arm's-length (called: *related party*) transactions. The IRS regards such transactions as being "structured" for tax avoidance by one or both of the related parties. No matter how clever the arrangement, a structured exchange is **not** of like kind. However, if each of the exchanged properties is held more than two years before further disposition, the exchange may be accepted as like kind.

Meanwhile, Part I is where most of the computer attention by the IRS is focused. Part I asks for the following information on the like-kind properties that have been exchanged:

1. Description of like-kind property given up.
2. Description of like-kind property received.

3. Date like-kind property given up was originally acquired (month, day, year).
4. Date you actually transferred your property to other party (month, day, year).
5. Date like-kind property you received was identified (month, day, year).
6. Date you actually received the like-kind property from other party (month, day, year).

The general instructions to Form 8824 summarize, as follows:

If you exchange business or investment property solely for business or investment property of a like kind, no gain or loss is [tax] *recognized under Section 1031. If, as part of the exchange, you also receive other (not like-kind) property or money, gain is recognized* [and taxed] *to the extent of other property and money received, but a loss is not recognized.*

Section 1031 does not apply to exchange of inventory, stocks, bonds, notes, other securities or evidence of indebtedness, or certain other assets.

Part III of Form 8824

Part III of Form 8824 consists officially of 14 computational lines. We list all of these lines for you in Figure 4.6. We've done only a modest amount of editing and abbreviating. For example, Part III uses the term "other property" to mean: *not like kind.* We prefer using the term "nonlike" as being less confusing than "other property." Nonlike includes equity cash and marketable boot. It does not include extraneous (and financially meaningless) property items thrown in to sweeten the deal.

Our Figure 4.6 is not intended to be a substitute for the official Part III. Therefore, by all means you must procure for yourself an official copy of Form 8824 and its 2,500 words of instructions. The official instructions are reasonably clear, and very informative examples are given. You really should read them.

SUMMARY OF VITAL 1031 EXCHANGE DATA			
Attach to Your Tax Return and Report on Form(s) Indicated			
Line	Description		Amount
1.	FMV of boot given (nonlike property)		
2.	Adjusted basis of boot given		
3.	Gain or (loss) on boot [Subtract 2 from1, enter on Sch. D]		
4.	Cash & boot received, plus net debt relief to you, LESS [not below zero] exchange expenses you paid		
5.	FMV of like-kind property received		
6.	Subtotal: ADD lines 4 and 5		
7.	Adj. basis of like-kind property conveyed, plus cash and boot paid to other party, plus expense NOT used on line 4		
8.	**Total Realized Gain or (Loss)** [Subtract 7 from 6]		
9.	Enter **smaller** of line 4 or line 8 [Not less than zero]		
10.	**Ordinary Income Recapture** [Enter on Form 4797] (see text)		
11.	**Capital Gain Income** [Subtract 10 from 9, but NOT less than zero. Enter on Sch. D, Form 4797, or Form 6252] (see text)		
12.	**Total Gain Recognized:** ADD lines 10 and 11		
13.	Deferred gain or (loss) [Subtotal 12 from 8]		
14.	**Basis of Property Received** [Subtract line 4 from sum of lines 7 and 12]		

Fig. 4.6 - Edited Version of Part III, Form 8824: Like-Kind Exchanges

Note that lines 1, 2, and 3 deal exclusively with nonlike property *given up* in the transaction. It is treated as an independent sale of that property unrelated to the exchange computations that follow. Any nonlike property *received* is an exchange computational matter.

Line 4 in Figure 4.6 is the aggregate of various items previously discussed. This item is the sum of—

- Equity cash received,
- FMV of nonlike property received, and
- Net liabilities (debt) assumed by other party.

Reduce this sum (but not below zero) by any exchange expenses you incurred. You need to do some side computations on your own on this. In this regard, Figure 4.5 should be helpful to you. Lines 5 and 6 in Figure 4.6 are self-explanatory.

Line 7 in Figure 4.6 is another aggregation of previous items that we have discussed. It consists of (a) adjusted basis of like-kind property conveyed, (b) net amounts paid to other party (cash, boot, amount of debt you assumed in excess of what the other party assumed of your debt), and (c) *plus* any exchange expenses not used on line 4. Lines 8 and 9 are self-explanatory.

Ordinary Income Recapture

Line 10 in Figure 4.6 raises a new item that we have not previously discussed, though we have alluded to it. Line 10 addresses: *Ordinary income recapture.* The idea behind recapture income is that certain properties enjoy statutory allowances (deductions against basis) which are treated as current operating expenses. The allowed/allowable basis deductions reduce the taxable amount of operating income. The result is a lower income tax during the years in which the property was held for productive use. When the property is transferred to a new owner (by sale or exchange), the basis deductions are recaptured. Depending on applicable rules, the recapture may be part ordinary income and part capital gain.

The most common example of the recapture principle is depreciable real property. The ordinary income recapture part is the excess amount of any accelerated depreciation taken, over and above that which would have been taken had straight-line depreciation based on conservative lifespans been used.

There are eight specific recapture rules in the Tax Code. They are prescribed by the following subsections, namely:

[1]. Subsec. 179(d)(10) — Election to expense certain depreciable assets (vehicles and equipment used in business).

[2]. Subsec. 280F(b)(2) — Limitation where certain property used more than 50% for personal purposes.

[3].	Subsec. 291(a)	—	Reduction in certain tax preference items for corporations (depletion, amortization, intangible drilling, mining exploration, real estate trusts, financial institutions, etc.).
[4].	Subsec. 1245(a)(1)	—	Ordinary income from dispositions of certain depreciable (tangible) property.
[5].	Subsec. 1250(a)(1)	—	Ordinary income from dispositions of certain depreciable realty.
[6].	Subsec. 1252(a)(1)	—	Ordinary income from disposition of certain farm land (re soil, water, and land clearing expenses).
[7].	Subsec. 1254(a)(1)	—	Ordinary income from disposition of interests in oil, gas, geothermal, or other mineral properties.
[8].	Subsec. 1255(a)(1)	—	Ordinary income from disposition of Section 126 property (re various statutory cost-sharing conservation programs).

Collectively, all of these references are called: *Recapture income rules*. If any of your 1031 menu of properties involves recapture income, you need to familiarize yourself with the applicable rule above. Or, at least seek professional counseling thereon. Were you not to do so, the fact that there is a dedicated line on Form 8824 for this one item alone means that the IRS could assess you a negligence penalty.

Bottom Lines & Forms

Lines 10 through 14 in Figure 4.6 (for Form 8824) are what we call "bottom lines." This is the information that the IRS will record in its computer summary of your exchange transaction. The official form provides at each of these lines self-guiding instructions on what to do. These instructions raise certain issues not previously addressed. For example, the instruction at line 10 says—

Enter here and on Form 4797, line 16.

Do you know what Form 4797 is, or its line 16? Probably not . . . unless you are a tax professional.

Form 4797 is titled: ***Sales of Business Property***. It consists of three parts: I — *Property Held More Than 1 Year*; II — *Ordinary Gains and Losses*; and III — *Gain from Disposition of* [Recapture] *Property*. Part I consists of lines for the entry of capital gains from like-kind exchanges, installment sales, and casualties or thefts. Part II consists of "line 16": *Ordinary gain or (loss) from like-kind exchanges*, and other lines for other recapture income (including installment sales). Part III is a full-length page for computing the total gain on the eight recapture-type properties cited above. The idea in Part III is to separate the ordinary gain (recapture income) from the total gain and transfer it to Part II. What is left on Part III is capital gain which is transferred to Part I. If you are going to be involved in 1031 exchanges on more than one occasion, you must acquaint yourself with the existence and purpose of Form 4797.

Line 11 in Figure 4.6 has been edited to read: *Capital gain income*. This differs from the small-print official instructions on that line which read—

Subtract line 10 from line 9. If zero or less enter -0-. If more than zero, enter here and on Schedule D [Form 1040] *or Form 4797, unless the installment method* [Form 6252] *applies.*

The installment method (Section 453) applies where an exchange receives nonlike property in the form of promised money via an installment contract. The applicable Form 6252: ***Installment Sale Income*** separates recapture income (ordinary gain) from capital gain on a year-by-year basis. You are then directed onto Schedule D (Form 1040).

As you surely already know, Schedule D (Form 1040) is titled: ***Capital Gains and Losses***. Schedule D contains entry lines with such captions as: *Gain from Form 4797, . . . Form 6252, . . . and*

Form 8824. The idea here is that all tax-recognized capital gain from any type of 1031 exchange winds up on Schedule D. From here, it is transferred to page 1 of Form 1040 where it combines with other sources of income, gain, or loss.

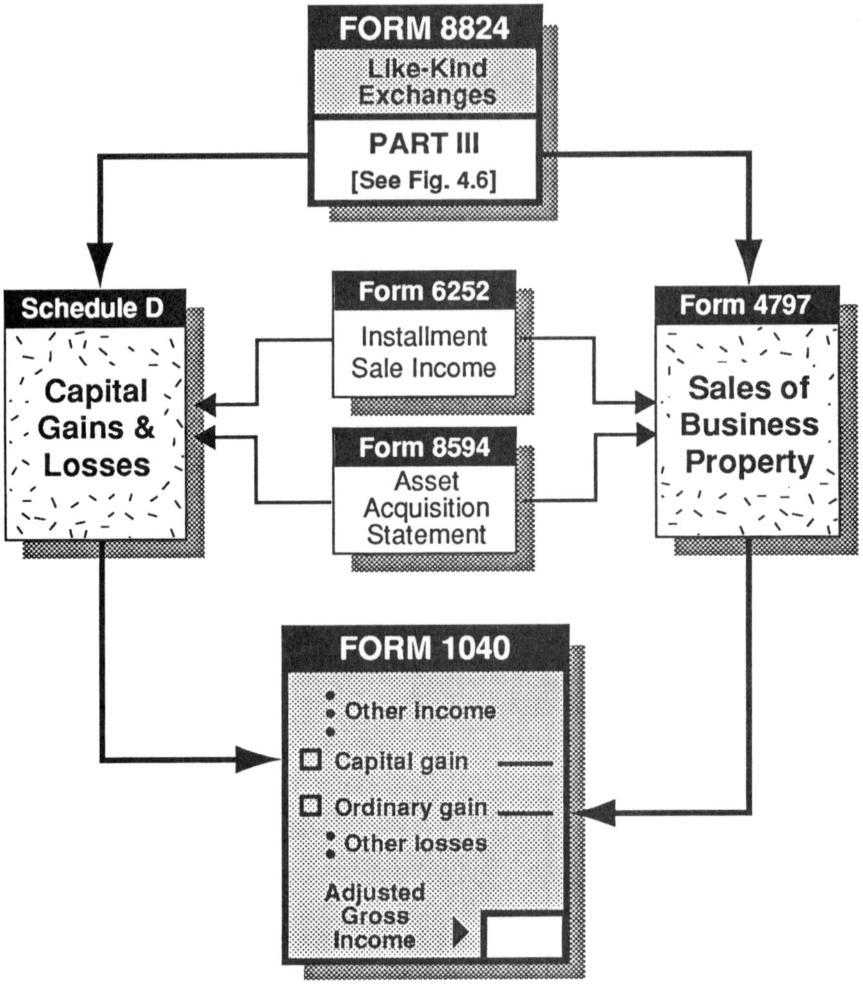

Fig. 4.7 - Tax Forms "Menu" When Making 1031 Exchanges

In Figure 4.7, we put the various tax forms (mentioned above) in perspective. For subliminal purposes, we also include Form

8594: ***Asset Acquisition Statement.*** You'll need this form when exchanging a business (which is not a unitary asset).

Basis of Property Received

Lines 12 and 13 in Figure 4.6 show arithmetical instructions which are self-guiding. However, we have done some editing of the official wording on Form 8824. Instead of line 12 being captioned: ***Recognized gain*** as on the official form, we prefer: *Total gain recognized (ordinary and capital).* This wording is to remind you that there are two components of recognized gain. Each is taxed quite differently.

Line 14 — the true bottom line in Figure 4.6 and on Form 8824 — is officially captioned as shown: ***Basis of like-kind property received.*** The self-guiding arithmetical instructions read—

Subtract line 4 from the sum of lines 7 and 12.

We don't think this instruction gives you a good feel of what is taking place when computing your ongoing tax basis in the property acquired by exchange. We can do better than the official instruction. We do so in step fashion in Figure 4.8.

We suggest you read through Figure 4.8 in its entirety, step by step. By doing so, we think you'll see the wisdom and, yes, the tax cleverness, which underlies the 1031 exchange concept. The basis in the property received (step 11) is a *direct continuation* of the adjusted basis in the property conveyed (step 1). Basis continuation through the exchange enables other pertinent adjustments-to-basis to be made. These adjustments are cash and boot, debt swapping, gain recognized, and exchange expenses (commissions, fees, costs, etc.). Nowhere in the 11 steps outlined is there any mention of the deferred capital gain (for which Section 1031 is so famous). So, where is it?

It's there — "floating in space," as it were. It is that deferred gain *floating in space* that allows you to make one exchange after another, more or less endlessly. Each exchange causes you to adjust the basis in each property you receive. When the time comes to execute a taxable transfer — as it invariably will — all of that

The "Ending Stage" of a Section 1031 Exchange

Step	Description	Amount
1.	Adjusted basis of property **conveyed**	
2.	Cash and boot **conveyed**	
3.	Debt assumed on property **received**	
4.	**Subtotal:** Add 1, 2, and 3	
5.	Cash and boot **received**	
6.	Debt relief on property **conveyed**	
7.	**Subtotal:** Add 5 and 6	
8.	SUBTRACT step 7 from step 4	
9.	**Gain recognized** on exchange	
10.	Exchange expenses **you** incurred	
11.	BASIS OF PROPERTY RECEIVED • ADD steps 8, 9, and 10	

Fig. 4.8 - Steps for Establishing Basis of Exchange Property Received

cumulative deferred gain will "pop out" as one target amount. It will do so in the sequence which follows:

Gross sales/transaction proceeds	$__________
LESS	
Cumulative adjusted basis	< >
LESS	
Expenses of sale transaction	< >
EQUALS	
Taxable cumulative deferred gain	==========

The taxable cumulative deferred capital gain will ultimately appear on Schedule D (Form 1040). There it will combine with other nonexchange-type capital gains and losses. Should there be a net/net long-term capital gain on your Schedule D, favorable tax rates will then apply. Capital gains tax rates are "favorable" in the sense that they are statutorily lower than ordinary income tax rates.

5

MULTIPARTY 1031 EXCHANGES

When There Are Three Or More Parties And Properties In A 1031 Exchange, One Must Anticipate Conflicts And Complications In Completing The Exchange Within 180 Days. If All Does Not Go Precisely As Planned, Each Conveyance Of Property Will Be Treated As A SALE, And Each Receipt Of Property Will Be Treated As A PURCHASE. To Prevent This Treatment, Four SAFE HARBORS Are Prescribed. The Best Overall Approach Is To Engage A "Qualified Intermediary." Such An Entity Holds Temporary Legal Title To All Properties Until All Terms Of The "Qualified Exchange Accommodation Arrangement" Are Fulfilled.

In Chapter 4, we focused entirely on two-party, one-property exchanges. That is, there were two unrelated exchangers A and B. Each had one item of like-kind property to exchange with the other. The exchange was done through an escrow agent, a broker, or an attorney who was the neutral party thereto. The time constraints of Section 1031(a)(3) — 45 days to identify and 180 days to complete — presented no problem. Except for ordinary miscommunication concerning FMVs, debt swapping, cash and boot, financial accounting, and legal disclosures, the process goes smoothly. This is the classical underlying premise of all Section 1031 exchanges.

Instead of a common two-party exchange, suppose there were three parties, four parties, or even as many as five parties to the exchange. Suppose that one or more of the parties has multiple properties (not of the same kind) to exchange. Suppose that two or more of the parties were closely related by business and family ties. And further suppose that, as time nears for completing the exchange, there are legal uncertainties concerning ownership of one or more of the properties involved. Would any of these or other variant situations affect the "smoothness" of the exchange process?

The answer is: **Yes**, most certainly!

If a multiparty exchange does not go smoothly, the IRS position is steadfast. What may have been characterized in contractual language as a 1031 exchange is treated as an array of sales and repurchases. In other words, no capital gain deferment whatsoever is allowed . . . to any of the parties.

Over the past 30 years or so, there have been many court rulings on the interpretive fine points of Section 1031. Some rulings have upheld the IRS's position; others have favored the taxpayer/exchangers. The overall effect has been some modest liberalization of the key mandates underlying Section 1031. These liberalizations constitute "safe harbors" against your participation being treated as a sale and repurchase rather than an exchange.

Consequently, in this chapter we want to familiarize you with the special situation, rules, and rulings that are applicable to multiparty exchanges. The moment that more than two serious-minded parties are involved, each with potential multi-type properties to exchange, things can get very complicated. There are added complications should two or more parties be closely related, or should consecutive exchanges be too closely connected in time. We want to introduce you to these complications in a way that you are not caught off guard and uninformed.

Related Person Resale Rule

Section 1031(f) is titled: ***Special Rules for Exchanges Between Related Persons***. A "related person" is any member of one's immediate family (grandparent, parent, child, brother, or sister), members of a family business, beneficiaries of a family trust, officers in a close corporation, and partners in a partnership. The common theme throughout all of these relationships is economic influence and lack of arm's-length deals. The premise is that property exchanges between related persons can be "structured" in a way to defeat the Congressional intent behind the *nonrecognition of gain* aspects of Section 1031.

The essence of Section 1031(f) is that, if the property received by a related person is *resold within two years*, the original exchange will **not qualify** as a Section 1031 exchange. Any gain not previously recognized must be recognized by either of the related parties, upon the property's disposition.

There are three exceptions to this special rule. As set forth in paragraph (2) of Section 1031(f), the exceptions are—

[1] The disposition was after the death of either of the related persons (whether family or business related).

[2] The disposition was an involuntary conversion, and the threat of conversion occurred after the exchange.

[3] You can establish to the satisfaction of the IRS that neither the exchange nor the disposition had tax avoidance as its principal purpose.

The specific intent of the related person resale rule is to thwart any "bending of the rules" between persons with reciprocal economic interests. The type of bending anticipated includes basis shifting, short sales, option protections, diminution of economic rules, and various silent understandings between private persons.

The more flagrant of such transactions goes something like this. An influential person owns property worth $1,000,000. His adjusted basis in that property is just $100,000. He wants to avoid all tax on the $900,000 capital gain. Through a "private exchange" (no escrow agent or broker), he acquires like property worth $900,000. In the arrangement is a reverse exchange agreement to reacquire the original property for $900,000. This (on paper) would increase his basis from $100,000 to $1,000,000. If he sold the property for $1,100,000, he would pay tax on $100,000 of gain rather than on his $1,000,000 true gain.

Really, now! Why do some influential property owners want everything? They do; it is called: *human greed.* Such persons exchange and exchange and exchange, and figure they'll pay no tax whatsoever. To the IRS, any such arrangement is an outright sham. Gross negligence and fraud penalties can be imposed.

Grouping Properties by Classes

In any multiparty exchange, there is inevitably the likelihood of multiple properties of different kinds and classes. Owner A wants to exchange his farm tractor for owner B's work horse; Owner B wants to exchange a small parcel of land for owner C's water-well drilling equipment; Owner C wants to exchange his hunting lodge in the mountains for a small rental house in the city. This is the way it is in real life. While all intended participants may have heard about like-kind exchanges, most are unaware of the existence of IRS Regulation § 1.1031(j)-1. This regulation is titled: ***Exchanges of Multiple Properties***. It comprises nearly 8,500 words, including numerous numerical examples.

Generally, Section 1031 requires a property-by-property comparison of the like-kindness of the properties involved. However, Regulation § 1.1031(j)-1 authorizes a variant to this general theme. The variant addresses the like-kindness on a grouping basis. That is, there is an *exchange group* for passenger autos; another exchange group for land; another for buildings; another for related-service equipment; and so on. The only requirement is that, within each group, there must be at least one property transferred and at least one (like-kind) property received. Any property transferred and received in a designated grouping is an "exchange." A single exchange group is valid so long as more than one property is transferred and received within that group. In multiparty exchanges, multiple exchange groups are the rule rather than the exception.

Thus, the first step in setting up a multiparty exchange is to group the properties by kind or class. You can't group cars and computers, or boats and land, for example. If there is no like-kind exchange match, the unmatchable item is assigned to a "residual group." A residual group consists of cash, promises of money, or other property (nonlike in kind). There is a separate residual group (where applicable) for each party to the exchange.

To illustrate the grouping of multiple properties, consider a two-party exchange between J and K. Each offers to the exchange process the following items (7 in number each):

J's Property		K's Property	
Computer	A	Computer	W
Computer	B	Printer	X
Printer	C	Real Estate	Y
Real Estate	D	Real Estate	Z
Real Estate	E	Grader	R
Scraper	F	Truck	S
Inventory		Cash	

There are three exchange groups here. Can you identify them?

Exchange group I consists of computer A, computer B, printer C, computer W, and printer X. They are all within the same General Asset Class.

Exchange group II consists of real estate D, E, Y, and Z. They are all of like kind.

Exchange group III consists of scraper F and grader R. They are both in the same Industrial Product Class.

Omitted from any of these three groupings are inventory, cash, and truck S. Inventory is an ineligible item for exchange as it is held primarily for sale to customers in a trade or business [Section 1031(a)(2)(A)]. Cash itself is never an item of exchange. Truck S is "other property" as it is clearly unlike that of any other property offered in the exchange pool. The residual grouping for either J or K cannot be established until the FMVs of all offered properties are determined . . . and compared. In the property listings above, transferor J is the taxpayer on whom we focus primarily.

Exchange Grouping "Next Step"

The next step in the exchange grouping process is to FMV each item in the exchange pool: the property transferred **and** the property received. We assume for the time being that there is no existing debt on any of the properties in the exchange pool. This simplifies matters by requiring that only the aggregate FMVs on both sides of the exchange be equal. Since transferor J is our tax focus, we need to indicate his adjusted basis in each item of property that he is offering to transfer.

With these points in mind, the following amounts are postulated:

	Property Transferred		*Property Received*	
	Adj. Basis	*FMV*		*FMV*
A.	$ 1,500	$ 5,000	W.	$ 4,500
B.	500	3,000	X.	2,500
C.	2,000	1,500	Y.	11,000
D.	11,200	12,000	Z.	14,000
E.	-0-	11,800	R.	2,000
F.	3,300	2,500	S.	1,700
Inventory	1,000	1,700	Cash	1,800
	$19,500	$37,500		$37,500

(Keep this listing in mind, particularly the adjusted basis amounts, as we'll be referring to them later.) Note that, in the aggregate, the FMVs of the seven properties transferred from J to K, and received by J from K, exactly match each other. Let's see what the FMV match is when we assign the properties and their FMVs to Exchange Groups I, II, and III (described above). We leave open the residual group for taxpayer J until other matters are described.

We present in Figure 5.1 the pertinent data for each of the three exchange groups identified above. We also show, where applicable, an exchange "surplus" or an exchange "deficiency." A "surplus" is when the transferor's aggregate FMVs in the qualified grouping exceed the aggregate FMVs of the property received. A "deficiency" is the reverse: the transferor receives more FMV than that which he transferred. The **per group** FMV surplus or deficiency determines how much gain is tax recognized . . . for *that* group. The overall net effect is that realized gain, recognized gain, and basis of replacement property are determined group by group, rather than property by property.

Group-By-Group Analysis

Taxpayer J gains from each of the three Figure 5.1 exchange groups as follows:

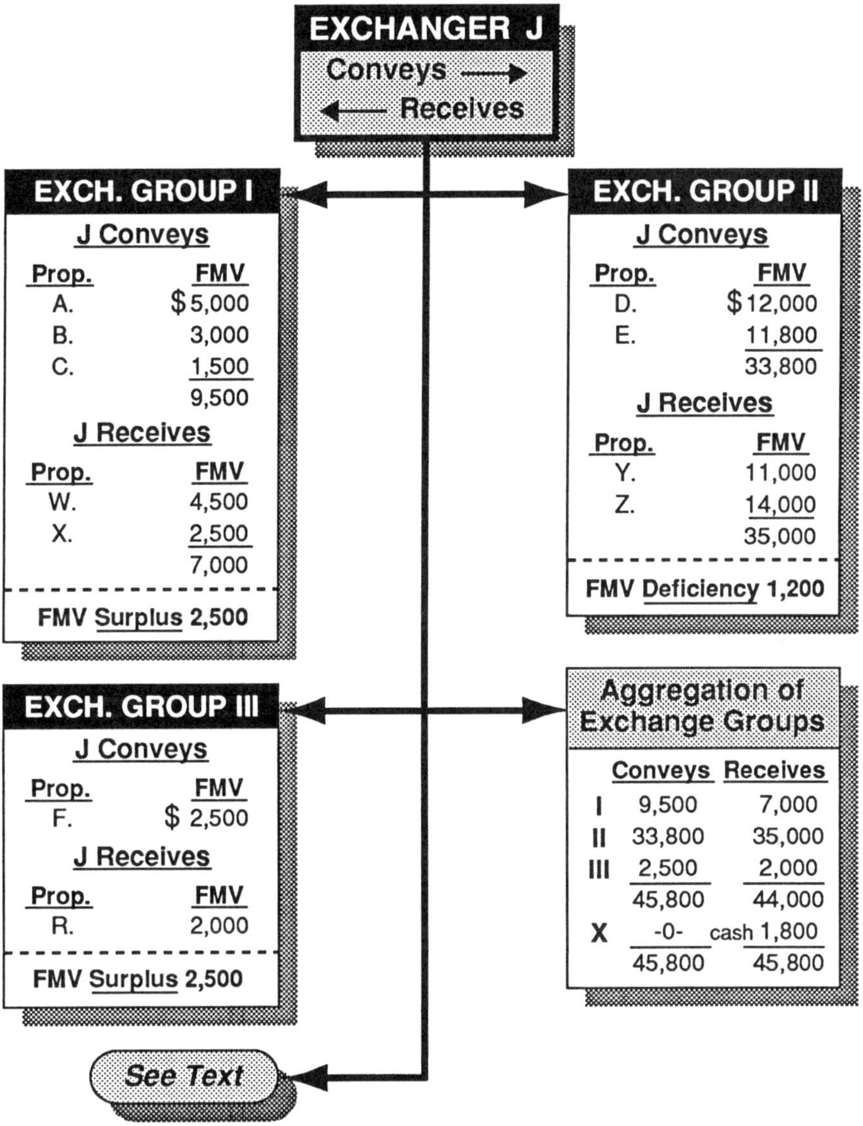

Fig. 5.1 - Like-Kind Property Groupings in a Multiproperty Exchange

As to Group I — The gain *realized* is the sum of the FMVs transferred (9,500) minus the sum of J's adjusted basis in those properties (4,000). Thus, the amount of gain actually realized is

$5,500 [9,500 – 4,000]. Because there is an FMV surplus of $2,500 [9,500 – 7,000] in Group I, this becomes the amount of gain recognized in that group. Gain recognized is always the LESSER of gain realized or the exchange group surplus in FMV. The amount of gain *deferred*, therefore, is $3,000 [5,500 – 2,500].

As to Group II — The amount of gain realized is the sum of the FMVs of the two real estate properties transferred (33,800) minus J's adjusted basis therein (11,200) or $22,600. As indicated in Figure 5.1 for Exchange Group II, there is no FMV surplus on J's part. Instead, there is an FMV deficiency of $1,200. By not having an FMV surplus, J recognizes no gain for that group. Thus, his entire $22,600 realized gain is all tax deferred.

As to Group III — There is a loss realized instead of a gain. Taxpayer J transfers property worth $2,500 in which his adjusted basis is $3,300. This constitutes a capital loss of $800 [2,500 FMV – 3,300 basis]. A loss is never tax recognized in a Section 1031 exchange. Although there was an FMV surplus of $500 [2,500 FMV transferred – 2,000 FMV received], said surplus is not less than the zero amount of gain realized. Therefore, there is no gain recognized in Exchange Group III.

In the FMV and basis tabulations above, there is "floating" in the exchange pool inventory worth $1,700 (with basis of 1,000) and a truck S also worth $1,700. Since these are clearly unlike properties (even though their FMVs are the same), they do not and cannot form an exchange group. Consequently, what may be thought of as an exchange (inventory for truck) is tax treated as a sale. Therefore, taxpayer J has to recognize tax on his full $700 of realized gain [1,700 FMV – 1,000 basis].

Inasmuch as we have accounted for all of J's properties in the J-K exchange pool, there is no residual group for J. There is, however, a residual group for K . . . in the amount of $1,800 cash. This is the amount owing to J to offset his net FMV surplus in the three exchange groups. For recap purposes, J's FMV surplus and deficiencies are: $2,500 surplus for Group I; $1,200 deficiency for Group II; and $500 surplus for Group III. These net out to be

$1,800 of FMV surplus in J's favor. In other words, in three 1031-type exchange groups, J has transferred to K $1,800 more in FMV than he has received from K. Therefore, K has to make up the difference with $1,800 in cash. We summarized all of this for you in the "Aggregation" box in Figure 5.1.

The residual grouping analysis is a tad more complicated when there is *existing debt* (or other encumbrance) on any of the properties in the three exchange groups. If, in the aggregate, J assumes more debt than that from which he is relieved, the excess debt assumed is treated as money paid to K. If J's aggregate debt relief is greater than his debt assumption, his excess relief is treated as money paid to him by K. A simple visualization of why this is so is presented in Figure 5.2.

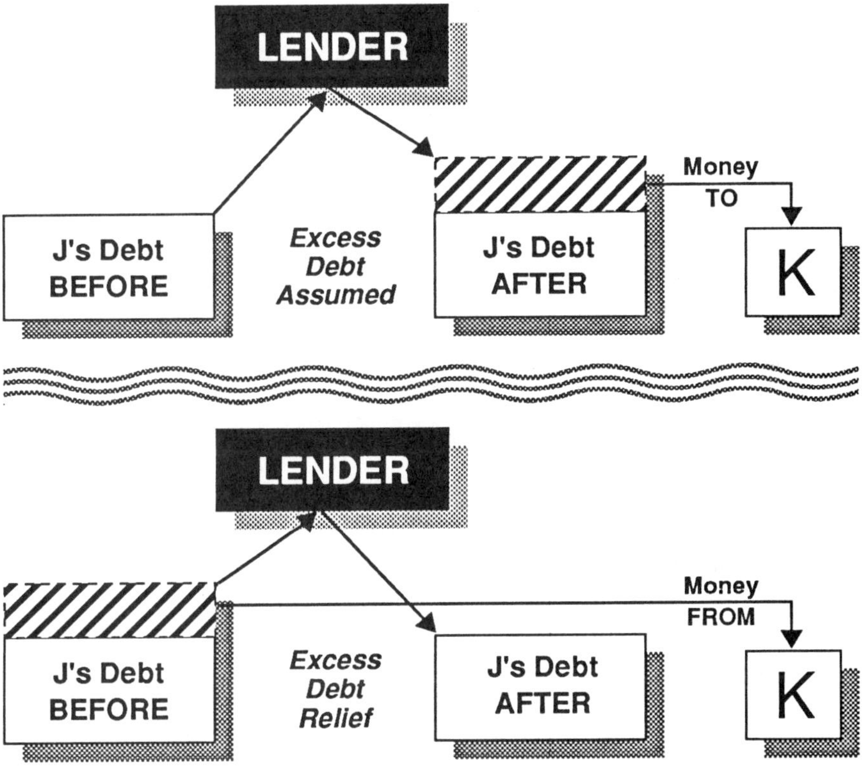

Fig. 5.2 - Comparison of Excess Debt Assumption vs. Excess Debt Relief

The basis of the replacement property acquired by J is also done on a group-by-group analysis. The principles follow along the lines that we have discussed previously (in Chapter 4) and which we'll discuss in more detail in Chapter 6. There are still further computational twists that we need to tell you more about.

Multiparty Arrangements Synopsized

When a 1031 exchange involves any combination of active business property, investment property, rental real estate, mining rights, timberland, or any other eligible like-kind property, the arrangements for such an exchange can become quite complex. More than the intent of any two parties is required. There are security provisions, financial guarantees, clear title assurances, specific dates for the relinquishment and replacement of properties, and other contractual terms to be met. Not every party to a multiparty exchange is an exchanger. One party may be a pure buyer; another party may be a pure seller; while the "exchanger" may want to part sell, part exchange, and part buy.

For example, suppose that party A wants to exchange his 10-unit apartment building for a 20-unit commercial mall held by party C. Party B wants to buy A's property; party C does not want to exchange with A. Instead, C wants to sell via an installment sale as part of his retirement planning. How do the parties go about accomplishing each of his separate goals?

The simplest solution is a three-party escrow exchange arrangement. A three-party contract is drawn up whereby A and C each "sells" into an escrow pool. Party B "buys" C's property which he immediately exchanges (within the escrow pool) for A's property. A gets the exchange property that he wants; B buys the property that he wants; and C gets the installment sale proceeds and long-term commitments that he wants.

But, suppose that party B does not want to participate in the C-to-A exchange arrangement. Party B has serious legal concerns about the matter, while C has serious financial concerns about his installment sale terms getting botched up. Party D comes along and wants to exchange two of his properties for that portion of party C's property which far exceeds the FMV of A's property. Add to all of these concerns the 45-day identity period and the 180-day replacement period imposed by Section 1031(a)(3). Now what?

Answer: There needs to be a fifth party. Such is called the *accommodation party* . . . or party "E" in our parlance. Party E may be a financial institution, a legal institution, or an exchange guarantor company. Such an arrangement is authorized by the IRS's ***Revenue Procedure 2000-37***, I.R.B. 2000-40,308 (published September 14, 2000). This approved procedure allows all parties (A, B, C, and D) who have bona fide property interests to present their offers, terms, and conditions for getting what each wants. In the meantime, party E becomes the **nonparty** *accommodation titleholder* of all properties (like and nonlike) and all monies and money equivalents needed. An effort to portray the facilitative role of party E is presented in Figure 5.3.

The "Constructive Receipt" Doctrine

In all multiparty 1031 exchanges, there is one tax disqualification trap that can shatter the best laid legal and financial arrangements. The trap is called: *constructive receipt*. This is a tax doctrine of long standing which ignores accounting gimmicks and circuitous legal wording that disguise one's rights to demand and receive money or property. In 1031 exchanges, the focus of this doctrine is on the transferor/conveyor of like-kind property. Should the transferor actually receive — or have the right to receive — any money, nonlike property, or money equivalents **before** his replacement property is received and settled, the transaction will be treated as a *sale*: NOT an exchange. This treatment holds even though the replacement property is ultimately received within the framework of the exchange accommodation contract. Such is the essence of IRS Regulation 1.1031(k)-1(f)(1),(2): ***Receipt of money or other property***; ***Actual and constructive receipt***. The idea is that all proceeds that accrue during the exchange process (the relinquishing and retitling of the properties) be **held in escrow** until all terms and conditions of all transactions are met.

There is no constructive receipt of money or other property by the transferor if its control or receipt is subject to substantial limitations and restrictions. The conditions must be spelled out in

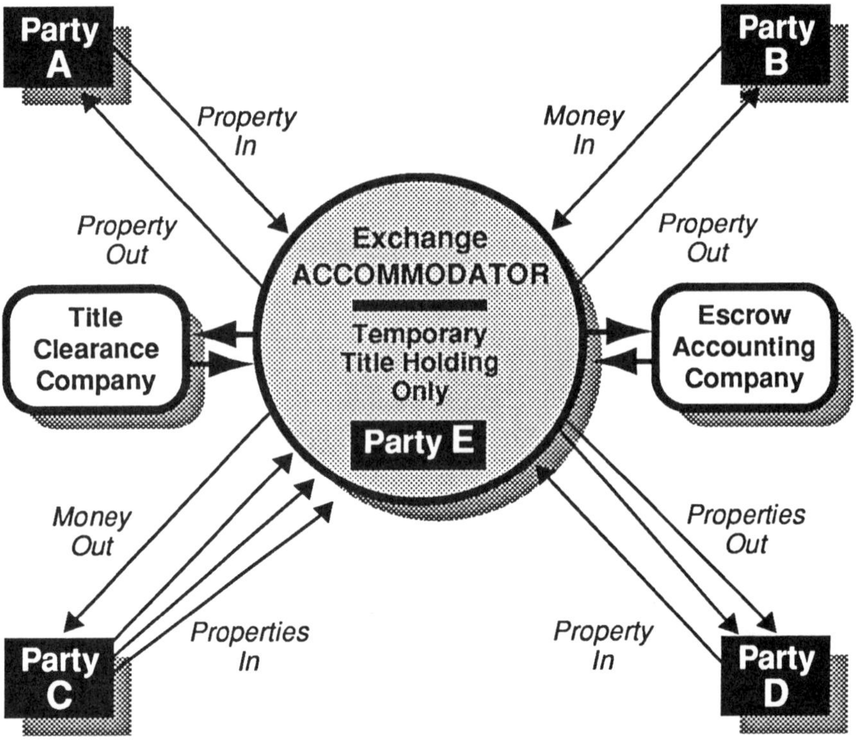

Fig. 5.3 - The Role of the "Accommodator" in a Multiparty Exchange

written form; must identify each transferor in the exchange; and may set forth those circumstances which are beyond the control of the transferor and/or the transferee. However, constructive receipt will be deemed to occur when the limitations and restrictions lapse, expire, or are waived. Actual or constructive receipt by the transferor's agent is treated as actual or constructive receipt by the transferor himself.

As you may recall from Chapter 3, there is a 45-day identification requirement and a 180-day replacement period imposed on a 1031 exchange. Because of many unforeseens in meeting these time constraints, transferors usually want some security arrangement or guarantee that, if the exchange falls through, they (at least) want their relinquishment to go through as a sale. Unless the wording of the exchange arrangement is carefully constructed, any rights to the sale proceeds will take preference over the intentions of making a qualified exchange As the consequence of so many unforeseens and changes-of-mind among participants in a multiparty exchange, the IRS and the courts have liberalized their positions on the meaning of "constructive receipt." These liberalizations are known as SAFE HARBORS for protecting the exchange intents within a multiparty agreement.

Safe Harbors Briefed

There are four safe harbors for protecting an exchange from being default-treated as a sale. The four approved by the IRS are:

[1] Security or guarantee arrangements;
[2] Qualified escrow accounts and qualified trusts;
[3] Qualified intermediaries; and
[4] Interest and growth factors.

Each of these four safe harbors is covered by a separate subregulation of its own. They are all umbrellaed under Regulation § 1.1031(k)-1(g): ***Safe harbors*** 1(g)(2) for [1], 1(g)(3) for [2], 1(g)(4) for [3], and 1(g)(5) for [4]. Of these four, the most practical is the use of *Qualified intermediaries*.

To satisfy a particular safe harbor, all of its regulatory terms and conditions must be met. More than one safe harbor can be used but, if so, the terms and conditions of each must be separately satisfied. The idea is to absolutely restrict a transferor's access to money, property, or security until all elements of the contractual arrangements are satisfied. All agreements must provide that each transferor (there may be more than one) cannot receive, pledge, borrow, or otherwise obtain any benefits of money or other property before the exchange time constraints have expired. All parties to the arrangement must agree that their property interests have been met, before the residual proceeds and nonlike properties are distributed.

Rather than trying to describe each safe harbor to you in its regulatory language, we try to abbreviate the essence of each in Figure 5.4. When scanning this figure, do keep in mind that the intent of each safe harbor is to assure that you do not trigger a constructive sale in lieu of your intended exchange.

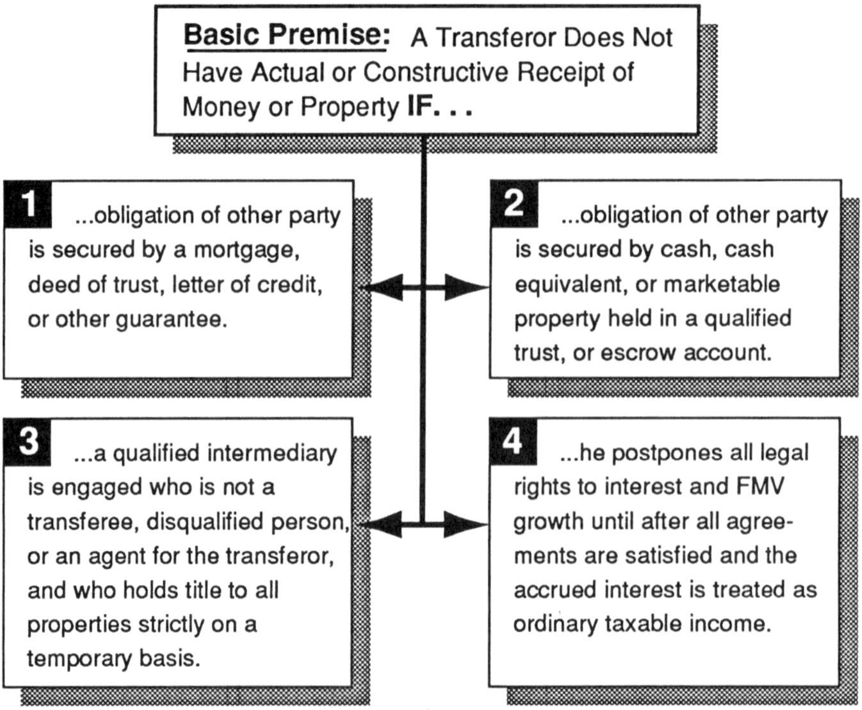

Fig. 5.4 - The"Safe Harbors" Against Constructive Receipts by Transferor

Using a "Qualified Intermediary"

Because of the complexities and unforeseens in a multiparty exchange, many such deals are consummated through a middleman. This does not cause a constructive receipt problem so long as the middleman is a *qualified intermediary*. The primary prerequisite for such a person (or entity) is that he NOT by the transferor, nor the transferor's agent, nor a "disqualified person." A disqualified person is any person related by family blood to the transferor or related to the transferor by financial interests holding a 10% or more ownership stake in a business enterprise. A person who is the transferor's employer, attorney, accountant, investment banker, broker, or real estate agent *within a two-year period* on the date of the transfer of the first of the relinquished properties is an agent. So, too, is any person who is an agent of the transferor at the time the exchange arrangement was first entered into. However, the performance of independent services regarding transactions intended to qualify as a like-kind exchange and routine financial, title insurance, escrow or trust services by a financial institution, title insurance company, or escrow company do not turn an otherwise qualifying person into an agent [Regulation § 1.1031(k)–1(k)(2)].

A qualified intermediary has no ultimate ownership interests in the properties that he is intermediating. He is a facilitator, pure and simple: a "straw person" (as it were). He acquires the relinquished property from the transferor, transfers said property to the transferee, acquires the replacement property and transfers it to the transferor. The intermediary is treated as acquiring and transferring properties if he does so through legal titles only, irrespective of general tax principles. He may also engage in title rearrangements between buyers and sellers who are neither transferors nor transferees, but peripheral participants to the exchange. He avoids all tax consequences via a process called "direct deeding" of titles, without access to any of the secured funds in the escrow account.

For a respectable fee, there are professional facilitators "out there." They call themselves **Exchange Guarantors**, to distinguish their functions from those of title insurers, escrow agents, mortgage companies, and brokerage firms. Exchange guarantors are not sales commission participants. They render a fee-for-service depending on the number of direct deeds (title transfers) that they are called upon to handle.

Time Constraints Reviewed

The core tax dilemma in almost every multiparty exchange is the 45/180-day time constraint imposed by IRC Section 1031(a)(3). This section is officially titled: ***Requirement that Property be Identified and that Exchange be Completed not more than 180 Days after Transfer of Exchanged Property***. The 45-day period is the time within which the replacement property is to be identified. The 45-day counting starts on the date that the relinquished property is transferred. It ends at midnight on the 45th day thereafter.

The 180-day period is called the exchange-completion time. It is that time within which the replacement property must be received (by the transferor). Both the 45-day identification period **and** the

180-day replacement period start when the relinquished property is transferred. That is, when its deed of title is transferred to someone or some entity (the exchange guarantor?) other than its ultimate recipient. Thus, under the right timing arrangements, a transferor could have up to as much as 225 days (45 + 180) to initiate and complete his 1031 exchange. One way to do this is to acquire the replacement property *before* giving up title to the relinquished property. This is quite feasible within a multiparty exchange accommodation arrangement.

There is a technical anomaly as to when the 180-day exchange period ends. The precise statutory language reads—

> *Any property received . . . after* ***the earlier of***—
>
> > *(i) . . . 180 days after the date on which* [it is] *relinquished in the exchange, or*
> >
> > *(ii) the due date (determined* ***with regard to*** *extension) for the transferor's return of tax . . . for the taxable year in which the transfer of the relinquished property occurs* [shall be treated as a sale]. [Emphasis added.]

In other words, if a transferor relinquished his property on December 16th, for example, he'd have only 120 days (to April 15th) to receive his replacement property [15 in December, 31 in January, 28 in February, 31 in March, and 15 in April]. If he applied for the automatic 4-month extension, his 180 days would end on June 14th [15 in April, 31 in May, and 14 in June]. Without an extension, the latest relinquishment date to get 180 days of exchange time would be October 17th [14 in October, 30 in November, 31 in December, and 105 from January to April 15th]. If a leap year were involved (February having 29 days), the latest relinquishment date (without an extension) would be October 18th.

The plain language of Section 1031(a)(3) is clear. It reads that—

> *For purposes of this subsection, any property received by the taxpayer* [transferor] *shall be treated as property which is* ***not like-kind if***— [the time constraints above are not met].

6

A TRUE LIFE 1031 EXAMPLE

Being So Popular As They Are, Section 1031 Exchanges Take On Various Multiparty/Multiproperty Arrangements. The Essential Ingredient To Success Is Engaging Early A QUALIFIED FACILITATOR/GUARANTOR By The Party Most Desiring The Exchange. Where The Aggregate FMVs Of The Properties Exceed $1,000,000, Extremely Thorough Planning And Preliminary Consultations Are A "Must." Many Diverse Monetary And Property Interests Are At Stake. It Is Always Best To Decide On Replacement Properties BEFORE Relinquishing The Exchanged Property. We Have For You A Fascinating True Life Example Of How Things Can Really Work.

When considering a 1031 exchange of property worth $1,000,000 or more, much preplanning and preliminary inquiries are required. Especially if you have a relatively low adjusted tax basis in that property. For example, if your adjusted basis was $100,000 and an independent appraiser valued the property at $1,000,000, your realized gain would be $900,000. The federal capital gains tax on this amount would be approximately $180,000 (20% x $900,000). If you were of retirement age (say around 65 or so), you might consider a 10- to 20-year installment sale contract. Doing so, you could pay the tax over the life of the installment contract and still have a comfortable income.

But if you were younger, say in the 40 or so age range, and you inherited property which is now in the $1,000,000 Fair Market Value (FMV) range, you certainly would want to investigate the tax and peripheral benefits of an exchange. Who knows, you might be able to parlay the $1,000,000 into a larger amount for a more comfortable retirement later.

We have the perfect example to relate to you in this regard. It's a "from rags to riches" affair. This author did all of the preliminary education of the exchanger, and did all of the final tax computations and reportings to the IRS. Without offering specific referral names, the author encouraged the exchanger to seek help from others, such as from real estate attorneys, real estate agents, real estate appraisers, and, above all, to engage a qualified intermediary/exchanger. The property to be exchanged was 16 acres of prime farmland being encroached on by rapidly expanding Silicon Valley companies at the southernmost end of San Jose, California.

Background on the Case

The exchanger — we'll call him Walt — was a 40-year-old farm mechanic. He had a 20-year-old truck fitted out with welding equipment and bins for the storage of parts and materials. He traveled within a 100-mile radius of his home to farms, orchards, and ranches where he repaired machinery and equipment. He also share-cropped the farm on which he lived. Between his two jobs, he grossed (in his best years) *under* $60,000 per year.

He was born on 16 acres of land in a home which his parents had built. The land was originally owned by the grandparents. When his grandparents and father died, there were eight heirs to the property (including Walt). After he married, he rebuilt and remodeled the old home to accommodate his wife and four children (all boys). The wife did not like living and working on a farm . . . and so left him and their four children. He borrowed money against his interest in the farm to meet his property settlement obligations to his ex-wife. Other family-related owners of pieces of the farm did not want to live on it either. They began offering to Walt their individual shares of the farm at the then market rates some 15 years ago. Within about 10 years, he owned 80% of the 16-acre farm. The two holdouts were his two sisters, who each owned 10%.

As the electronics industry expanded southward in the Santa Clara valley, and pressure for residential acreage grew, the City of

San Jose rezoned the area, demanded easements on the property for utilities and roads, and placed restrictions on the types of crops that could be grown. The farmland was in an unincorporated area of the county which the city was planning to annex under its power of eminent domain. The city offered to buy the property from Walt and his two sisters for 15% over their cost basis. The sisters were willing to go along, but Walt — the 80% owner — was not.

Walt engaged several attorneys to fight "city hall" for his right to sell his land at its best FMV price. In order to grant this right, the city required that the property be resurveyed in its entirety; that it be rezoned according to its plan; and that all utility easements (water, power, sewage, and access right of ways) be staked off for development. At this point, a developer became very interested. The developer and Walt separately engaged professional appraisers. The "compromise" FMV agreed upon was $5,289,000 (that is 5 *million* plus). By this time, Walt's basis in his 80% had grown to $386,500. This amount *included* $49,550 in attorney fees and $18,130 in surveying fees. Is there any wonder why Walt refused to accept the city's offer to buy the entire 16 aces of prime farmland for just 15% over its inherited cost basis? He had the prospects of becoming a millionaire.

The Next Hurdle

The developer wanted to buy the entire 16 acres of prime land free and clear of all entanglements. He had big plans for the area: light industry, commercial, and residential. Sisters X and Y were willing to go along. But brother Walt wanted to make a 1031 exchange for his 80% portion. The developer wanted no part of the exchange process. Furthermore, he wanted commitment on releasing the 16 acres to him as soon as possible, so that he could start his own planning.

The first tax advice given to Walt was that he engage a qualified exchange guarantor, and that he instruct the intermediary to begin looking for replacement properties. The rule on point is a 45-day identification period. Subrule (1) is that *three* properties of any fair market value be so identified. Or, subrule (2) permits any number of replacement properties to be identified so long as their aggregate

FMV not exceed 200 percent of FMV in the property to be relinquished. Walt's interest in the property was $4,231,200 (80% of $5,289,000). His two sisters wanted no part of the exchange. Each wanted her share out in cash, after proration for sales commissions and closing costs. The year was 1997.

Within a short time after it became known in multiple-listing realty circles that there was a serious exchanger looking for $4,000,000 or so worth of property, offers came pouring in. Walt visited each offered property, accompanied by the sales agent representing each owner thereof. He decided on the following three properties:

A	— a 22-unit commercial mall: FMV	$2,640,000
B	— a 7-unit light manufacturing complex: FMV	925,000
C	— 200 acres of low grade timberland: FMV	500,000
	Aggregate FMVs	$4,065,000

After verifying these FMVs with his own appraisers, exchanger Walt relinquished his 80% of the 16 acres to the Exchange Guaranty Company. His two sisters also relinquished their 20% to the same exchange guarantor. In the end, since each sister was a pure seller, each received $47,647 cash out of the deal (after allocable expenses). This left Walt as the sole exchanger who could not close the deal until all replacement property terms had been satisfied.

Personal Residence Dilemma

On the 16 acres of prime farmland was the primary residence of Walt and his four sons. The developer intended to demolish the house. Were he to do so immediately, Walt and his sons would have no place to live. Besides, if he could sell the house separately, he could have gotten a $250,000 *exclusion of gain* under Section 121(b)(2): ***Exclusion of Gain from Sale of Principal Residence.*** That law went into effect on May 7, 1997. This was eight months *before* the exchange arrangement was approved by all parties thereto. The developer did not want the house sold separately, as he would have to buy out the new owner in order to demolish it. In addition, the exchange of a personal residence does **not** qualify under Section 1031. Personal residence exchanges formerly qualified under Section 1034, but that section was repealed on May 6, 1997. It was replaced by Section 121.

Was there a solution to Walt's personal residence exchange dilemma?

Answer: Yes . . . if Walt acted promptly and decisively. Walt did so. The result, schematically, is depicted in Figure 6.1.

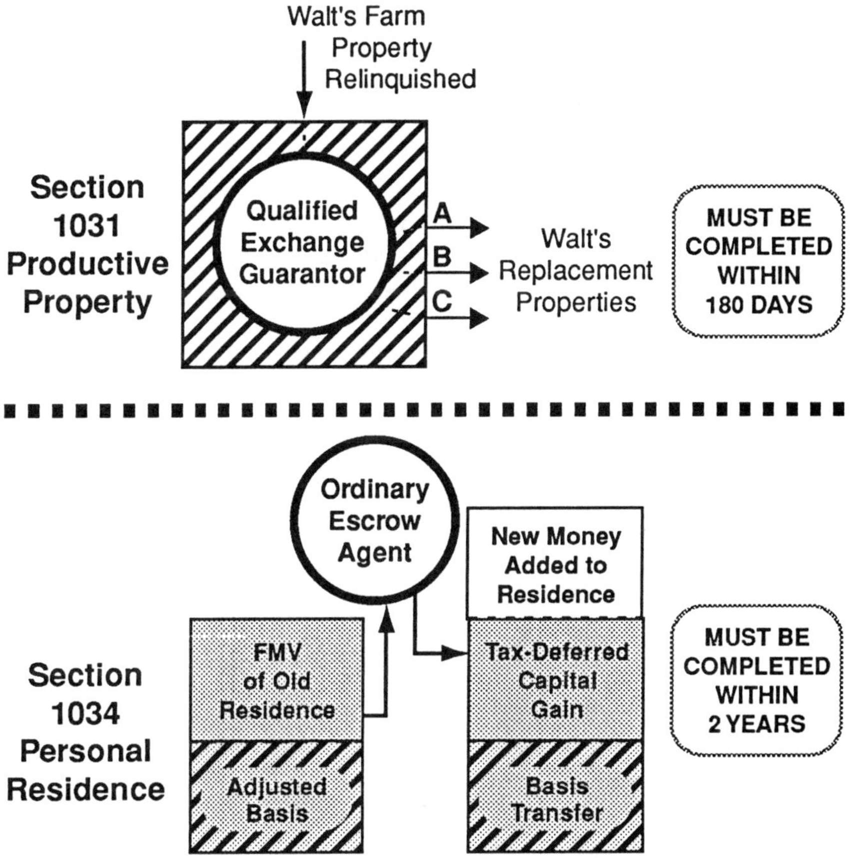

Fig. 6.1 - Each Tax Code Exchange Section is Independent of All Others

Note that Walt had engaged in *two* separate exchanges: Section 1031 **and** (old) Section 1034. This was perfectly tax legal.

For Walt, a special, one-time, transitional rule applied, namely: Section 121(f): ***Election to have Section not Apply***. (Walt was tax informed of this feature well before the 1031 exchange agreement was entered into.) A homeseller could elect out of the Section 121 exclusion benefit if — on or before August 5, 1997 — he entered into a **binding contract** to purchase or build a replacement home within two years following the enactment of Section 121.

This is exactly what Walt did. He selected the most accessible corner of his 200 acres of scrub timberland and engaged a contractor to construct a $1,000,000 home thereon (including access roadways and utilities). This arrangement qualified as a *transitional* 1034 exchange. It was not part of the 1031 exchange process. The new residence contract was finalized on August 4, 1997. It called for completion on or before May 6, 1999: the 2-year period required.

The 1031 exchange concluded on January 22, 1998 when title to the 200 acres of low-grade timberland was quieted by the exchange guarantor. Thereafter, Walt and his four sons had to move off the property which no longer belonged to them. Fortuitously, they had a couple of old camping trailers and motor homes which they had used for family recreational activities. They converted these vehicles to temporary living quarters at the site where their new home was to be built. Walt then turned his full attention to the 1031 process.

Setting up the 1031 Exchange

In Figure 6.2, we present an overall depiction of the preliminary events that had to be resolved before the 1031 process could go forward. Once resolved, the entire exchange process was completed in 114 days: from date of relinquishment of the 16 acres of primeland (9-30-97) through quieting of title to the 200 acres of scrubland (1-22-98). Section 1031(a)(3) allows 180 days.

The technical focus of the 1031 exchange for Walt was his exchanging 12.8 acres of prime farmland (80% of 16 acres) for properties A, B, and C. A and B were already income-producing properties. Property C was undeveloped and unused. It contained an abundance of low-grade timber and much scrub undergrowth used as a habitat for wild pigs, wild turkeys, and other smaller animals. He converted it to modest income by offering day-hunting

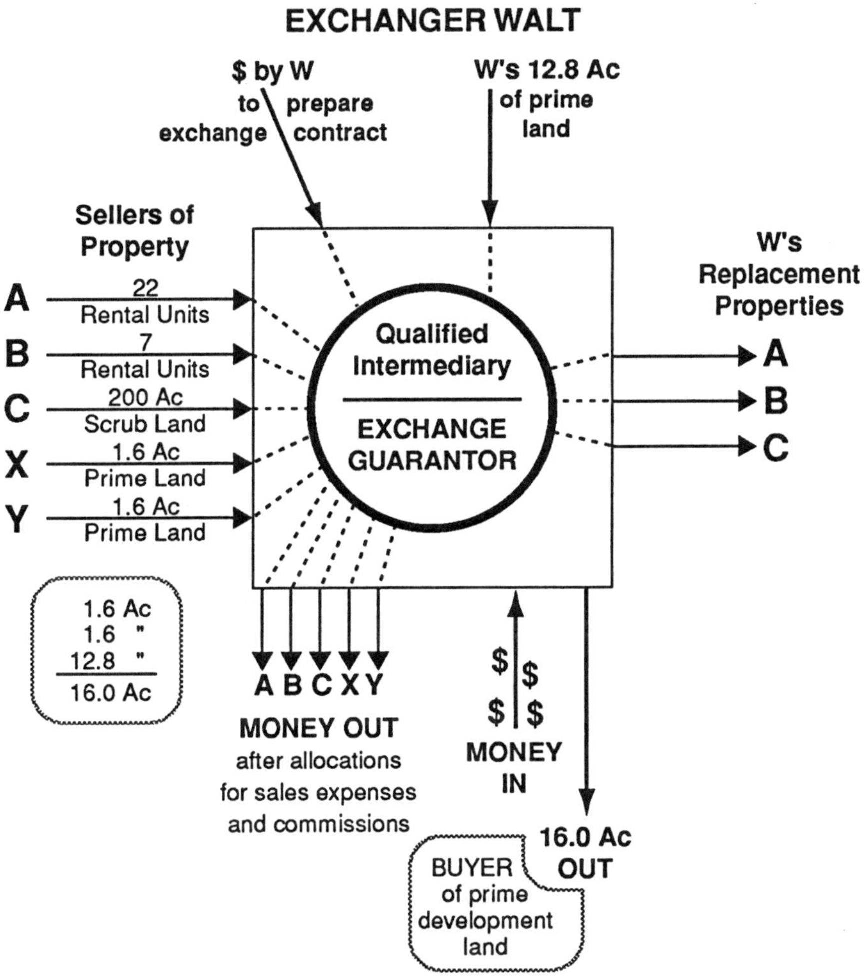

Fig. 6.2 - Setup for Text-Presented Multiparty/Multiproperty Exchange

permits and timber cutting rights to those who had their own off-road vehicles and equipment. He also offered monthly grazing and foraging rights to cattle growers and goat growers in the surrounding agricultural areas.

Walt's 12.8 acres of prime land FMVed at $4,231,200 (80% of the developer-agreed FMV of $5,289,000). Of Walt's FMV land share, his former primary residence had to be separately FMVed for Section 1034 purposes. It had no value whatsoever to the 16-acre developer. Nevertheless, based on comparable homes in the area, it appraised at $578,546 (with an adjusted tax basis of $50,515). The 1031 exchange value of Walt's land thus became $3,656,654 [$4,231,200 land – $578,546 house]. His basis in the 12.8 acres of land was $335,985 [$386,500 total basis – 50,515 house basis].

In other words, exchanger Walt was conveying $3,652,654 in land value and receiving $4,065,000 of value in three separate like-kind 1031 properties, namely:

Property A	=	$2,640,000	FMV
Property B	=	925,000	FMV
Property C	=	500,000	FMV
		$4,065,000	

Balancing the Equities

The first computational phase of any 1031 exchange is to balance the equities between the properties being exchanged. Since Walt was receiving more in FMV than that which he was exchanging, he either had to make up the difference with cash, assumed debt, or other property. As a condition for engaging an exchange guarantor, Walt had to immediately put up $7,580 in cash. Property C had a $36,007 mortgage on it, which Walt assumed. He had to borrow against properties A and B.

The results of the equity balancing computations went like this:

	Property CONVEYED	Property RECEIVED
FMV of property exchanged	$3,652,654	$4,065,000
Existing mortgage	-0-	<36,007>
Existing equities	3,652,654	4,028,993
Boot		
Cash	7,580	-0-
Purchased money (deeds of trust)	-0-	<368,759>
Other nonlike property (boot)	-0-	-0-
Equities balanced	$3,660,234	$3,660,234

This is called an "up exchange": the value of the property received is greater than that which is conveyed. If an existing mortgage on property received is not too great, generally, in an up exchange, all of the capital gain realized on the transaction is tax deferred. Let's see how this works out, using actual numbers.

Gain Realized/Gain Recognized

Whether a sale or an exchange, the amount of gain realized is always the amount of consideration received *minus* the amount of consideration paid.

The amount of consideration received is determined as follows:

1. FMV of property received	$4,065,000
2. Cash (if any) received	-0-
3. FMV of boot (if any) received	-0-
4. Mortgage/debt relief on property conveyed	-0-
Total consideration received	$4,065,000

The amount of consideration conveyed is determined as follows:

5. Adjusted basis of property conveyed	$ 335,985
6. Cash (if any) conveyed	7,580
7. Adjusted basis of boot (if any) conveyed	368,759
8. Mortgage assumed on property received	36,007
9. Exchange expenses	40,374
Total consideration given	$ 788,785

Therefore, the total capital gain realized on the exchange is:

	$4,065,000 received
MINUS	788,785 conveyed
EQUALS	$3,276,215

How much of this realized gain is tax deferred?

Answer: **All** of it! The reason is that there is no net cash or boot received, after subtracting exchange expenses, and after adding any net mortgage relief on property conveyed. In this particular illustrative (true life) exchange case, Walt recognized no capital gains tax whatsoever on his $3,276,215 of realized gain! Some day, either he or his four boys will pay all of the deferred-gain tax . . . most likely in piecemeal fashion.

Aggregate Basis in Replacement Properties

Recall that exchanger Walt received three separate properties: A, B, and C. Also recall in Chapter 2 (at Figure 2.2 on page 2-8), how we depicted the transfer of adjusted basis in the exchanged property to the replacement property, and on to the next replacement property . . . ad infinitum. After the direct transfer to the replacement property, basis adjustments were made depending on how much "new money" is added. That is, basis adjustment to the replacement property depends strictly on the amount of new money that has been added to that property. When more than one property is acquired in the exchange or, conversely, when more than one property is conveyed, we have to work (initially) on the *aggregate basis* concept.

In our true life example above, the 12.8 acres of prime farmland relinquished in the exchange had an adjusted basis of $335,985. Recall our computation on page 6-8 in this regard. To this amount, what new money was added?

Ordinarily, new money is the excess of that which is conveyed over that which is received, plus the taxable portion of any gain recognized, plus those exchange expenses borne by the exchanger. Money received is cash (if any), boot other than cash, and debt relief (if any). In our particular case, no cash, no boot, and no debt relief were received. The primary reason for this is that the arrangement was an up exchange and the conveyed land was free and clear of all debt. Hence, we need only focus on the new money conveyed. Walt's conveyance of new money consisted of the following items:

		$ Amount
1.	Cash conveyed	$ 7,580
2.	Adj. basis of boot conveyed (2 deeds of trust)	368,759

3. Mortgage assumed on property received		36,007
4. Exchange expenses		40,374
	Total "new money"	$452,800

The "boot conveyed" was borrowed money in the form of a deed of trust for $300,000 against property A, and a further deed of trust for $68,759 against property B. Property C already had a mortgage on it for $36,007, which Walt assumed. Always keep this one principle in mind: debt assumed is treated as money paid; debt relief is treated as money received; and borrowed money, when recorded as a "deed of trust" against property received is treated as money paid. Recall Figure 3.5 on page 3-20 in this regard.

Now, what is the aggregate exchange basis in the three replacement properties acquired?

Answer: $788,785. This is the sum of the adjusted basis of the property conveyed ($335,985) PLUS the total amount of new money conveyed ($452,800). Thus, the *aggregate basis* total is $788,785 [335,985 + 452,800].

Basis Allocation Among Properties

Knowing the aggregate basis in three newly acquired (replacement) properties is one thing. Allocating this basis to each property received, and allocating it among the items within each property, is another ballgame. In fact, there are two computational ballgames. Game 1 is a property-by-property allocation; game 2 is an item-by-item allocation within a property allocation. Game 1 is first. That is, the amount of basis to be allocated is $788,785 (as established above).

Property-by-property allocation of the aggregate basis is done by fractionizing the FMV of each property, in terms of the aggregate FMVs of all properties: A, B, and C. Once a property's allocation fraction is determined, that fraction is applied to the aggregate basis of all the properties.

Let us illustrate the mechanics of the process with property A. Its FMV is $2,640,000 (recall from above). The aggregate FMV for all three properties is $4,065,000 (also recall from above). Therefore, its basis allocation fraction is

2,640,000 ÷ 4,065,000 = 0.6494 (to 4 decimals)

Using this decimal fraction, apply it to the $788,785 aggregate basis of all properties. The result is—

0.6494 x 788,785 = $512,237.

This is the allocable basis to property A only.

Doing the above for all three properties en masse, we get the following results:

	Property FMVs	Fraction of Aggregate FMV		Basis Allocation Each Property
A =	$2,640,000	0.6494	⟶	$512,237
B =	925,000	0.2276	⟶	179,527
C =	500,000	0.1230	⟶	97,021
Aggregate	$4,065,000	1.0000	Aggregate	$788,785

Item-by-Item Allocations

Now comes game 2: item-by-item allocation of basis within each property: A, B, and C. To accomplish this, we need the latest applicable data from the Office of the County Assessor. All U.S. states, bar none, impose a property tax on each parcel of real property located within their political borders. They do so by assigning each parcel of land an APN: ***Assessor's Parcel Number***. Then they assign separate values to land and to improvements. An "improvement" is any structure, building, or complex of buildings and structures fixed to the land that is APN identified. Most property tax years extend from July 1st through June 30th. Thus, for our true life case, the exchange period started on 9-30-97 and ended on 1-22-98. The valuations used by the Assessor were those that existed on July 1, 1979. As a consequence, the official assessment year for each of the three properties was '97-'98.

The '97-'98 Assessor valuations for each of the three replacement properties were:

	{Land:	1,129,618}
A = $2,767,566 =	{	}
	{Bldgs:	1,637,948}
	{Land:	193,800}
B = 561,000 =	{	}
	{Bldgs:	367,200}
	{Land	200,000}
C = 200,000 =	{	}
	{Bldgs:	-0- }
$3,528,566		

The Assessor's valuations and the agreed FMVs between buyer and seller often are unrelated. Over time, however, as the same or similar property is sold repeatedly, the Assessor's value — because of his interest in property tax revenues — approaches the FMV.

Note, in the Assessor's data above, that each of properties A and B has two items separately valued: land and building structures. Now we must allocate item by item the property-by-property basis allocation derived on page 6-12. We do this for properties A and B separately, as follows:

Property A		Allocation Fraction		Basis in Item as Allocated
Land	= 1,129,618	0.4082	→	209,095
Bldgs	= 1,637,948	0.5918	→	303,142
	2,767,566	1.0000		
		Property A's basis		512,237

Property B		Allocation Fraction		Basis in Item as Allocated
Land	= 193,800	0.3455	→	62,027
Bldgs	= 367,200	0.6545	→	117,500
	561,000	1.0000		
		Property B's basis		179,527

Property C has only one item, namely land. Hence, no item-by-item basis allocation is necessary. It takes the same basis that we established earlier, namely: 97,021.

Now, the Depreciation Surprise

As you know, when you have income-producing property, such as properties A and B above, you are allowed a depreciation deduction against the basis of the structures and equipment used for producing that income. With this point in mind, let us recap the allocated basis items above. Doing so, we have—

Property A: 22 commercial rental units

Land basis	209,095	Nondepreciable
Bldgs. basis	303,142	**Depreciable**

Property B: 7 commercial rental units

Land basis	62,027	Nondepreciable
Bldgs. basis	117,500	**Depreciable**

Property C: minimal income from hunting, camping, grazing

Land basis	97,021	Nondepreciable
Bldgs. basis	None	

TOTAL BASIS = $778,785 (same as established earlier)

Of this $778,785 amount, how much is depreciable (as a deduction) for income tax purposes?

Answer: $420,642 [303,142 for property A and 117,500 for property B]. Furthermore, being commercial rental units, the mandatory depreciation allowance is straight-line over 39 years. You have to use 39 years whether the property is one year old or 139 years old. This means that the maximum allowable depreciation deduction is just over $10,000 per year [$420,642 ÷ 39 yrs = 10,786]. For a property owner with over $4,000,000 in productive property, the depreciation allowance of $10,000 per year is a shocker. If (hypothetically) it were all depreciable , the yearly depreciation would be $104,230 per year [4,065,000 ÷ 39 yrs].

To most exchangers, the depreciation allowance comes as a big surprise and disappointment. Many "howl and scream" — literally — when they review, study, and haggle over the basis computations on their replacement properties. They want to depreciate everything: the full market value of each property acquired. They forget, as in our example case, that over $3,000,000 ($3,276,215 to be exact) was tax deferred. The attitude often is: "That's all tax free; isn't it? So why can't I depreciate it?" The exchange rules say, in effect, that you have to take the bad with the good.

Income Greatly Enhanced

Another surprise overtook our exchanger. His gross income shot up astonishingly. By 1031 exchanging his 12.8 acres of prime (though semi-productive) farmland for 29 commercial rental units (properties A and B), his income tax accounting attention abruptly shifted. His average rental income from each of the 29 units came in at roughly $22,500 per year. This meant that his gross income jumped from just under $60,000 (including his farm income) per year to over $650,000 per year [$22,500 per unit x 29 units = $652,500]! His income from property C (for hunting, camping, and grazing) is not significant to our discussion here. In other words, after the 1031 exchange, Walt's gross income jumped more than 10-fold over that which he derived before the exchange. And he paid no capital gains tax! He paid ordinary income tax only.

His expense offsets against his $650,000 income boiled down to just four items: property insurance, property taxes, mortgage interest, and depreciation allowance. His fire insurance on the buildings approximated $40,000; his property taxes approximated $44,000. His mortgage interest approximated $30,000 [a $300,000 trust deed on Property A; a $68,759 trust deed on property B]; and an assumed mortgage of $36,007 on property C: each at about a 7.5% rate of interest per annum]. As pointed out earlier, his depreciation allowance was about $10,000 per year. Altogether, his fixed expenses came to around $124,000 per year [40,000 + 44,000 + 30,000 + 10,000].

All utilities and tenant-caused repairs and tenant-sought improvements were paid for by the tenants. Walt did all the minor repairs himself, as this was what he was accustomed to do on his own farm and on the farms of others. Recall from our introductory description of Walt that he was a self-employed farm mechanic with four dependent sons. Prior to the exchange, his total income tax (from self-employment and net farm proceeds) was *less than* $10,000 per year. In some years it was substantially lower.

Now, with 29 units of rental income after the exchange, his income tax situation changed dramatically. Without refinements for his standard deductions and child exemptions, his new tax structure looked something like this:

Gross rental income	$650,000
Allowable expenses (4)	124,000
Net taxable income	526,000
x 35% ordinary tax rate	$184,000!

In other words, his *federal* income tax jumped 18 times over that which he experienced before the exchange. Add another $46,000 of California income tax, and his total income tax was approximately $230,000 for the year. This still left him with an after-tax benefit of nearly $300,000 for the year. This compares with about $30,000 after tax before the exchange. This is what we mean when we described the exchange as: *from rags to riches*. This is truly a true case. It illustrates quite vividly how a well planned and well executed Section 1031 exchange can produce remarkable financial results.

7

INVOLUNTARY CONVERSIONS

Property That Is Destroyed In A Disaster, Or Taken By Condemnation, Is Addressed In Section 1033. If ALL Reimbursement Proceeds (Insurance, Court Awards, Public Assistance) Are Used To Acquire REPLACEMENT PROPERTY "Similar Or Related In Service Or Use" To That Converted, No Gain Is Tax Recognized. There Are, However, Adjustments To Basis In The Replacement Property. Depending On Circumstances, Replacement Is Required Within 2, 3, Or 4 Years After The First Taxable Year "In Which Any Part Of The Gain" Is Realized. For Business Or Investment Property, The Purchase Of Corporate Stock May Qualify As Replacement Property.

There are situations in which one is compelled to give up his property and seek another. No sale or exchange takes place involving the free choice or will of the owner. He is deprived of the use of his property under compulsion and conditions over which he has no control. These transactions are tax-termed *involuntary conversions*.

Involuntary conversion results primarily from destructive forces and condemnation powers. These are not like-kind "exchanges" in the customary sense. It is for this reason that special tax treatment applies. Since there is no special tax form that can be used to report the conversion, a taxpayer-designed "statement" attached to one's return is required.

Conversion by destruction covers all cases of physical damage caused by violent and external means. Examples are lightning, storm (tornado, hurricane), flood, earthquake, volcanic eruption, landslide, tidal wave, fire, and the like. Conversion by condemnation (or under the threat thereof) is the taking of property for public needs such as for freeway construction, airport expansion, public housing projects, etc. The resulting destruction or condemnation may not be 100%. But it must be of such magnitude as to render the property no longer usable: beyond ordinary repair. Usually, restoration/replacement funds are sought through insurance claims and disaster loans from the government.

The involuntary conversion of one's property may result in conversion into a replacement property, or into money and other property. Whatever the cause, there is possibility of gain. This is due to the excess of awards, proceeds, and/or reimbursement over one's tax basis in the converted property. Whenever there is a gain — whether under compulsion or not — there is accountability for tax. While the conversion law is compassionate in this respect, there is no tax forgiveness for involuntariness.

Establishing the amount of gain under involuntary conversion conditions is tricky and time consuming. Insurance companies and government agencies do not pay promptly. Any reimbursement you get is quite unlike the closing escrow process in a Section 1031 exchange. It usually takes several years before the full amount of the realized gain is known. Explaining the rules for establishing this gain plus explaining those rules where the gain is not taxed, is what this chapter is all about.

Highlights of Section 1033

We urge that you take a moment and flip back to page 1-8 to recall Figure 1.2. Of the nine exchange laws listed there, note that Section 1033: ***Involuntary Conversions***, is second in importance only to Section 1031. It is second in importance both in the number of professional text pages devoted to it and in its professional word count. Its actual statutory word count is approximately 4,000 words. It is a patchwork of numerous amendments since its enactment nearly 50 years ago. It is not exclusively applicable to any one special kind of property. It applies equally to personal residences, rental real estate (of all types), business property, farm assets, mining rigs, livestock, excess acreage, outdoor advertising displays, maritime vehicles, aircraft, and so on.

Section 1033(a) consists of two general rules, namely: (1) ***Conversion into Similar Property***, and (2) ***Conversion into Money***. General rule (1) is the shorter (48 words). So let us cite it to you, essentially in full. It reads—

> *If property . . . is compulsorily or involuntarily converted . . . into property* ***similar or related in service or use****, no gain shall be recognized.* [Emphasis added.]

Note immediately the divergence from the like-kind-replacement-property concept of Section 1031. In lieu thereof, we have the term: "similar or related in service or use." Not at this moment, but shortly below, we are going to explain this term more fully.

General rule (2) is more complicated than the above. Its preamble words read—

> *If property . . . is compulsorily or involuntarily converted . . .* ***into money or property not similar*** *or related in service or use to the converted property, the* ***gain (if any) shall be recognized*** *except to the extent hereinafter provided.* [Emphasis added.]

The "extent hereinafter provided" covers another 850 words of special conditions. One of these conditions, subparagraph (A), permits a taxpayer to replace his property, then "elect" to have any excess proceeds over replacement cost be treated as recognized gain. A second condition, subparagraph (B), requires that one start computing his gain—

> *2 years after the close of the first taxable year in which any part of the gain upon conversion is realized, or*
> *at the close of such later date as the* [IRS] *may designate on application by the taxpayer.*

Gain starts to be realized the moment one recovers his full capital basis in the property converted. For example, suppose the adjusted basis in your converted property was $100,000. And, further, suppose that the fair market value of your property at the time of its destruction or condemnation was $600,000. After suing the insurance company or whomever, you are awarded $500,000 as compensation for the conversion. The moment you receive $101,000 you come under the *conversion to money* rule of Section 1033(a)(2). Every payment you receive thereafter has to be accounted for in the tax domain as "realized gain." The amount of gain *recognized* is the extent to which the compensation award exceeds the purchase cost of the replacement property.

In Figure 7.1 we present an overview distinction between subsections (a)(1) and (a)(2) of Section 1033. The real substance of Section 1033 is its rule (2) within which rule (1) is the nonrecognition part. The replacement property may be higher or lower in value than the property converted.

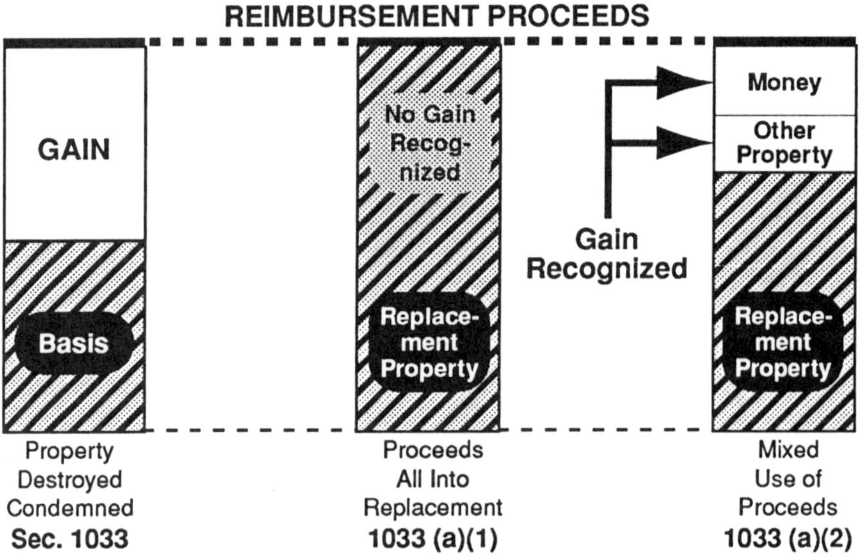

Fig. 7.1 - Treatment of Sec. 1033 Gain from Reimbursement Proceeds

Destruction in Whole or Part

Section 1033(a) includes a parenthetical phrase which we intentionally excluded above. The excluded phrase is: "If property—

(as a result of its destruction in whole or in part, theft, seizure, or requisition or condemnation or threat or imminence thereof)—

is compulsorily or involuntarily converted . . ." This parenthetical phrase raises many pertinent questions. What is meant by: "destruction in whole or in part"? What is meant by: "theft, seizure, requisition . . ." etc. As you would expect, these and other pertinent questions are addressed in various IRS Regulations and IRS Revenue Rulings. We'll give you the gist of these as we go along.

Destruction in whole or part is that which is caused by a *casualty*: an event beyond the knowledge, timing, or control of the property owner. Usually, a casualty arises from some sudden, unexpected, or unusual cause. Good examples of causes of such damage to property are hurricane, fire, flood, quarry blast, arson (except to one's own property), sonic boom, earthquake, earthslide, the battering of waves and winds, an unusual or unprecedented drought or freeze, shipwreck, or other. The IRS (in Rev. Ruling 66-334) cites an "other casualty" as salt water pollution of an underground fresh water supply by a leaky salt water storage tank used in an oil drilling operation. Yet in another Rev. Ruling (74-532), the IRS treated the demolition of a building as a "voluntary conversion," as was the sale of property that was the target of repeated vandalism. Though the vandalism certainly defaced the property, it was not serious enough to warrant being treated as "destruction in whole or in part." The "in part" portion of destruction has never been expressly defined. The connotation is that the extent of destruction must be sufficient to render continued use of the property inadequate for its established purpose.

Theft of another person's property is a clear-cut indication of involuntary conversion. The term "theft" covers any appropriation of another's property for use by the taker, without the owner's knowledge and permission. It includes all forms of swindling, false pretense, and outright guile. As an example of guile, Rev. Ruling 66-355 points out that theft occurred when a financial manager pledged the stock of his clients as collateral for his own personal loans, and the bank sold the stock to satisfy the manager's overdue loans.

Seizure is clearly an involuntary conversion. This occurs when a governmental agency takes physical possession of private property for a public purpose, without first obtaining court approval or paying compensation. Rev. Ruling 79-269 gives an instructive example of nonseizure. When the trustee appointed by a bankruptcy court sold stock and other assets of the bankruptee, the proceeds were not used for a public purpose. Instead, the proceeds were used to pay the creditors of the bankruptee. Bankruptcy is usually a financial event, and not something caused by physical compulsion.

Condemnation: "Threat or Imminence" Thereof

The cited Section 1033(a) parenthetical phrase above also includes the terms: *requisition or condemnation or threat or imminence thereof.* The general concept here is that a governmental or quasi-governmental body legally takes private property for public use — without the owner's consent — but upon the award and payment of just compensation. This is quite different from those situations where sales, exchanges, distributions, or divisions of property between private parties are mandated by legislation, court order, reclamation laws, certain government agency orders (FCC, SEC, or others), or due to threatened or actual foreclosure proceedings. It's the "threat or imminence" of governmental action that requires special heeding.

The *threat or imminence* provision requires that the governmental or quasi-governmental agency—

1. Must have the legal power to condemn or to requisition, and
2. Must, in fact, make a threat of condemnation or make it known that condemnation is indeed imminent.

The disposition of one's property under the above two conditions qualifies as an involuntary conversion. This is so regardless of whether condemnation proceedings, if undertaken, would be successful. The factual threat by a government body with the power to enforce its threat is sufficient.

Condemnation is threatened or imminent when a property owner is "informed," orally or in writing by a representative of a governmental body or by a public official authorized to acquire property for public use, that such body or official has "decided" to acquire his property. Some verification of the decision via an official memorandum or minutes of a public hearing is required. Based on such information, together with news reports and notices in public media, the property owner has reasonable grounds to believe that condemnation will begin unless he sells voluntarily.

If condemnation is merely being "considered," rather than having been decided, there is no threat or imminence. Considerations and deliberations (of condemnation) go on all the time in the public arena. It is not until specific decisions have been made that threat or imminence looms.

If, in fact, threat or imminence does prevail, it is sometimes better to dispose of one's property prior to its actual condemnation. The politics of condemnation, the inertia of bureaucracy, the greed of attorneys, and the delays of justice, can result in net proceeds to the property owner much less than a pre-condemnation "sale."

Unfortunately, it is often difficult to "negotiate" with a condemning authority. Such an authority can be arrogant and intimidating, especially if some sharpie legal firm has been engaged to do the negotiating. As a precaution against being completely taken, *two* independent, impartial, professional appraisers (not attorneys) should be employed by the property owner. Both appraisers should be present at the negotiating conference.

One of the likely benefits of a negotiated sale to a condemning authority is that the monetary proceeds may be available immediately upon transfer of title. If so, this can save valuable time and anguish in seeking suitable replacement property.

Eligible Replacement Property

To be eligible for nonrecognition of capital gain under Section 1033(a), the replacement property must be—

similar or related in service or use to the property . . .

involuntarily converted.

In other words, there must be "sufficient relatedness" to the property destroyed or condemned. Whether the relatedness is sufficient depends in large part on whether the taxpayer (claiming nonrecognition of gain) is an ***owner-user*** or an ***owner-lessor***. The fact that replacement costs are not the same as those used to compute insurance or other award proceeds does not affect the nonrecognition of gain. If the cost of replacing property is greater than the recovery proceeds, the excess cost adds to one's capital basis in the replacement property.

For an owner-user, the property acquired must have a close functional similarity to the property converted. This means that the replacement property must have *closely similar physical characteristics and end uses* to the property that was involuntarily converted. For example, under the close functional similarity test, a corporation that lost its headquarters office building to fire could replace it with another office building (miles or cities apart). However, the test would not be met if the company replaced its destroyed parking garage with a warehouse. A warehouse, where product inventory is stored until customer orders are received, is income-functionally different from that of a parking garage where paying customers are in and out daily.

For an owner-lessor [investor-landlord], focus is on the similarity of the relationship between services and uses of the original and replacement properties. The relationship can be sufficiently similar even though the use by the respective tenants changes. For example, the original property may be rented to attorneys and doctors; the replacement property (if a building with rental spaces) is similar if it is rented to repair technicians and auto mechanics. The mere fact of simply renting the original and replacement properties in and of itself is not sufficient. The similarity of replacement is determined by the following inquiries:

(1) Are the properties similar in *physical nature*?
(2) Are the *business risks* associated with the properties similar?
(3) Are the *demands of tenants* similar with respect to property management, services made available, and safety and insurance requirements?

In Figure 7.2, we try to synopsize the principal features of eligible 1033 replacement property. Many of these features derive from various court rulings and IRS rulings. The general idea is that, both before and after the conversion, the property owner's economic interests and management participation must continue much the same.

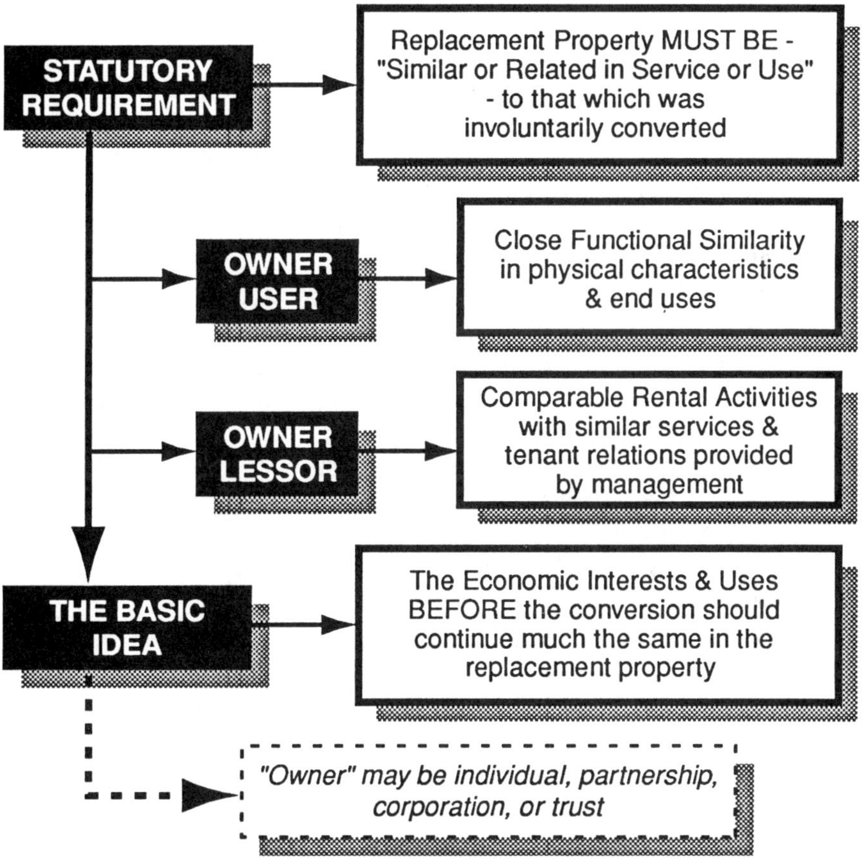

Fig. 7.2 - Tests for Eligibility of Replacement Property Under Sec. 1033

Complete Outline of Section 1033

Now that we have given you a taste of what involuntary exchanges are all about, we want to give you a complete outline of the coverage within Section 1033. As we do, keep in mind that even though an exchange may be "involuntary," there is a tax accounting process for the *conversion gain.* This gain is computed like any other form of capital gain [gross proceeds – (cost or other basis plus expense of conversion)]. Our point is that, even if your property is destroyed or condemned in its entirety, and you receive any insurance proceeds or court awards, you have to make a full accounting thereon. In essence, this is what Section 1033 is all about.

In Figure 7.3, we list *all* of the official captions that index the contents of this very important — and compassionate — tax law. The caption list cites each subsection, each paragraph of that subsection, and each subparagraph thereof. Particularly note the alphanumeric designation of each caption: (a) for subsection, (1) for paragraph, and (A) for subparagraph. There are 53 captions listed.

We urge that you take a few moments at this point to skim-read the entire list of captions. This skim reading alone will enhance your in-depth knowledge of the statutory provisions for involuntary conversions. Note that we show the word count (in increments of 10): 2,650 in total. Each page of this book averages about 350 words (without figures). Thus the statutory word length of Section 1033 is about the equivalent of seven to eight page-lengths of this book. We give you this comparison to impress on you that Section 1033 is a complex law which addresses complex real-life involuntary situations.

A quick "analysis" of Figure 7.3 reveals that ***Conversions into Money***: Subsection (a)(2), involves many more accounting rules than does *Conversion into Similar Property*: subsection (a)(1). This applies to both the conversion process and basis accounting in the replacement property. Although the captions alone do not tell so, the replacement periods may be two years, three years, four years, or longer (upon approval by the IRS). Compared to the 180-day replacement period for Section 1031, you should sense instantly that there are special reasons for the longer periods in Section 1033. We'll explain these reasons below.

A further "analysis" of Figure 7.3 reveals that subsections 1033 (c), (d), (e), and (f) are devoted to livestock businesses and certain farmlands. We'll touch on these matters shortly. We'll also

IRC SECTION 1033 : INVOLUNTARY CONVERSIONS		
Subsec. & Para.	Official Captions	Word Count
1033 (a)	General Rule	30
(a) (1)	Conversion Into Similar Property	20
(a) (2)	Conversion Into Money	30
(a) (2) (A)	Nonrecognition of Gain; (i), (ii)	210
(a) (2) (B)	Period Within Property Must be Replaceed; (i), (ii)	120
(a) (2) (C)	Time for Assessment of Deficiency Attributable to Gain Upon Conversion; (i), (ii)	140
(a) (2) (D)	Time for Assessment of Other Deficiencies Attributable to Election	110
(a) (2) (E)	Definitions; (i), (ii)	100
1033 (b)	Basis Of Property Acquired Through Involuntary Conversion	10
(b) (1)	Conversions Described in Subsection (a) (1)	30
(b) (1) (A)	Decrease in Amount	50
(b) (1) (B)	Increases in Amount	30
(b) (2)	Conversions described in Subsection (a) (2)	90
(b) (3)	Property Held by Corporation the Stock of Which is Replacement Property	10
(b) (3) (A)	In General	50
(b) (3) (B)	Limitation	60
(b) (3) (C)	Allocation of Basis Reduction; (i), (ii), (iii)	70
(b) (3) (D)	Special Rules; (i), (ii)	80
1033 (c)	Property Sold Pursuant to Reclamation Laws	50
1033 (d)	Livestock Destroyed by Disease	40
1033 (e)	Livestock Sold on Account of Drought, Flood, or Other Weather-Related Conditions	80
1033 (f)	Replacement of Livestock with Other Farm Property Where There Has Been Environmental Contamination	90
1033 (g)	Condemnation of Real Property Held for Productive Use in Trade or Business or for Investment	10
(g) (1)	Special Rule	80
(g) (2)	Limitation	20
(g) (3)	Election to Treat Outdoor Advertising Displays as Real Property	10
(g) (3) (A)	In General	80
(g) (3) (B)	Election	20
(g) (3) (C)	Outdoor Advertising Display	60
(g) (3) (D)	Character of Replacement Property	80

Continued on Next Page ▶

Fig. 7.3 - Complete Listing of All Captions to Section 1033

Subsec. & Para.	Official Captions	Word Count
(g) (4)	Special Rule	20
1033 (h)	Special Rules for Property Damaged by Presidentially Declared Disasters	10
(h) (1)	Principal Residences	20
(h) (1) (A)	Treatment of Insurance Proceeds; (i) (ii)	130
(h) (1) (B)	Extension of Replacement Period	20
(h) (2)	Trade or Business and Investment Property	60
(h) (3)	Presidentially Declared Disaster	60
(h) (4)	Principal Residence	40
1033 (i)	Replacement Property Must be Acquired From Unrelated Persons in Certain Cases	10
(i) (1)	In General	70
(i) (2)	Taxpayers to Which Section Applies	40
(i) (2) (A)	C Corporations	-
(i) (2) (B)	Partnerships	40
(i) (2) (C)	Other Taxpayers	30
(i) (3)	Related Persons	30
1033 (j)	Sales or Exchanges to Implement Microwave Relocation Policy	10
(j) (1)	In General	40
(j) (2)	Qualified Sale or Exchange	80
1033 (k)	Cross References	-
(k) (1)	Holding Period	20
(k) (2)	Treatment of Gains	20
(k) (3)	Principal Residence Exclusion (old)	20
(k) (4)	Principal Residence Exclusion (new)	20
	Total Word Count: 2650	

Fig. 7.3 (Continued) - Complete Listing of All Captions to Section 1033

comment further on the special treatment of real property held for productive purposes or for investment [subsection (g)], special rules for Presidentially declared disasters [subsection (h)], replacement property from related persons [subsection (i)], and on other matters in passing.

Replacement Property Time Frames

The length of time between the beginning and ending of the replacement property period depends on the character of the property and its conversion cause. Real property is treated more favorably than other forms of property which are involuntarily converted. It also makes a difference whether the property is converted by destruction or theft, or by condemnation or seizure.

For destroyed or stolen property, the replacement *begins* on the date of destruction or theft. This date is readily ascertainable either from media accounts, official reports, or insurance claims. The "date of destruction" is the date on which the casualty that caused the destruction ceases: when the storm is over, as it were. The date of theft is the date on which the theft or embezzlement is actually discovered. That is, when you discovered it and reported it to someone else — hopefully in writing.

For property subjected to condemnation or seizure, the *earliest* of the following three dates triggers the start of the replacement period:

(1) the date on which the property was condemned or seized;
(2) the date on which the property was first subjected to threat or imminence of condemnation or seizure; or
(3) the date on which the property was sold or exchanged under threat or imminence of condemnation or seizure.

Depending on the character of the property, the replacement period *ends* 2, 3, 4, or more years—

> . . . ***after the close of the first taxable year in which any part of the gain upon the conversion is realized*** [Subsections 1033(a)(2)(B)(i); 1033(g)(4); 1033(h)(1)(B); and 1033(a)(2)(B)(ii)].

What does this phrase: "after the close of the first taxable year," etc. mean?

Answer: It is that year in which you receive the first dollar of compensation that exceeds your adjusted basis in the property converted. For example, suppose that your basis in property converted is $60,000 and that your expected compensation proceeds are to be $150,000 in two equal payments of $75,000 each. Your first payment is in 2003 and the second payment in 2004. Since the first payment represents $15,000 of realized gain (75,000 – 60,000 basis), the close of the first taxable year in which *any part* of the gain is realized is December 31, 2003. Such close of the first taxable year is the "beginning of the ending."

With this fundamental accounting point in mind, we present in Figure 7.4 a summarized depiction of the replacement time rules above. Note that in addition to the 2, 3, or 4-year replacement periods, we show a "permitted extension" period. Either of the applicable 2, 3, or 4-year periods may be extended upon application to the IRS on Form 2688: ***Application for Additional Extension of Time to File U.S. Individual Income Tax Return*** (or comparable form for corporations and other entities). You must explain the hard reality why the extension is necessary: such as construction delays, counter lawsuits, or other circumstances entirely beyond your control.

How Nonrecognition Election Made

The nonrecognition of gain allowed by Section 1033 is NOT automatic. Whether replaced by similar property, other property, or money, the nonrecognition rules of subsections (a)(1) and (a)(2) must be elected. This is contrary to that which could be interpreted by a casual reading of these subsections. Therefore, you have to take specific overt action on your own to elect the applicable options and to so notify the IRS. How does one do this?

Answer: You do so the "first year" in which *any gain* is realized. In other words, until you realize at least $1 or more in gain (proceeds minus basis), there is no tax reporting required on your part. We tried to focus attention on this first year in Figure 7.4 as well as in our example above re year 2003.

The *first year in which gain is realized* becomes the "marker year" for attaching an election statement to your return. We suggest doing this by using Schedule D: ***Capital Gains and Losses***, for the type of return you are preparing (individual, corporation, partnership, or trust). Use, as appropriate, the first line of either Part I or Part II of that schedule. Part I is for assets held one year or less; Part II is for assets held more than one year. Fill in columns (a), (b), and (c) only. Column (a) is captioned: *Description of property.*

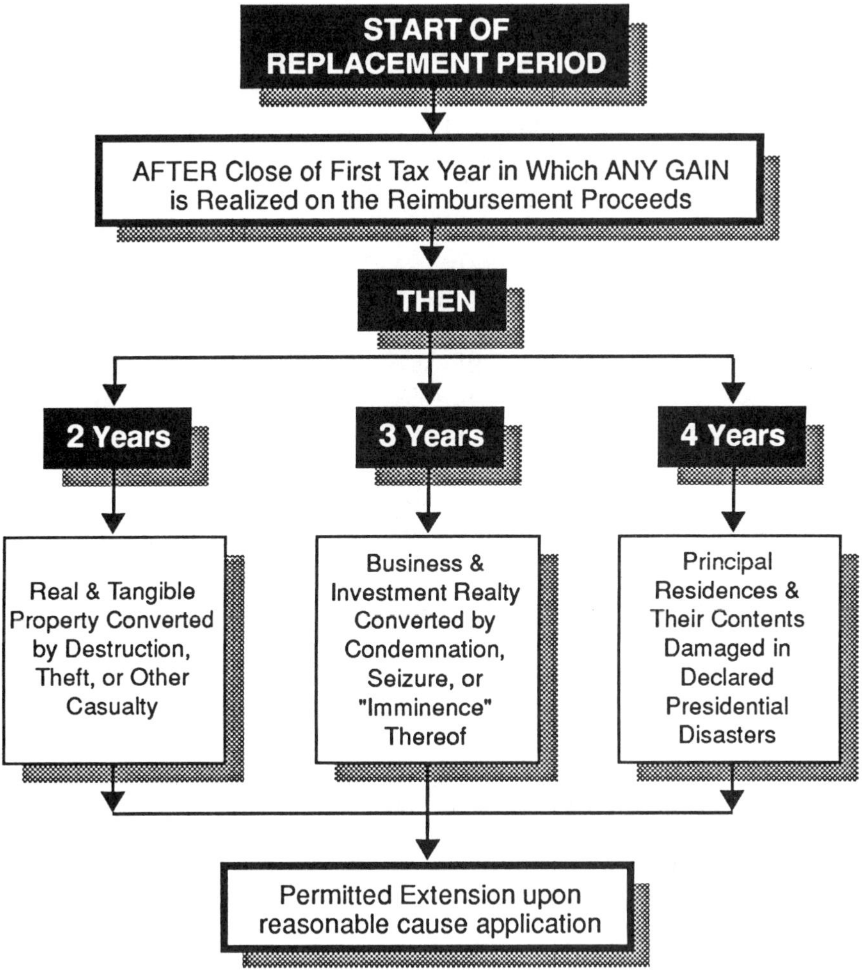

Fig. 7.4 - Replacement Periods for Property Involuntarily Converted

Enter: INVOLUNTARY CONVERSION. Columns (b) and (c) are captioned, respectively: *Date acquired* and *Date sold*. The date "sold" is that date (month, day, year) on which the first dollar of gain was realized.

Columns (d), (e), and (f) ordinarily require dollar amount entries. Make no such entries the first year of gain. Instead, type or print across them: **See Election Statement Attached**. Title your statement: "Section 1033 Election Statement" (show your name,

Tax ID, form number, and tax year). Then provide the following specific information in the format of your choice—

[1] A complete description of the conversion event and its date of occurrence.
[2] The nature, character, location, and regular use of the property converted.
[3] Computation of the realized gain for the first year, and indicate whether additional gain or other proceeds are anticipated (and how much).
[4] Your intention to replace the property with similar and/or nonsimilar property within the appropriate 2, 3, or 4-year periods indicated in Figure 7.4.
[5] Your election of the nonrecognition-of-gain provisions of subsections 1033(a)(1) or (a)(2) as applicable.
[6] A description of the intended replacement property that fulfills the statutory requirements of Section 1033.
[7] Your intention to recognize any excess portion of the gain over that necessary to acquire the replacement property, OR your intention to *reduce* the adjusted basis of the converted property by any excess gain realized.

Each year after the first year, attach to your return an amended copy of your statement with the new information then available. Cross reference your subsequent year statement on Schedule D. If the replacement property is consummated within the Figure 7.4 time frames — the replacement year — attach a final statement. Show all computations of the total gain realized, cost of the replacement property, and all necessary basis adjustments to the property acquired If you fail to do this convincingly and correctly, the IRS can assess you a tax deficiency. The deficiency dates back to the first year in which any part of the gain is realized. Now you know why the correct first year is so important.

Replacement with Corporate Stock

Involuntarily converted business or investment property can be replaced with corporate stock under certain conditions. The principal condition is that the corporation whose stock is purchased as replacement property itself must own property "similar or related in service or use" to the converted property. Furthermore, the corporation must own the replacement property **before** its stock is purchased by the owner of the property converted. In other words, the replacement property cannot be acquired by the corporation after its controlling stock is purchased. This is the substance of a Federal Appeals Court ruling [*Taft Broadcasting Co.*, CA-6, 91-1 USTC ¶ 50,189] for interpreting subsection 1033(a)(2)(A): ***Nonrecognition of gain***, when the replacement property is corporate stock.

The statutory language on point is—

> *If the taxpayer . . ., for the purpose of replacing the property so converted, purchases other property similar or related in service or use . . .,* ***or purchases stock*** *in the acquisition of control of a corporation owning such other property, . . . the gain shall be recognized only to the extent that the amount realized upon such conversion . . . exceeds the cost of such other property* ***or such stock****.* [Emphasis added.]

For purposes of nonrecognition of gain, the acquisition of qualified corporate stock must result in a controlling interest in the target corporation. A "controlling interest" means ownership of at least 80% of **all** voting and nonvoting stock of the corporation (which already has the replacement property). Acquisition of control must result from the direct purchase of stock, by using the actual proceeds from the converted property. The advancement of estimated proceeds from the other monetary sources, or from personal or commercial loans, does not count.

Figure 7.5 is a visualization of what should be taking place with the corporate stock option. The idea is that the converted and replacement properties are "similar or related" regardless of their forms of ownership whether before or after the conversion event.

Many properties held for productive use in a trade or business, or for investment, are held in corporate form. Thus, the corporate stock option adds flexibility to replacement property choices. Subsection 1033(g)(1) adds additional flexibility in the event that the converted property is real estate. In such case, the "like-kind" rule

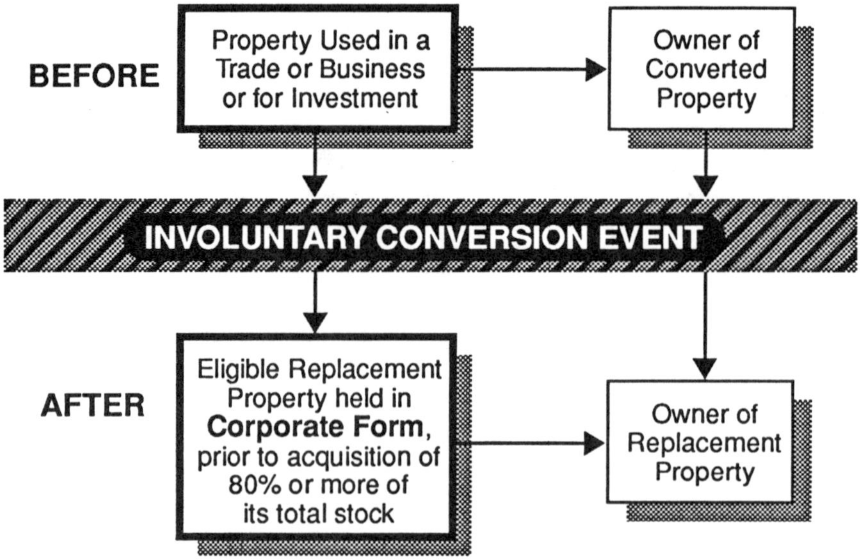

Fig. 7.5 - The Corporate Stock Option for Replacing Converted Property

can apply in lieu of "similar or related in service." For example, if a warehouse and its underlying land are condemned, seized, or requisitioned, it may be replaced with an office building and its underlying land.

Buying Replacement from Related Persons

The term "related persons" means individual family members **including** related entities (corporations, partnerships, trusts). The term is defined more specifically in Section 267: ***Transactions between Related Taxpayers***. There, in subsection 267(b): ***Relationships***, 13 combinations of individuals and entities are prescribed. Restrictions on related party transactions apply because of the likelihood that "special deals" can be arranged. The most influential participant (in terms of wealth and economic control) usually wants to rig the transaction for his/her/their/its exclusive tax benefit. Fair market give-and-take and arm's-length negotiations are put aside. Hidden somewhere in the deal is a tax avoidance scheme of some sort.

Being aware of this likelihood is what subsection 1033(i) is all about. Its title is: ***Replacement Property Must Be Acquired from Unrelated Person in Certain Cases***. The "certain cases" are:

(1) a C corporation,
(2) a partnership in which one or more C corporations own more than 50% of its capital or profits interests, and
(3) any other taxpayer whose realized gain on the converted property exceeds $100,000.

The essence of subsection (i) is that—

> [Nonrecognition of gain] *shall not apply if the replacement property or stock is acquired from a related party.* [However, this] *sentence shall not apply to the extent that the related person acquired the replacement property or stock from an unrelated person during the applicable* [replacement] *period.*

In other words, if a related person acquires the replacement property from an unrelated person within the time frames of Figure 7.4, and retransfers it above-board to a related converted property owner, the arrangement is allowed. The premise here is that a related party may act as an intermediary. That is, so long as the replacement property was not previously owned by the intermediary (before the conversion event).

Somewhat obscure above is the meaning of the $100,000 *de minimis* exception. Where the aggregate realized gain on involuntarily converted property does not exceed $100,000, replacement with property acquired from a related person (**other than** C corporations and partnerships with majority corporate partners) is allowed. In the case of an ordinary partnership or an S corporation, the $100,000 rule applies to both the partnership and each partner and to both the S corporation and each shareholder.

Replacement Options for Farmers, Etc.

Subsections 1033(c), (d), (e), and (f) focus on involuntary conversions of commercial livestock and certain land used in farming, ranching, and dairying. The respective titles of these subsections are:

(c) Property Sold Pursuant to Reclamation Laws.
(d) Livestock Destroyed by Disease.
(e) Livestock Sold on Account of Drought, Flood, or Other Weather-Related Conditions.
(f) Replacement of Livestock with other Farm Property where there has been Environmental Contamination.

These titles alone pretty much define what constitutes involuntary conversion for farmers, ranchers, and others breeding, growing, using, and selling livestock (other than poultry). Subsection (e) specifically excludes poultry from the term "livestock."

Livestock destroyed by disease, or sold or exchanged because of disease, are disposition treated as deferral of gain, if indeed any gain is realized. Replacement animals must be acquired within two years after the disease has been eradicated. If there is no realized gain, the losses are treated as ordinary losses under Section 1231: ***Property Used in a Trade or Business and Involuntary Conversions*** (special rule for determining capital gains and losses). Other animal losses such as from old age and natural causes are subject to the customary loss rules under Section 165: ***Losses*** (for individuals and corporations).

When livestock is sold as a result of drought, flood, or other weather-related condition (eligible for federal assistance), the deferral-of-gain rule applies only to excess sales. The term "excess sales" means those in excess of the number of head that normally would have been sold, were it not for the drought, flood, etc. For example, suppose a farmer or rancher normally sells 100 head of livestock each year. Instead, because of drought, etc., he sells 135 head. His excess sales are 35 head. He may elect to defer the gain on these 35 head to the following tax year. If he involuntarily sold 235 head, he may elect to recognize gain on 100 head in year 1, another 100 head in year 2, and the remaining 35 head in year 3. With each election, he must establish that the excess sales would not have occurred but for adverse weather conditions.

Because of soil or other environmental conditions, a farmer may not be able to reinvest the proceeds from his involuntarily converted livestock into similar or related-in-use livestock. In this case, he may reinvest the proceeds in other property (including real property) used for farming.

The sale, exchange, or other disposition of excess land lying within an irrigation district to conform to acreage limitations imposed by federal reclamation laws, qualifies for nonrecognition/deferment of gain. Excess land is irrigable land in excess of that to which a farmer (or other owner) is entitled to receive water. If the disposition includes other land or other property, only the "excess lands" (within an irrigation district) are considered.

Presidentially Declared Disasters

Ordinarily, involuntary conversions are one, two, or three property owner events. But, in the case of wildfires, floods, hurricanes, tornadoes, earthquakes, etc., multiple property owners — hundreds, often thousands — are simultaneously involved. In such cases, special replacement rules apply if the affected area is designated by the President as a federal disaster (warranting public assistance). A federal disaster area generally covers multiple counties in a given state, and, often, various counties in adjacent states. The Federal Emergency Management Agency (FEMA) issues public notices listing each county involved, the type of disaster, and its date of occurrence. The occurrence of a federal disaster may last anywhere from two days to 30 days or more.

The special rules to which we allude are those prescribed in subsection 1033(h): ***Special Rules for Property Damaged by Presidentially Declared Disasters***. In the broad general sense, these rules relax the replacement property requirements and use similarities. The most immediate relaxation is that the replacement period is extended to four years. When a widespread disaster occurs, local cleanup businesses, building material suppliers, and reconstruction contractors are inundated with requests for services. Consequently, it becomes self-evident that more time is needed to rebuild or acquire suitable replacement property.

The relaxation of the replacement rules focuses on two classes of property. These two are: (1) principal residences, and (2) business and investment property. The primary relaxation difference is the treatment of insurance proceeds.

In the case of one's principal residence (whether as a home owner, renter, or other dwelling occupant), no gain is recognized on the receipt of insurance proceeds for personal items (furniture, furnishings, fixtures, kitchenware, etc.) that was part of the contents of the residence. Thus, *all* insurance proceeds whether for the loss of personal items or for the dwelling unit itself are treated as a common pool of funds for replacing the dwelling unit that was destroyed. This "common pooling" idea also applies to the sale of land on which the dwelling unit was erected or parked. The IRS ruled in 1996 that the receipt of insurance proceeds and proceeds from the sale of underlying land to the destroyed dwelling unit constitutes a single conversion transaction for replacement rule purposes.

In the case of productive business and investment property, a distinction between the types of insurance proceeds is tax important. If an insurance policy (or part of the policy) insures against loss of profits or other fixed charges, as distinguished from loss of use of the property, the profit loss proceeds are taxable as ordinary income. The rationale is that such proceeds merely replace the net profits that would be fully taxable, absent the involuntary conversion. Insurance proceeds for lack of use and occupancy of business and investment property are treated as realizable gain for nonrecognition, if replaced by "property of a type" previously used. This is a less stringent replacement rule than "similar or related in service or use" property.

Basis in Replacement Property

Establishing your basis in replacement property follows the general principals discussed back in Chapter 2: Importance of "Tax Basis." That is, you start with the adjusted basis of the property disposed of — whether voluntarily or involuntarily — and transfer that basis to the newly acquired property. In the case of involuntary conversion by destruction (fire, flood, earthquake, etc.) the prior property basis records may not be readily available. Said records, together with the property itself, may also have been destroyed by the conversion event. In such case, a reconstruction of those records (by the best means practical) becomes necessary.

With the prior property basis information at hand, subsection 1033(b) applies. This subsection is titled: ***Basis of Property Acquired through Involuntary Conversion.*** Its three pertinent paragraphs are:

(1) *Conversions described in subsection (a)(1)*
— replacements similar or related in service or use;

(2) *Conversions described by subsection (a)(2)*
— replacements with **money** or property **not** similar or related in service or use; and

(3) *Property held by corporation the stock of which is replacement property.*

If the replacement property is "similar or related in service or use" to that property which was converted, your new basis is—

Adjusted basis of converted property
PLUS any gain tax recognized (on the insurance proceeds or other compensation),
MINUS any loss tax recognized (under the rules of Section 165: Losses),
MINUS fair market value (FMV) of any nonsimilar or nonrelated-in-service property acquired.

If direct money is received (whether cumulatively or in lump sum) as a consequence of the conversion event, and that money is used to **purchase** replacement property, the basis rule is slightly different. If replacement property is purchased outright, your basis in that property is—

Its cost (FMV)
DECREASED by the amount of gain not recognized on the transaction.

For example, suppose a building with an adjusted basis of $100,000 is totally destroyed by fire. The insurance proceeds and other compensation for the loss is $150,000 (paid in money). A replacement building is purchased for $130,000. The realized gain in this case is $50,000 (150,000 – 100,000 basis) of which $30,000 is tax deferred (not recognized). Hence, the replacement basis is $130,000 cost decreased by the $30,000 of deferred gain. The result is the same $100,000 basis as was in the prior property before it was involuntarily converted.

If 80% or more of stock in a corporation owning qualified replacement property is acquired (by purchase), the basis in that stock must be decreased by any realized gain on the conversion that is not tax recognized. The acquirer's stock basis then becomes: purchase cost minus gain deferred. Simultaneously, the **corporation** also must reduce the adjusted basis of its asset by the same amount. The reduction, however, cannot produce an adjusted basis in the corporate asset below zero. The idea here is that the acquired corporate replacement asset should have the same basis as the converted property.

Consider, for example, that taxpayer A owned a building with an adjusted basis of $100,000 when it was involuntarily converted. He received $1,000,000 in insurance proceeds. He used this money to purchase all of the stock in corporation X which had a qualified replacement building. The corporation's adjusted basis in that building was $800,000. Since A elected to defer the tax on his $900,000 of realized gain, he had to reduce his basis in X's stock by the same amount. Thus, A's basis in X's stock was $100,000. Yet, X's basis in the building was $800,000. This is not economic replacement reality. Consequently, the X building had to have its basis adjusted downward by $900,000 . . . but not below zero. The net result was that A's basis in X's stock was $100,000 while X's basis in the replacement building was zero. Should, later, the building be sold to a third party for $1,000,000 simultaneously upon A's total liquidation of his stock, he would have a taxable gain of $900,000. This is the same amount that he did not pay tax on previously.

8

CERTAIN REACQUISITIONS

When A Buyer Of Real Property Defaults On A Seller-Financed Mortgage (Secured By The Property Sold), THREE Tax-Accounting Events Arise. One, Certain Pre-Reacquisition Gain Is Recognized (On The Amount Of Principal Received). Two, No Gain Or Loss Is Recognized To The Seller-Reacquirer (When All Indebtedness Is Canceled). And, Three, The Buyer-Defaulter Treats The Cancellation Of Debt As Income. The Tax-Deferred Exchange Is Event Two Only: The Note Of Indebtedness For The Property Itself. After Establishing The Resulting Basis Of The Property Reacquired, It May Be Resold To An Unrelated Party.

Our chapter heading is a shortened version of the official title to Section 1038: ***Certain Reacquisitions of Real Property***. These title words clarify partially what "certain reacquisitions" means. The exchange aspects (for deferment of gain) apply only to the reacquisitions of real estate. What type or types of real property are eligible for (partial) nonrecognition of gain upon reacquisition? Neither Section 1038 nor its regulations say. Therefore, any type of real property — commercial, industrial, residential, investment, agricultural, mining, etc. — is eligible so long as other qualifying conditions are met.

Foremost among the "other qualifying conditions" is that the nonrecognition of gain upon reacquisition applies only to the **owner-seller** of the real property. Said owner-seller holds all of the indebtedness (mortgage) on the property sold, and, subsequently, the buyer defaults thereon. Upon default, the seller reacquires the property — either by agreement or by legal process — and repositions himself for its resale. The seller-reacquirer may be an individual or an entity (partnership, corporation, trust) so long as he/it owned the property at the time of its sale.

As you'll see shortly, Section 1038 targets only seller-financed indebtedness where the owner-seller holds the mortgage on the property. That is, the seller finances the entire mortgage arrangement and thereby holds an ongoing security interest in the property sold. This targeting rules out commercial lending institutions which rarely own the property on which they advance the mortgage money. However, if a commercial lender forecloses on the property, and he becomes the legal title holder thereof, he is not denied the benefits of Section 1038.

Accordingly, in this chapter we want to unveil the beneficial features of Section 1038. We also want to explain why (and how) partial gain is recognized when a seller-financed arrangement terminates before maturity (full payoff) of the debt. In the process of doing so, we have to introduce you to the *installment method* of gain-on-sale accounting (Section 453) and the treatment of cancellation of debt when formerly-owned real property is reacquired. A number of computational steps and basis adjustments are needed before the reacquired property can be resold. It is the **reacquisiton** aspect that is treated as a tax-deferred exchange: not the resale itself.

General Rule on Reacquisitions

On the subject of reacquisitions, subsection 1038(a): ***General Rule***, says—

> *If— (1) a sale of real property gives rise to indebtedness to the seller which it secured by the real property sold, and*
> *(2) the seller of such property reacquires such property in partial or full satisfaction of such indebtedness,*
> *Then, **except as provided** in subsections (b) and (d), **no gain or loss shall result** to the seller from such reacquisition, and no*

debt shall become worthless or partially worthless as a result of such reacquisition. [Emphasis added.]

The above is the full text (about 85 words) of subsection (a). Note the cross reference to subsections (b) and (d). Subsection (b) is titled: ***Amount of Gain Resulting***, whereas subsection (d) is titled: ***Indebtedness Treated as Worthless Prior to Reacquisition.*** These are the two exceptions to the "no gain or loss shall result" from the reacquisition.

Meanwhile, there are three other subsections to Section 1038 which we should mention for familiarization purposes, namely:

(c) Basis of Reacquired Real Property;
(e) Principal Residences; and
(g) Acquisition by Estate, Etc. of Seller

As to subsection (c): *Basis*, we'll definitely address this matter later in this chapter. But we will not address subsections (e) and (g). Subsection (e): *Residences*, permits a deviation from the computational aspects of subsection (a) if the reacquisition of the seller's principal residence is resold within one year. Subsection (g): *Estates*, says that the rules of subsection (a) still apply even after the original seller is deceased. Either his/her estate, or heirs, or trust can benefit from the reacquisition process.

Only a specific portion of the Section 1038(a) reacquisition process qualifies as the tax-deferred exchange. We try to depict in Figure 8.1 that portion which constitutes the "exchange." The idea is that the owner-seller who financed the mortgage indebtedness has a security interest (by means of a Deed of Trust) recorded against the property sold. If the buyer defaults on the mortgage payments (usually, for 90 days or more) and the security holder repossesses the property, the remaining unpaid balance on principle is canceled. The cancellation is treated as the exchange of a security interest (in real property) for an ownership interest in that property. This exchange arrangement has many of the elements of a like-kind Section 1031 exchange, discussed in previous chapters. The result is that no gain or loss is recognized on the reacquisition-exchange portion only.

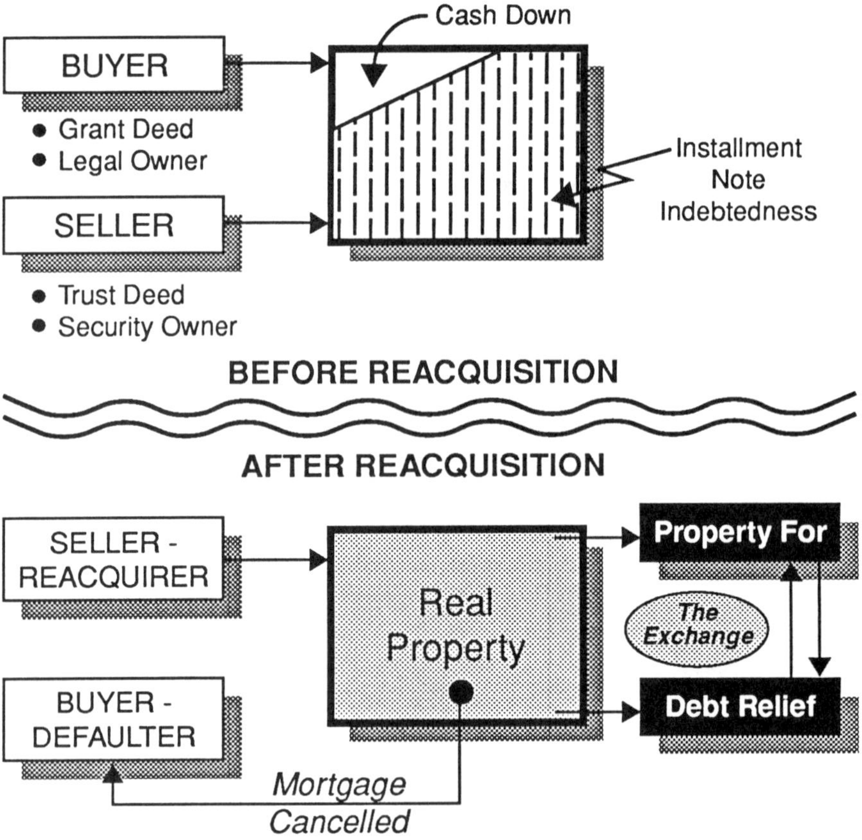

Fig. 8.1 - The "Property-for-Debt" Exchange Portion of Section 1038

Installment Sale Accounting

Periodic payments on a mortgage obligation are traditionally identified as payment of principal PLUS payment of interest (for the use of borrowed money). The interest portion is handled as a separate tax accounting matter, unrelated to the subject herein.

In contrast, the payments on principal have to be separated into two distinct tax elements: (a) return of capital and (b) capital gain. The return-of-capital portion of the principal is not taxed; it is after-tax money being returned to the seller. The capital-gain portion is taxed (or at least tax accountable); it is part of the profit earned on the sale transaction. The requirement to separate these two portions of the payments on principal is particularly important to owner-sellers who finance the mortgage on the property sold. For such seller-financing, installment-sale accounting is mandatory.

For installment-sale accounting, a separate tax law (independent of Section 1038) applies. We are alluding to Section 453: ***Installment Method.*** Its subsection (b)(1) defines an "installment sale" as—

> *a disposition of property where at least one payment is to be received after the close of the taxable year in which the disposition occurs.*

Installment sales are primarily beneficial to real estate transactions. This is because a relatively large amount of principal is owed, on which payments are made over a long period of time: 10, 20, or 30 years. The benefit to an owner-seller who finances the disposition is that his gross profit (capital gain) is spread out over the life of the installment obligations In an installment sale, the portion of capital gain received each year is taxed. There is no deferment of tax whatsoever on each yearly portion of the gain received. How does one determine the taxable portion of payments received on principal each year?

Answer: The seller-financer uses IRS Form 6252: ***Installment Sale Income.*** This form consists of three parts, namely—

Part I — Gross Profit and Contract Price;
Part II — Installment Sale Income; and
Part III — Related Party Installment Sale Income

Other than explaining the underlying features which are relevant to this chapter, we will not go into Form 6252 in any detail. We just want you to be aware of its existence and relevance to Section 1038.

Gross Profit Percentage

The core feature of Form 6252 is its computation of Gross Profit Percentage (GPP). In a nutshell, the **GPP** is

$$\text{Gross Profit Percentage} = \frac{\text{Gross Profit}}{\text{Contract Price}}$$

The "gross profit" is the total capital gain to be realized upon disposition of the property, as though it were a cash sale instead of an installment sale. Gross profit is the gross selling price reduced by your adjusted basis in the property plus all expenses of the sale.

The "contract price" is the gross selling price less any mortgage or other debt existing on the property (prior to its sale) and *assumed by the buyer*. Do not confuse any existing mortgage with a seller-financed mortgage. It is not until a gross selling price is agreed upon that a seller-financed mortgage attaches to the property. If the buyer assumes an existing mortgage (in addition to the seller's mortgage), the debt relief afforded the seller is treated as cash paid to the seller. The result is a "contract price" which is correspondingly less than the selling price. If there is no existing mortgage, or if it is paid off by the seller at time of sale, the contract price and the selling price are one and the same. Part I of Form 6252 is devoted to 14 lines of computations for establishing separately the gross profit and the contract price.

Once you have computed the gross profit **and** the contract price, you simply divide the former by the latter to arrive at your GPP. You are expected to establish this ratio to four decimal places. For example, a GPP of 0.3826 would mean that your gross profit (total capital gain) is 38.26% of the contract price. Once established, the GPP remains constant throughout the life of the installment obligations . . . or until there is default.

To illustrate the "mechanics" of Form 6252, let us assume that you receive the following payments on principal, after which the buyer defaults: \$20,000; \$15,000; and \$10,000. Using the GPP of 38.26% above, the capital gain you would have received is—

Year 1:	\$20,000	x 0.3826 =	\$ 7,652
Year 2:	15,000	x 0.3826 =	5,738
Year 3:	10,000	x 0.3826 =	3,826
	\$45,000		\$17,216

Part II of Form 6252 shows you how the capital gain amount is computed each year, then instructs you to enter said amount on Schedule D: ***Capital Gains and Losses***. You pay income tax on the Schedule D amount. This is **not** part of the 1038 exchange.

So much for Form 6252 and its GPP process. Now, let's get back to subsection 1038(a) re the nonrecognition of gain or loss on a property reacquisition exchange.

Amount of Gain Resulting

Ordinarily, when a seller finances the sale of his previously owned property, he does not want the property back. He wants the mortgage contract honored so that he can use that money for other investments. Nevertheless, when a seller has to take his property back, it is tax treated as a reverse sale. This is because it is a capital transaction — change of legal ownership — just like any other sale or exchange. The method of reacquisition, whether by mutual consent or process of law, has no effect on the transactional treatment. If the reacquirer incurs out-of-pocket expenses for the repossession, these are taken into account when establishing the amount of gain (if any) that results from the repossession.

Subsection 1038(b)(3): ***Gain recognized***, states very clearly that any gain . . . *resulting from a reacquisition to which subsection (a) applies shall be recognized.* Keep in mind that the subject has shifted to gain upon reacquisition rather than gain upon the original sale.

Subsections 1038(b)(1) and (b)(2) prescribe how the amount of recognized gain is to be computed. Rule (b)(1) is the "lesser of" approach, whereas Rule (b)(2) sets a limitation on the amount of gain under Rule (b)(1).

Rule (b)(1) prescribes that the amount of gain resulting from the reacquisition is the ***lesser of***—

[A] Deposit and installment received before the reacquisition *minus* that amount of gain reported as income during the pre-reacquisition period,

OR

[B] Gain on original sale (as though it were fully consummated) reduced by that gain reported as income for the pre-reacquisition period, and further reduced by any repossession costs (and legal expenses) incurred by the seller for reacquiring his former real property.

The net effect of Rule (b)(1) is to tax that portion of the down payment plus mortgage payments that had been treated as tax-free recovery of capital under the installment method. In the numerical example above, the original sale resulted in $45,000 being collected on principal. Of this amount, $17,216 was reported and taxed as capital gain income. The difference between these two amounts, $27,784 (45,000 – 17,216), is now subject to reacquisition tax in whole or part. The rationale is that once the property is reacquired it can be resold. When resold, a whole new set of gain computations goes into effect at that time. To allow the $27,784 to remain tax free would provide a tax benefit never intended by Section 1038.

Rule (b)(2) says, in effect, that the taxable amount of the prior untaxed recovery of capital (the $27,784 amount above) is limited. It is limited by the total remaining gain that the seller would have recognized had the buyer made *all* payments without defaulting on the mortgage.

In Figure 8.2, we try to depict why certain pre-reacquisition gain has to be recognized. The reality is that reacquisition is not an opportunity to haul in tax-free money at the expense of the defaulting buyer. Reacquisition is strictly an opportunity to make a tax-deferred **exchange** only. The exchange occurs at the time the mortgage debt still outstanding is canceled, and title to the property (which secured the mortgage) is revested with the seller.

A More Comprehensive Example

Let's go through a step-by-step analysis on how the gain on recapture is determined. For this, consider the following facts. You sold a building for $500,000 in which your adjusted basis was $350,000. Thus, your taxable gain (ultimately) would be $150,000 (selling price minus basis). Correspondingly, your GPP (gross profit percentage) would be 150/500 or 30%. The buyer paid you

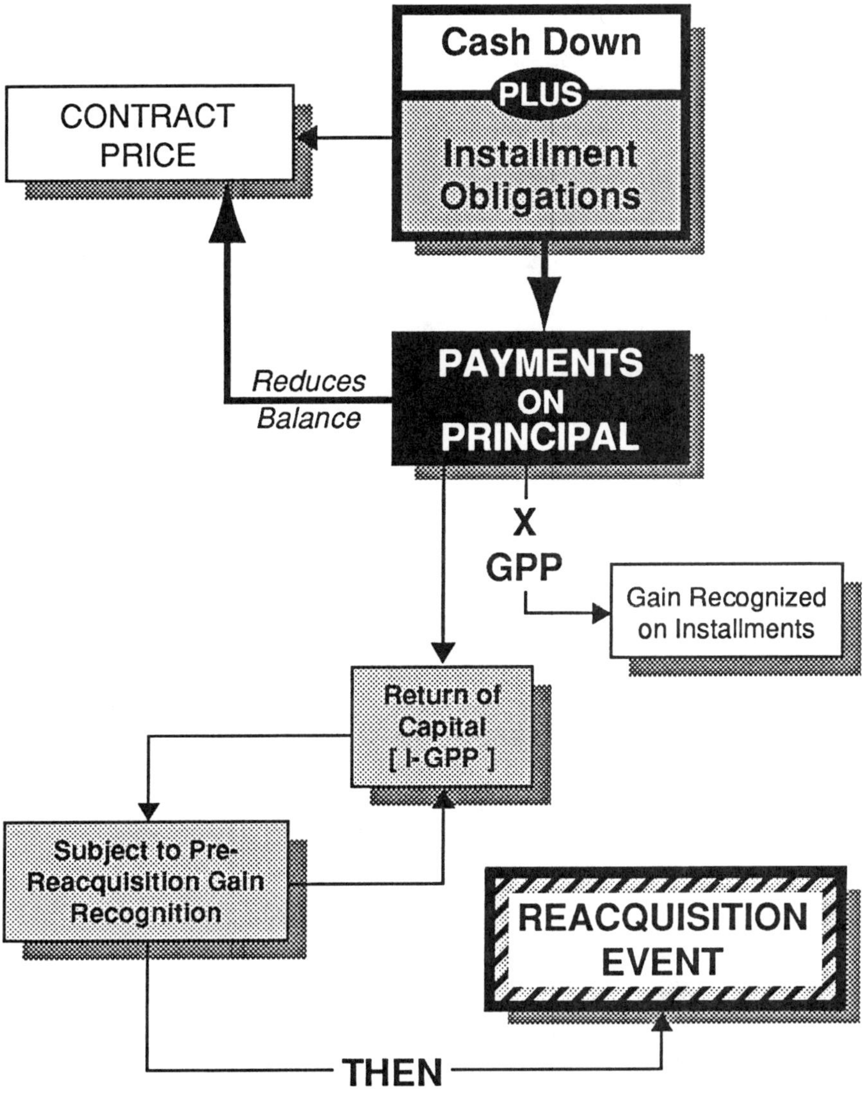

Fig. 8.2 - Depiction of Pre-Reacquisition Payments on Gain Recognition

$100,000 as a down payment (year 1) and you financed the remaining $400,000 with a mortgage secured by the property itself. In year 2, the buyer paid $10,000 on principal; in year 3, he paid $15,000. In year 4, without making any payments, the buyer defaulted. You paid $10,000 to repossess the property through legal foreclosure procedures. Upon reacquisition, how much gain are you required to tax recognize?

Answer: By plodding through the following steps—

[1] Payments on principal received prior to reacquisition [100,000 + 10,000 + 15,000] $125,000

LESS

[2] Total pre-reacquisition gain recognized under the installment method [125,000 x GPP] .... <37,500>

[3] Pre-reacquisition amount treated as tax-free return of capital [125,000 x (1 – GPP)] 87,500

OR

[4] Gain on original sale of property, had all mortgage payments on principal been made...... 150,000

LESS

[5] Pre-reacquisition gain previously recognized..... <37,500>

[6] Repossession costs .... <10,000>

[7] Remaining gain that would have been recognized had all mortgage payments been made [step 4 less steps 5 and 6] 102,500

Therefore,

[8] GAIN RECOGNIZED upon reacquisition is .... $ 87,500 [the *lesser* of step 3 or step 7]

Reporting Pre-Reacquisition Gain

Now, the question arises, how do you report your pre-reacquisition gain on your tax return? There is no preprinted tax form for this specific purpose. This means that you have to provide your own "computation of reacquisition gain" along the lines that we stepped you through above.

After your computations are made, you report the net result (gain recognized) on Schedule D: ***Capital Gains and Losses***. As an individual, such would be on Schedule D (Form 1040); as an estate or trust, it would be on Schedule D (Form 1041); as a partnership or LLC, it would be on Schedule D (Form 1065); as a C corporation, it would be on Schedule D (Form 1120); and as an S corporation, it would be on Schedule D (Form 1120S). In all cases, Schedule D consists of six columnar entries as follows:

Col. **(a)** — *Description of property*
Col. **(b)** — *Date acquired*
Col. **(c)** — *Date sold*
Col. **(d)** — *Sales price*
Col. **(e)** — *Cost or other basis*
Col. **(f)** — ***Gain or (loss)***

In column **(a)** enter: ***Sec. 1038 Reacquisition***. In column **(b)** enter the date on which you consummated the seller-financed arrangement (installment note re the original sale of real property). In column **(c)** enter date of reacquisition and cancellation of all installment debt (due from buyer). Across columns **(d)** and **(e)** enter: SEE STATEMENT. Such statement should be along the lines of the 8-step numerical example that we presented above. Make sure that step [8] is clearly marked: GAIN RECOGNIZED. Then enter such dollar amount in column **(f)** as GAIN.

Keep in mind that the holding period of assets for the purpose of Schedule D (Capital Gains and Losses) is the holding period of the seller-financed installment note (mortgage). It is **not** the holding period of the underlying real property. Because the mortgage is secured by the real property from which it derived, it is tax treated as an intangible capital asset. This is much the same way that stock in a corporation is treated.

For all forms of ownership of property, Schedule D is in two parts: I — ***Short-Term*** (one year or less) and II — ***Long-Term*** (more than one year). Rarely does the reacquisition of real property legally sold occur within one year of such sale date. Almost invariably, it is more than one year (hence, Part II of Schedule D). It takes a certain amount of practical time to establish legal default. Various written demands for payment have to be made. It takes additional time to work through the foreclosure process and retitle the property in the original seller's name.

Basis of Property Reacquired

Once the legalities of the repossession process are completed, the reacquirer can turn his attention to the reselling of the property. Before doing so, however, the basis in the property has to be recomputed. A seller-reacquirer cannot use the prior basis that was used when determining his GPP (gross profit percentage) on the original sale. Instead, he starts with *adjusted basis of debt before repossession*, and then adds certain items to it. It is as though the reacquirer is repurchasing his previously sold property for the exact amount of unpaid debt that he is canceling.

The basis computation methodology is addressed head-on in subsection 1038(c): ***Basis of Reacquired Real Property***. The essence of subsection (c) is that—

> *If subsection (a) applies to the reacquisition of any real property, the basis of such property . . . shall be the* ***adjusted basis of the indebtedness . . .*** *(determined as of the date of reacquisition),* ***increased*** *by the sum of—*
>
> *(1)* *the amount of gain* [recognized] *from such reacquisition, and*
>
> *(2)* *the amount of money and* [FMV] *of other property . . . paid or transferred by the seller in connection with the reacquisition.* [Emphasis added.]

To put the reacquisition basis in perspective, let us use some illustrative numbers. Consider that the original seller-financed mortgage was $400,000 of which $80,000 was paid by the buyer before defaulting. The seller's GPP was 30%. The gain recognized upon reacquisition was $54,000 and the cost (to the seller) of repossession was $12,000. What is the new basis in the reacquired property?

Answer: Calculate as follows—

1.	Remaining unpaid principal .... [$400,000 original debt – $80,000 payments]	$320,000
	LESS	
2.	Unreported profit .... [GPP (30%) x $320,000]	<96,000>
3.	Adjusted basis of debt before repossession	224,000
	PLUS	
4.	Gain recognized before reacquisition .... [given]	54,000
5.	Repossession costs [given]	12,000
6.	BASIS in reacquired property	$290,000

The very last sentence in subsection (c): ***Basis***, etc. says—

If any indebtedness to the seller . . . is not discharged upon the reacquisition, the basis of such indebtedness ***shall be zero****.* [Emphasis added.]

In other words, all remaining unpaid principal owing to the seller by the buyer (the $320,000 above) is canceled outright. The amount canceled becomes the starting point for establishing a new basis in the property reacquired. The net effect is that the canceled debt to the buyer is basis treated as a purchase-type payment by the seller.

Effect of Debt Cancellation on Buyer

So much for the treatment of debt cancellation by the seller-reacquirer. What about the treatment of such cancellation by the buyer?

Answer: The buyer has to report the cancellation as *income*! This is so prescribed by Code Section 61(a)(12): ***Income from Discharge of Indebtedness***. This means that the defaulting buyer has to go through a tax accounting process of his own. The rationale is that where there is a discharge of indebtedness (other than in bankruptcy) it is like someone paying you money and you use that money to pay off your debt. See Figure 8.3. This is like any other money which you would have to report as income. In the case of real property indebtedness, it is more likely than not that the income would be a deductible loss. We have a real-life illustration of this point.

The buyer-defaulter (husband and wife) purchased a bowling alley and restaurant business for $650,000. The purchase price was allocated as follows: (1) building $275,000 (42.31%); (2) equipment $115,000 (17.69%); (3) goodwill $180,000 (27.69%); and (4) land $80,000 (12.31%). The buyers paid $115,000 cash down from the sale of their residence. The seller financed the $535,000 balance with an installment note secured by the business and its real estate. The terms of the note required that, if there were any defaults on payments of principal, the associated unpaid interest would be capitalized and added to the principal balance. No payments on the note were made whatsoever. Within 18 months the business was insolvent, whereupon the original seller reacquired his former property. At the time of reacquisiton, the unpaid principal had grown to $565,000. When the business and its real estate were retitled in the name of the former owner, the installment note was canceled.

The total debt relief in the case above was $565,000. As Section 61(a)(12) income, how does the buyer-defaulter report this on his tax return?

Answer: He uses Form 4797: ***Sales of Business Property***, and shows his gross sales proceeds as $565,000 on line 1 thereof. Then he allocates his "sales price" (discharge of indebtedness)

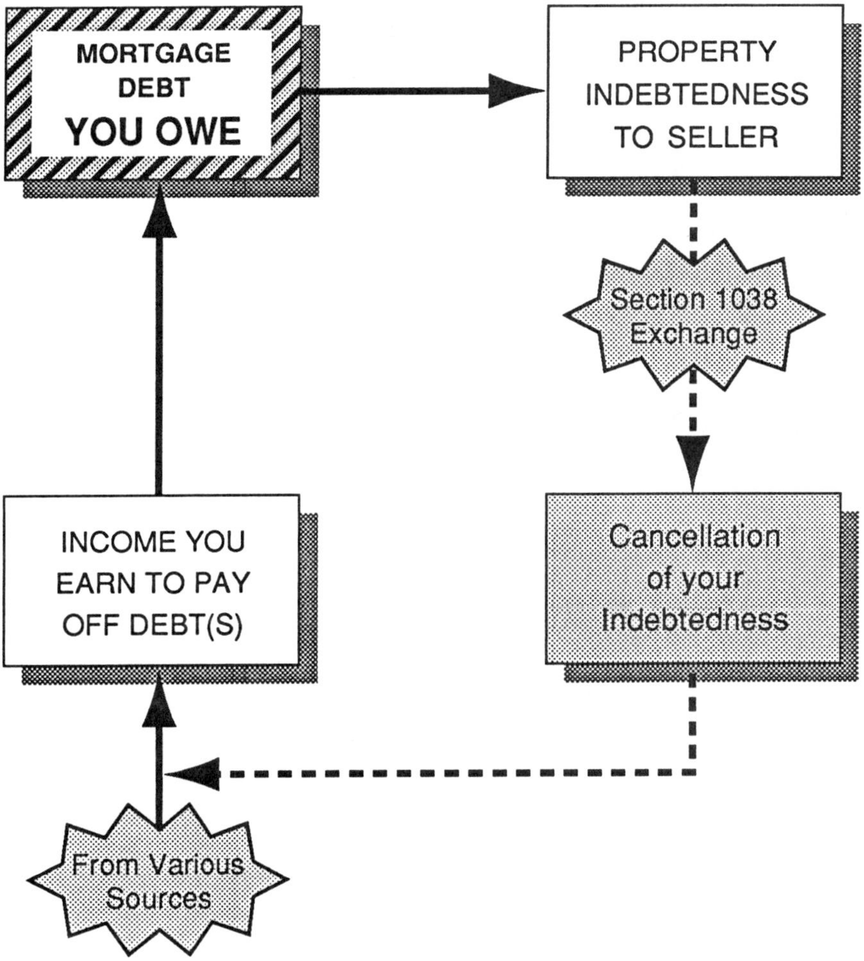

Fig. 8.3 - The "Tax Effect" When Debt is Cancelled

among the four assets that he purchased for $650,000. He allocates using the same percentage proportions that he used when purchasing the business. Thus, the $565,000 discharge of indebtedness is allocated as follows:

(1)	Building	[42.31%]	$239,050
(2)	Equipment	[17.69%]	99,950
(3)	Goodwill	[27.69%]	156,450

(4)	Land	[12.31%]	69,550
		100.00%	\$565,000

Assets (1), (2), and (3) are depreciable items when used in a trade or business. As such, a depreciation deduction is allowed for the period of time used in the business before its reacquisition (18 months or 1.5 years in the example above). Whatever amount is allowed, it is all *recaptured* when the business is sold or surrendered for debt relief. Because of differences in "class lives," each of the three assets has its own depreciation schedule. For 18 months, straight line, the approximate depreciation allowances are:

(1)	Building	[30 yrs]	\$ 14,000
(2)	Equipment	[7 yrs]	24,000
(3)	Goodwill	[15 yrs]	18,000
			\$ 56,000

Aggregating all of the above, the buyer-defaulter has a deductible business loss. The amount of said loss is

(\$565,000 + 56,000) – \$650,000 = <\$29,000>

By virtue of Section 1231(a)(2): ***Property Used in the Trade or Business and Involuntary Conversions***, a business capital loss converts into an ordinary loss. This means that the \$29,000 loss can be used by the defaulter to offset all other forms of positive income he may have.

9

DIVORCE SETTLEMENTS

Transferring Marital Property Between Divorcing Spouses Has Long Been A Contentious Issue Over Who Pays Any Applicable Capital Gain Tax. Section 1041 Attempts To Resolve This Issue By Decreeing That: "No Gain Or Loss Shall Be Recognized" . . . Etc. The Idea Is To Treat All Intraspousal Transfers As Tax-Free GIFTS. The Transferee (Recipient) Spouse Then Takes On As His/Her Basis That Which The Transferor Had. This BASIS CARRYOVER Can Often Cause Unintended Tax Inequities, Especially When Property Is Over-encumbered With Debt, When There Are Redemptions Of Stock, And When There Are Transfers Into Trust.

Most persons do not think of marital property settlements as tax-deferred exchanges — but they are. In a given year, divorce exchanges are far more common than are Section 1031 exchanges. This is because, in the U.S., nearly 50% of all marriages end in divorce within five to ten years of the wedding vows. At the blissful time of marriage, property acquisitions and property settlements are dreamworlds apart.

When the first signs of marital disharmony and the prospects of physical separation set in, the spouses become locked in an emotional struggle. There are conflicting intertwinings of what should be entirely separate decisional matters: alimony, child support, and property settlement. Each of these three separate matters is tax treated differently. Where ordinary business give-and-take should prevail, it all vanishes into thin air. Emotional bickering seems to be the norm, regardless of the intellectual or economic level of the spouses. In this environment, property settlement issues are the last item on the divorce agenda.

Because of the scheming and deceiving associated with marital property settlement matters, very few spouses — **and their attorneys** — fully comprehend or fully comply with the provisions of IRC Section 1041. This special section of the Internal Revenue Code is titled: ***Transfers of Property between Spouses or Incident to Divorce.*** The miscomprehensions surrounding Section 1041 are due, in large part, to the fact that divorce attorneys are state law practitioners: not practitioners in federal tax law. With regard to federal income tax matters, Section 1041 takes precedence over attorney interpretations under state property law, state contract laws, and state divorce laws.

The Essence of Section 1041

Section 1041 consists of approximately 180 statutory words. The essence of the intent of these words lies in its 36-word subsection (a): ***General Rule.*** This general rule reads in full as follows:

> ***No gain or loss shall be recognized*** *on a transfer of property from an* ***individual*** *to (or in trust for the benefit of)—*
>
> *(1) a spouse, or*
> *(2) a former spouse, but only if the transfer is incident to divorce.* [Emphasis added.]

We suggest that you reread these words again. Concentrate on the fact that the focus is on two types of taxpayers only: spouses **or** former spouses. These are **individual taxpayers**. Section 1041 does not apply to corporations, partnerships, trusts, or other entity forms. It applies only to the transfers of property between spouses incident to divorce or to other separation arrangements. It does not apply to alimony payments, spousal support, child custody, or to child support arrangements. Nor does it apply to any income that the transferred property may generate.

If you have not already surmised by now, divorce proceedings, if any, do not have to be finalized before the advantage of subsection (a)(1) can be taken. In other words, spouses while legally married (even though physically separated) can arrange and agree among themselves as to their property settlement terms. They can do this strictly on their own without ever consulting an attorney. They could, but very few spouses do.

One reason they do not do so is that they are unaware of the existence of Section 1041. Regular income tax returns being filed annually do not call attention to this special section of the tax code. Tax professionals know about it, but the spouses have to be alert enough to ask intelligent questions. Divorce attorneys are not the best sources for tax information.

For example, a tax professional would also know about subsection 1041(d): ***Rule where Spouse is Nonresident Alien.*** This one-sentence rule reads—

> *Subsection (a)* ***shall not apply*** *if the spouse (or former spouse) of the individual making the transfer is a nonresident alien.* [Emphasis added.]

A nonresident alien is both a non-U.S. citizen **and** a non-U.S. resident. Such persons are beyond the reach of U.S. tax laws.

There is a basic underlying implication in the no gain/no loss rule of subsection (a). Being a tax-deferred exchange of property between spouses (or former spouses), at some point downstream there will be a taxable transaction. This will occur when the *transferee spouse* (recipient of the subsection (a) property) sells or otherwise retransfers said property to an unrelated third party. If the transferee spouse were a nonresident alien, any downstream taxable transaction would be unenforceable by the IRS. Congress did not intend to allow this; hence, subsection (d).

Meaning of "Incident to Divorce"

Subsection (a)(2) above (re a former spouse) uses the phase: ". . . if the transfer is incident to the divorce." So, what does "incident to divorce" mean?

The answer lies in subsection (c) **and** Regulation § 1.1041-1T(b), Q/A-7. [The "Q/A" is Question/Answer.] These two on-point rules read as follows—

> **Subsec. (c)** — ***Incident to divorce.*** *For purposes of subsection (a)(2), a transfer of property is incident to the divorce if such transfer—*
>
> *(1) occurs within 1 year after the date on which the marriage ceases, or*
> *(2) is related to the cessation of the marriage.*
>
> **Reg. § 1.1041-1T(b)(7)** — *A transfer of property is treated as related to the cessation of the marriage if the transfer is pursuant to* ***a divorce or separation instrument*** [including an annulment] . . . *and occurs not* ***more than 6 years*** *after the date on which the marriage ceases. A divorce or separation instrument includes a modification or amendment to such decree or instrument.* [Emphasis added.]

Both subsection (c) and regulation (b)(7) use the term: *transfer of property*. This raises the question: What kind of property is covered by Section 1041?

Answer: Any kind of spousal property that has marketable value to an unrelated third party. This includes real estate, business ownership, investment property, corporate stock, tangible items (cars, boats, sports equipment, works of art, collectibles), and so on. Mostly such property is that which is already in possession of one or both spouses during the marriage. However, a transfer of property acquired within six years after the marriage ceases may also qualify for subsection (a) treatment.

Basis Transfer: Two "Tax Traps"

The no gain/no loss provisions of subsection 1041(a) are quite liberal. Especially so, since the transfer of property interest can be agreed to at any time—

[1] during the marriage,
[2] within one year after the divorce or separation instrument, or
[3] within 6 years after the marriage ceases.

This all sounds great — until we tell you about the two tax traps that emerge. Where are they? They are buried behind the wording in subsection 1041(b).

Subsection (b): ***Transferee has Transferor's Basis***, reads essentially in full as—

> *In the case of any transfer of property described in subsection (a)—*
>
> *(1) the property shall be treated as acquired by the transferee by* ***gift****, and*
>
> *(2)* ***the basis*** *of the transferee in the property* ***shall be*** *the adjusted basis of the transferor.* [Emphasis added.]

You do not see the two tax traps, do you? They are right there in paragraphs (1) and (2), respectively.

Trap (1) is that, when property is treated as acquired by gift, the "transfer of basis" rule applies. This means that there is no step-up in basis for, in effect, buying out the other spouse's property interests. Prior to 1984 when Section 1041 was enacted, transferee spouses got a step-up in basis when "buying" the property from the other spouse. Not so now.

Consider, for example, a husband and wife owning jointly (50/50) their marital residence which has a market value of $400,000. Their joint basis in that residence is $100,000, or $50,000 each. The wife wants to retain the residence, to which the husband agrees if the wife will buy his half for $200,000. The house is jointly refinanced, and a check for $200,000 is made payable to the husband. Technically, he would have a $150,000 tax accountable gain ($200,000 "sales price" — $50,000 basis). Under the provisions of subsection (a), he walks away with the $200,000 totally TAX FREE. The wife, on paper only, gets a $50,000 "basis transfer" from the husband . . . **NOT** the actual $50,000 itself.

If, subsequent to their divorce, the former wife sells the house for $400,000, she has a tax accountable gain of $300,000 ($400,000 – $100,000 basis). Theoretically, in this $300,000 gain is the $150,000 on which the former husband did not pay tax. Who pays this unpaid tax? The transferee spouse (former wife) does. She also pays tax on her own $150,000 share of the gain. We think that this is a gross inequity. In fairness to both spouses, the former wife should only pay tax on her portion of the gain. Congress, however, intended this inequity — Tax Trap (1) — to stand.

As clear evidence of this, let us cite the substance of Regulation § 1.1041-1T(d)(10): ***Tax consequences of transfers*** [between spouses]. Its Q/A-10 reads—

> *The transferor of property under section 1041 recognizes no gain or loss on the transfer* ***even if*** *the transfer was in exchange for the release of marital rights* ***or other consideration****. This rule applies* ***regardless of whether*** *the transfer is of property separately owned by the transferor or is a division (equal or unequal) of community property.* [Emphasis added.]

This regulation seems pretty clear to us. The transferor spouse walks away tax free, regardless of whether he/she has realized gain in the property transferred or not. Why do you suppose Congress did this? There *is* an explanation.

Why the Inequity Exists

Circa 1939, Congress codified the concept of a joint federal income tax return for a husband and wife. The income jointness prevailed even though one of the spouses had no income nor deductions. The premise then was, as it is today, that a husband and wife constitute *a single economic unit.* As a consequence, the spouses acquired "marital property" from the date of marriage to the date of legal separation. As long as the property was used as a marital and family residence, or for income production purposes, it was treated as an inherent form of co-ownership. This federal thesis flew in the face of state property laws which addressed the division of property between divorcing spouses in a radically different way.

For years thereafter, the federal tax treatment of divorce property settlements followed state property laws.

Then, in 1962, came the landmark U.S. Supreme Court case of *T.C. Davis*, 370 US 65, 62-2 USTC ¶ 9509, 82 S Ct 1190. In said case, the Court ruled that a transfer of appreciated property to a spouse (or former spouse) *in exchange for* the release of marital claims results in the recognition of gain to the transferor. The spouse receiving the property (the transferee) receives a basis in that property equal to its fair market value. The Court rejected Davis's contention that the transaction was comparable to a nontaxable division of property between co-owners. The Court based its decision on the fact that the wife's marital and dower rights (after the husband's death) were "unperfected." Her name was not included on the recorded title to the property, which it would have been for it to be considered co-owned or jointly owned.

In 1967, in its own Revenue Ruling 67-221, the IRS ruled that a wife who exchanges her marital rights for property realized no gain or loss. Her rights are taken to be equal to the value of the property received. In this and other of its rulings, the IRS was trying to uniformize the tax treatment of marital property settlements throughout the U.S. But this attempt proved very difficult. Much tax litigation resulted. State law differences re separate property, community property, joint tenancy property, tenants-in-common property, and tenancy-by-the-entirety property all flashed back to the *Davis* case for recognition of gain and step-up in basis. To make matters worse, ex-spouses as taxpayers rarely ever reported their divorce property gains or basis adjustments to the IRS. When queried on that matter, hostile ex-spouses whipsawed the IRS back and forth by having no records and pointing tax fingers at the other spouse. Rarely could the "other spouse" be pinned down.

Finally, in 1984, Congress, the courts, and the IRS had had enough. Congress intentionally enacted Section 1041 to take precedence over the *Davis* case and the turmoil that ensued. Section 1041 provides that the transfer to a spouse, whether or not incident to divorce, will be treated for income tax purposes in the same manner as a gift. A few years earlier (in 1981), Congress had decreed (via Section 2523: ***Gift to Spouse***) that intraspousal transfers of property were gratuitous nontaxable gifts. This means that no gain or loss is recognized by either spouse within the time framework prescribed.

Now back to our "inequity" allegation earlier: the $400,000 marital residence example. The rationale underlying Section 1041 is that any transfer of property between spouses (or former spouses) is a division of property among co-owners. This is so, whether the division is equal, unequal, equitable, or inequitable. Had the spouses been able to cut the $400,000 residence in half, the husband would take his half and the wife would take hers. The fact that the wife chose to buy her husband's half for $200,000 does not change the legislative premise of Section 1041. A more equitable arrangement, perhaps, would be for the wife to discount the $200,000 by the amount of capital gains tax (federal and state) she will ultimately have to pay on the husband's $150,000 untaxed gain.

For summary purposes at this point, we depict in Figure 9.1 the premise and principles underlying Section 1041. Fortunately, most income taxing states today accept this federal law in the spirit of treatment uniformity among divorcing spouses. However, when it comes to post-divorce ownership and rights, all states adhere to their own property laws.

Transferor's Adjusted Basis

Meanwhile, there is Tax Trap (2) with which to contend. As mentioned earlier, this trap is the transferor's "adjusted basis" in property which he/she transferred to the other spouse. This often becomes a very contentious issue when property interests other than the marital residence are transferred. Business interests, investment property, stock holdings, works of art and collectibles, and the like, require up-to-date adjustments to the transferor's tax basis in such properties. Subsection (b)(2), previously cited, clearly implies this.

Regulation § 1.1041-1T(e)(14): **Notice and recordkeeping requirement**, is more emphatic than subsection (b)(2). This Q/A-14 regulation says, in pertinent part, that—

> *A* ***transferor*** *of property under section 1041* ***must****, at the time of the transfer,* ***supply the transferee with records*** *sufficient to determine the adjusted basis and holding period of the property*

*as of the date of the transfer. . . . Such records must be preserved and kept accessible **by the transferee**.* [Emphasis added.]

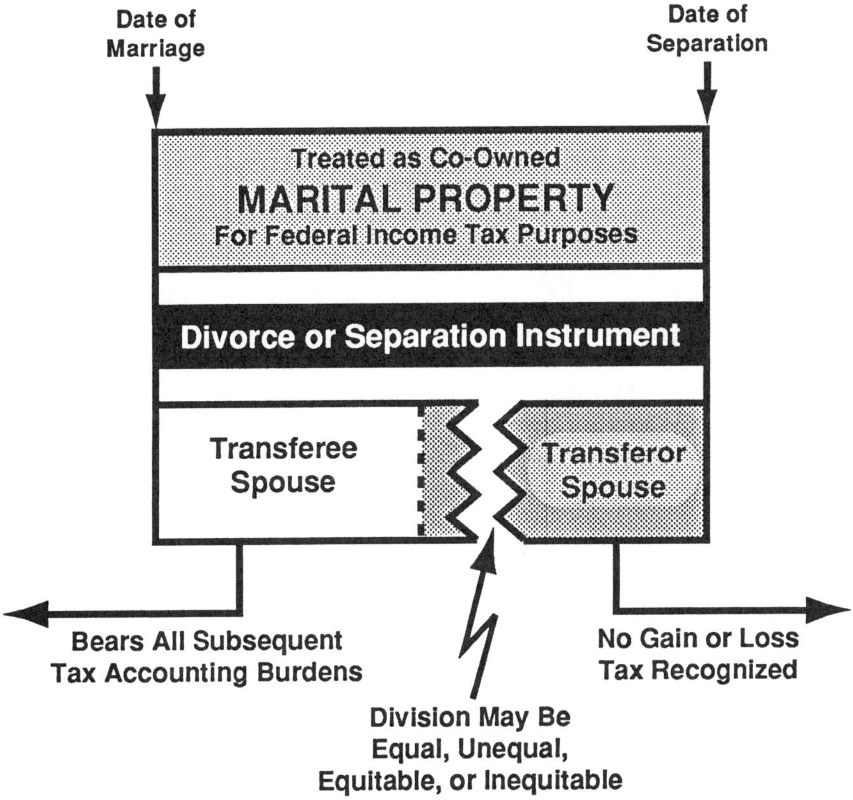

Fig. 9.1 - Transfer of Property Principles Under Code Section 1041

As you can sense from this regulatory wording, the burden for basis recordkeeping is entirely on the transferee: none on the transferor. Oh, yes, the regulation does say that the transferor "must supply" his basis records to the transferee, but what if he/she does not do so?

Let us be realistic. Spouses in the throes of settling their property interests at time of divorce are usually hostile, embittered, and distrustful of one another. The transferor spouse simply doesn't care and will not cooperate in furnishing his/her basis records to the transferee. Our experience in these matters is that basis records, if they exist at all, are poorly kept and hopelessly garbled. Intentionally — and vindictively — the transferor schemes to cause the transferee to "twist in the wind" with respect to the IRS. As per its policy of long standing, when records are poor or nonexistent, the IRS asserts a basis of ZERO. This is guaranteed to cause maximum tax and trauma downstream for the transferee.

The agony of Tax Trap (2) can be minimized with prudent forethought. When the divorce decree or separation instrument is being prepared, the transferee must insist on a clause therein that the transferor's obligation pursuant to IRC Sec. 1041(b)(2) and IRS Reg. 1.1041-1T(e)(14) be honored. The transferee should also indicate what he/she believes the basis should be. And, further, the transferee must insist that, if adequate basis records and information are not forthcoming, a judicial hearing on the matter be held. The IRS will generally accept a state court's ruling on evidential matters. This is called: "presumptive evidence." It is the transferee spouse who has to be the moving party in this regard: not the transferor. We try to depict this situation for you in Figure 9.2.

Transfers Via Third Party

On its face, Section 1041 does not address transfers of property to third parties on behalf of a spouse or former spouse. There is only an implication to this effect in the term "for the benefit of" in subsection (a). However, the concept is more clearly addressed in Regulation § 1.1041-1T(c): ***Transfers on behalf of a spouse***. The regulation Q-9 reads:

> *May transfers of property to third parties on behalf of a spouse (or former spouse) qualify under Section 1041?*

The response is regulation A-9. In introductory part, the regulation reads:

> *Yes. There are three situations in which* [such transfers] *will qualify under section 1041, provided all other requirements of the section are satisfied.*

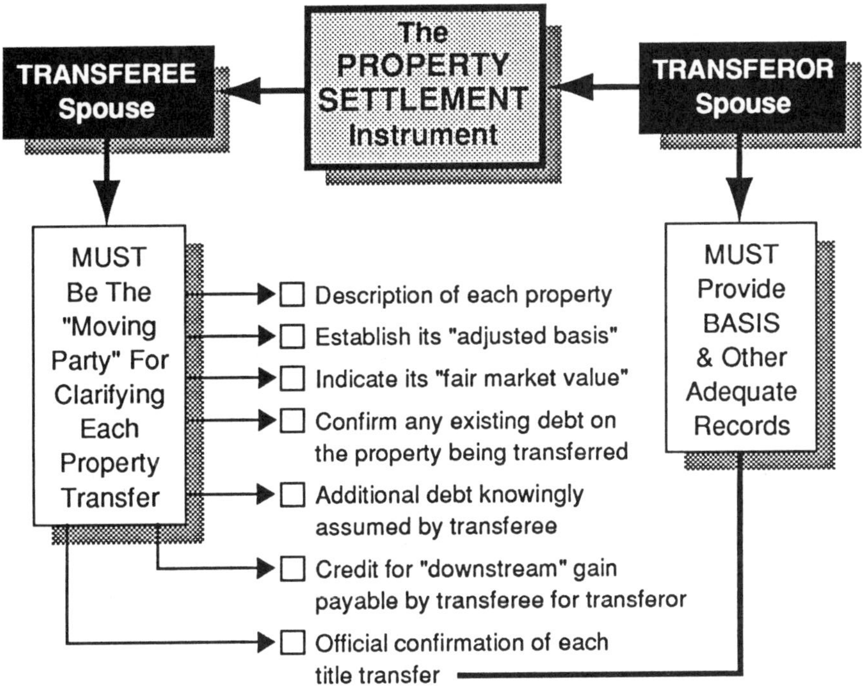

Fig. 9.2 - Precautions When "Finalizing" Spousal Property Settlements

Transferring property to a third party for the benefit of (or on behalf of) a spouse must meet three qualifying rules of its own. These rules are enumerated in the above-identified regulation, which we paraphrase as follows:

One. The transfer must be required by the divorce decree or separation instrument.

Two. The transfer must be made at the specific written request of the nontransferring spouse (or former spouse).

Three. The transfer must be consented to or ratified (in writing) by the transferring spouse who must also state that the spouses intend that the tax treatment under Section 1041 shall apply. In addition, the transferring spouse must have acquired the property for transfer prior to the transferor's filing his/her tax return for the year in which the transfer was made.

These rules make sense in that both spouses must consent to the third-party arrangement. Unfortunately, the last two sentences of the regulation (not paraphrased above) create ambiguity as to the clear intent of Congress. You can sense this ambiguity from the two sentences that read—

> [Under the three rules above], *the transfer of property will be treated as made directly to the nontransferring spouse (or former spouse) and the nontransferring spouse will be treated as immediately transferring the property to the third party. The deemed transfer from the nontransferring spouse (or former spouse) to the third party is* ***not a transaction that qualifies for nonrecognition of gain*** *under section 1041.* [Emphasis added.]

This last sentence: *the deemed transfer* . . . etc., is a flat-out contradiction to the no gain/no loss aspect of Section 1041(a). This is because there is no direct transfer between spouse A and spouse B. There is an intervening third party which in and of itself has no participation in the divorce wranglings. The problem is particularly acute when the property being deemed transferred is stock or other interests in a closely-held family business. Various courts have ruled that both spouses are taxable . . . in different ways. Much depends on the language of the divorce instrument. The result is along the lines that we depict in Figure 9.3.

Transfers into a Trust

In the leadoff sentence of Section 1041(a): No Gain/No Loss Recognition, there is a parenthetical clause which reads—

> . . . *(or in trust for the benefit of)* . . .

This clause is preceded by the phrase: *transfer of property from an individual to* . . . a spouse or former spouse. Beyond this, except

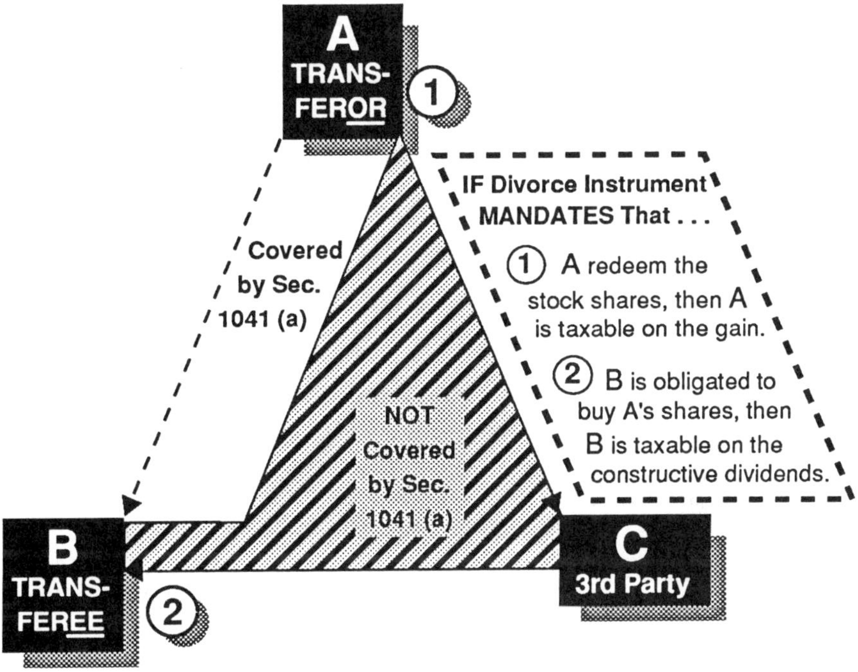

Fig. 9.3 - The "Deemed Transfer" Rule With 3rd Party Stock Redemptions

for subsection (e), neither Section 1041 nor any of its regulations specifies exactly what the cited parenthetical clause means.

When a tax law is silent on a specific application, the courts have long held that the "plain language" of the wording prevails. Therefore, in the case of property transfers into a trust, the transfer**or** must be an ***individual.*** No corporation or other transferring entity can be involved. This rids the transfer(s) of uncertainties that can occur when third parties intervene.

The "for-the-benefit-of" clause clearly means for the **exclusive** benefit of the transferee spouse or former spouse. In the ordinary sense, a "benefit" is a charitable act to assist someone in time of need. A "time of need" occurs when the transferee is unwilling or unable to manage the property prudently. A transferee would be unwilling/unable to manage his/her own affairs during prolonged illness, mental incompetency, physical handicap, emotional distress, unemployment, spendthrift habits, Alzheimer's disease, or for other valid causes. The reason(s) for a transferee's inability to manage his/her property affairs should be identified in the divorce decree or separation instrument.

Furthermore, each spouse needs to be aware that a trust, once funded with property assets, is a separate tax accounting entity of its own. If the assets generate income, that income has to be separated from any property distributions to the transferee. The income is taxable to the distributee whereas the property distributions are not taxable.

Potential for Trust Abuses

When property interests exceeding $1,000,000 (1 million) are transferred into a trust, the transferor often becomes tax aggressive. He uses Section 1041(a) as a "cover" for his tax avoidance tactics. The most prevalent form of this is to heavily encumber the property with new mortgages and other debt prior to its legal conveyance to the transferee. Then, through various legal shenanigans, he forces the unsuspecting transferee to assume responsibility for all liabilities outstanding on the property. Usually, the transferee is quite unaware of what is taking place.

For example, suppose the property settlement instrument requires the husband to transfer $3,000,000 (3 million) of assets into a trust for the benefit of his unwary wife. Also, suppose that the tax basis in the property is $150,000 which has an existing debt on it of $100,000. The equity in the property (value minus debt) is $2,900,000 [$3,000,000 value minus $100,000 debt]. Using the property as security, the transferor encumbers it with a new mortgage in the amount of $2,500,000 (2.5 million). He pockets the 2.5 million dollars and claims it to be tax free pursuant to Section 1041(a). Can he get away with this?

Answer: Absolutely not! Section 1041(e) mandates that the overencumbered portion be taxed to the transferor. The term "overencumbered" officially means: *Where liability exceeds basis*. In the postulated example above, the amount of liability exceeding basis is $2,450,000 [$100,000 existing debt pus $2,500,000 new debt less $150,000 basis]. This is the amount of constructive gain that has to be tax recognized by the transferor.

Section 1041(e): ***Transfers in Trust where Liability Exceeds Basis***, reads in full as—

> *Subsection (a)* ***shall not apply*** *to the transfer of property in trust to the extent that—*
>
> > *(1) the sum of the amount of the liabilities assumed, plus the amount of the liabilities to which the property is subject,* ***exceeds***
> >
> > *(2) the total of the adjusted basis of the property transferred.*
>
> ***Proper adjustment*** *shall be made under subsection (b) in the basis of the transferee in such property to take into account gain recognized by reason of the preceding sentence.* [Emphasis added.]

This "proper adjustment" sentence means that the transferee gets a step-up in basis to the extent of gain recognized by the transferor. Thus, in the numerical illustration above, the adjusted basis to the transferee would be $2,600,000 [$150,000 carryover plus $2,450,000 step-up]. This is certainly a **more equitable** basis transfer than that ordained by subsection (b): ***Transferee has Transferor's Basis***.

Notification to IRS by Transferor

Nothing in Section 1041 says anything about how the IRS is to be notified when divorcing spouses transfer property between themselves. Ordinarily, when there is a transfer of title to property, it is treated as a tax accountable disposition. As such, it is reported on Schedule D (1040): ***Capital Gains and Losses***. Certainly, a transaction governed by subsection (e): ***Transfers in Trust***, etc., would be reported this way. But, what about transfers governed by subsection (a): ***General Rule; No Gain or Loss***?

Regulation § 1.1041-1T(18) appears to address this question in an oblique way. It does so as though the spouses have to ELECT to have Section 1041 apply. Towards this end, the regulation specifically reads—

> *In order to make an election under Section 1041 for property transfers . . ., both spouses (or former spouses)* ***must elect*** *the application of the rules of Section 1041.* [They do so] *by attaching to the* ***transferor's*** *first filed income tax return* [Form 1040] *for the taxable year in which the* ***first transfer*** *occurs,* ***a statement signed by both spouses*** *(or former spouses) which includes each spouse's social security number and* [other appropriate information]. [Emphasis added.]

We urge the use of Schedule D (Form 1040) to notify the IRS of your "Section 1041 Election." Do this by entering as follows:

Col. (**a**): *Description of property* — Section 1041(a)
Col. (b): *Date acquired* — as appropriate, and
Col. (**c**): *Date sold* — date of official title transfer to transferee.

Then across columns (d), (e), and (f) write:

SEE SECTION 1041 ELECTION STATEMENT, ATTACHED.

The statement should signify that both parties understand the provisions of Section 1041, and that they have worked out (through recorded proceedings) any tax inequities reflected in the adjusted basis of the property transferred. There also should be a short description of **each** property item transferred, its fair market value, and the amount of debt on said property which the transferee assumes. Recall Figure 9.2.

In those situations where transfers of property are made over a period of years, a separate statement — and a separate transferor reporting on Schedule D — should be made each year in which property is transferred.

10

STOCK SALES TO ESOPs

A Unique Form Of Exchange Is The Sale Of Employer Securities To A Qualified ESOP. If, Prior To The Sale, The Securities Were Held For At Least 3 Years, You Have The Option Of Electing NONRECOGNITION OF GAIN On The Sale. If You So Elect, You Must Attach A "Statement Of Election" To Schedule D Of Your Return, Followed By A "Statement Of Verification" By The ESOP Administrator. The Election Is Valid ONLY If You Purchase Qualified Replacement Securities Within 3 Months Before Or Within 12 Months After The Sale. Basis Adjustments Are Required. When The Replacement Securities Are Subsequently Sold, All Gain (If Any) Is Tax Recognized.

The acronym ESOP stands for: Employee Stock Ownership Plan. This is a plan owned by employees of their employer's stock. More specifically, an ESOP is defined as—

> *A stock bonus plan or a* [combination] *stock bonus and money purchase plan which is qualified under Section 401(a) and which is designed to invest primarily in qualifying employer securities* [Section 4975(e)(7)].

Note the cross-reference to Section 401(a). Said section is titled: ***Qualified Pension, Profit-Sharing, and Stock Bonus Plans***. Its subsection (a) is titled: ***Requirements for Qualification***. Though not all apply to ESOPs, there are 34 separate qualification requirements in subsection (a) — yes, 34! This is probably the longest single *subsection* of the entire Internal Revenue Code. It consists of about 8,500 words and has been amended 27 times since its inception in 1954.

Needless to say, we have no intention of explaining the requirement for a qualified ESOP plan. Qualifying an ESOP, and keeping it so, is the obligation of the employer. Essentially, an ESOP is a stock bonus plan (all the securities of which are held in trust) for the exclusive benefit of employees when they retire, die, or terminate participation in the plan. There are tax advantages to the employer in that the corporation pays no income tax on the dividends earned on employee securities in the plan. There are tax advantages to the employees in that, while they pay tax on the dividends, they pay no social security/medicare tax, nor do they pay any capital gains tax until the stock is distributed to them.

So much for ESOPs. Our primary objective in this chapter is to acquaint you with the features of Section 1042 and its tax-deferment exchange advantages. The idea behind Section 1042 is to allow a taxpayer (other than a C corporation) to sell certain of his/her/its stock holdings to an ESOP without immediately paying tax on any capital gains therewith. The sale becomes a tax-deferred exchange when qualified replacement securities are purchased within three months *before* or 12 months *after* sale to an ESOP. When the replacement stock is subsequently sold, tax is then paid. There are some "details" that we need to explain.

Overview of Section 1042

The full official title of Section 1042 is: ***Sales of Stock to Employee Stock Ownership Plans or Certain Cooperatives.*** This tax law comprises approximately 3,000 words. These words are grouped into seven subsections as follows:

(a) Nonrecognition of gain.
(b) Requirements to qualify for nonrecognition.
(c) Definitions; special rules.
(d) Basis of qualified replacement property.
(e) Recapture of gain on disposition of qualified replacement property.

(f) Statute of limitations.
(g) Application of section to sales in agricultural refiners and processors to eligible farm cooperatives.

A glance at these subsectional captions reveals quickly certain overview-type features. Foremost is the fact that nonrecognition tax treatment (at time of sale to an ESOP) applies only to stock with a realized gain. Selling of loss stock to an ESOP is a "No-No." An ESOP is not a dumping ground for penny stock, underperforming stock, or interests in speculative ventures which have gone sour. Any stock sold to an ESOP must be that which is issued by a *domestic* C corporation and which is readily tradable on an established securities market.

Note use of the term: "Qualified replacement property." Actually, the word "property" is a little misleading. It implies that the replacement of stock sold to an ESOP can be any form of property. This definitely is not the case. The term qualified replacement property specifically means—

> *any* ***security*** *issued by a domestic* ***operating corporation*** *which* . . . [subsec. (c)(4)(A)].

An "operating corporation" is one which actively pursues a trade or business with the intent of making a profit, year after year, for its shareholders. Specifically, more than 50% of the assets of the corporation must be used "actively." There are other qualifications for replacement securities which we'll get to later.

Another unusual feature of Section 1042 is its subsection (f): ***Statute of Limitations***. Most tax-deferred exchange laws do not highlight the limitation period which bars the IRS from assessing a deficiency in tax. But because stock in a corporation is such an intangible asset — it is a "piece of paper" only — it invites tax gamesmanship by cavalier corporate officers who seek to use an ESOP as their secret tax haven. To assure that tax gamesmanship does not get out of hand, subsection (f) extends the normal 3-year statute of limitations to three years AFTER the IRS is notified that the seller has purchased qualified replacement securities. Said notification is via expressly required statements attached to one's income tax return.

Must "Elect" Nonrecognition

Section 1042(a): ***Nonrecognition of gain***, is an elective option. It is elective simply because, if the amount of capital gain potential is not significant enough, why go through all of the qualifying restrictions for replacement securities? For example, if the amount of potential gain is $100, it is better to pay the tax and be done with it. On the other hand, if the amount of potential gain is, say, $10,000, it is very tempting to be silent about a tax-deferred sale to an ESOP. Prescribing that the exchange benefits are elective means that the IRS has to be notified. If no written election is attached to one's tax return, all "silent elections" are null and void.

All of which brings us to the statutory wording of Section 1042(a). This subsection specifically reads as—

> *If—* *(1)* *the taxpayer or executor* ***elects*** *. . . the application of this section with respect to any sale of qualified securities,*
>
> *(2)* *the taxpayer* ***purchases*** *qualified replacement* [securities] *within the replacement period, and*
>
> *(3)* *the requirements of subsection (b) are met* ***with respect to such sale,***
>
> ***then*** *the gain (if any) on such sale which would be recognized as long-term capital gain shall be recognized* ***only to the extent that*** *the amount realized on such sale exceeds the cost to the taxpayer of such qualified replacement* [securities]. [Emphasis added.]

To help you grasp the exchange idea more quickly, we present Figure 10.1. Of the various activities therein, particularly note that the exchange portion is limited to the *sale* of qualified employee securities and their *replacement* with other qualified securities. To accomplish **The Exchange**, there are necessary associated features which we depict in Figure 10.1.

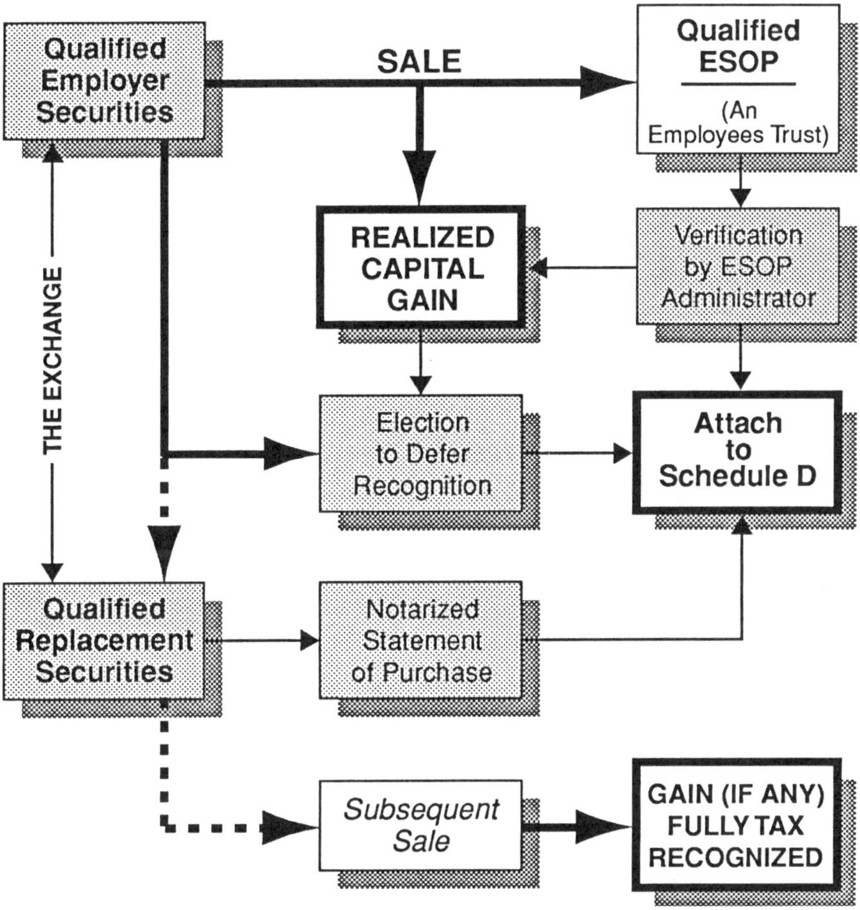

Fig. 10.1 - Generalization of the Exchange Features of Sec. 1042

Qualified Securities Defined

There are two categories of qualified securities for Section 1042 purposes. Category One comprises those which are eligible for **sale** to an ESOP. Category Two are those which are eligible as **replacements** to those sold in Category One. As you'll see shortly below, Category One securities are those which are issued by the employer who sponsors the ESOP, but are held by persons or entities other than the issuing employer. Since an ESOP is an employee stock ownership plan, the inference is that only the employer's securities (primarily its common stock) are eligible for ownership by the ESOP.

More specifically, Section 1042(c)(1): ***Qualified Securities***, defines such securities as—

> ***employer securities*** *. . . which—*
>
> *(A) are issued by a domestic C corporation that has no stock outstanding that are readily tradable on an established securities market, and—*
>
> *(B) were* ***not*** *received by the taxpayer in—*
>
> > *(i) a distribution from a* [qualified pension, profit-sharing, or stock bonus] *plan, **or***
> > *(ii)* [were not received by] *a transfer pursuant to an option or other right to acquire stock* [in connection with performance of services, incentive stock options, employee stock purchase plans, or corporate reorganizations, liquidations, etc.].

The clear implication here is that whatever capital stock has been authorized for issue by the employer corporation must be **purchased outright** by its shareholders (be they persons or entities). Employer securities acquired in any other way do not qualify as eligible securities for sale to an ESOP. Note that only C corporations (not S corporations) can sell qualified securities to shareholders. An "employer corporation" includes any member of the same controlled group of C corporations.

Further note that whatever amount of capital stock is authorized for issue must have been sold or committed to investors such that no stock remains outstanding. The idea here is to assure that all available stock is being readily and actively traded on securities markets. The idea is also to prohibit the employer corporation from selling its own stock directly to its own-sponsored ESOP. All eligible stock must be sold first to an investor who then sells it to an ESOP. Also included in the term "employer securities" are those issued by eligible worker-owned cooperatives, farmers' cooperatives, and processors of agricultural or horticultural products.

Requirements for Nonrecognition

Recall earlier our citation of subsection (a) of Section 1042: ***Nonrecognition of Gain***. Its paragraph (3) expressly said that any sale of qualified securities (to an ESOP) must meet the requirements of subsection (b). This referenced subsection is titled: ***Requirements to Qualify for Nonrecognition of Gain***. This subsection is paragraphed as follows:

(1) ***Sale to employee organizations.***

(2) ***Plan must hold 30 percent of stock after sale.***

(3) ***Written statement required.***

(4) ***3-year holding period.***

All four paragraphs are preceded by the clause—

A sale of qualified securities meets the requirements of this subsection if—

The paragraph (1) requirement completes the "if" portion of the umbrella clause by prescribing that if said securities . . .

are sold to—
(A) an employee stock ownership plan, or

(B) an eligible worker-owned cooperative.

Paragraph (2) sets forth the second requirement in that—

The plan or cooperative referred to in paragraph (1) owns . . . immediately after the sale at least ***30 percent*** *of—*

(A) Each class of outstanding stock of the corporation, or

> *(B) the total value of all outstanding stock of the corporation . . .*
>
> ***other than*** [preferred] *stock . . . which is not entitled to vote* [and] *which does not participate in corporate growth to any significant extent.*

In the case of the sale of stock of a qualified refiner or processor to an eligible farmers' cooperative, the cooperative must own **100** percent (instead of 30 percent) of all stock outstanding. [Section 1042(g)(4)(B)]. This is to validate the true cooperative principle of farmers' marketing associations.

Paragraph (3) of Section 1042(b) requires a **written verification** by the employer corporation, or by the eligible cooperative, that a sale to its ESOP indeed took place: its date and amount. The verification must also consent to the imposition of a 10 percent tax on any prohibited distribution of its ESOP shares, and to a 50 percent tax on any misallocation of its ESOP shares to charitable trusts. These prohibitions are designed to prevent the use of ESOPs as private tax shelters for wealthy investors and top executives of the employer or cooperative.

And, finally, paragraph (4) is the fourth requirement for nonrecognition of gain. This requirement reads in full as—

> *The taxpayer's holding period with respect to the qualified securities is at least 3 years (determined as of the time of the sale)* [to an ESOP].

The idea here is to assure that there is long-term capital gain, which is indicative of growth in the employer's (or cooperative's) business enterprise. The idea also is to thwart the tax mischief of day traders, stock brokers, and commercial underwriters.

Reporting Sales to IRS

When qualified securities are sold to an ESOP, the disposition of those securities is a tax accountable event. Note that we use the term: *tax accountable.* We do not say "taxable," nor do we say "tax deferred." These are matters that develop later, when replacement securities are purchased. The "accounting" task on your part is that which you report to the IRS. How does one do this?

Answer: You report each disposition event on Schedule D: ***Capital Gains and Losses***, Part II thereof — ***Assets Held More than One Year.***

Be aware that there is a Schedule D (**1040**) for individuals; a Schedule D (**1041**) for estates and trusts, a Schedule D (**1065**) for partnerships and limited liability companies; and a Schedule D (**1120**) for C and S corporations. In all of these Schedules D, the seven entry columns are the same. However, you need make a specific entry in the first three columns only. These columns are:

Col. (a) — *Description of property* ......Section 1042(a)

Col. (b) — *Date acquired* ....as appropriate

Col. (c) — *Date sold* .... to an ESOP

Then across columns (d), (e), (f), and (g) enter:

SEE ELECTION STATEMENT ATTACHED

The election statement is required by IRS Regulation § 1.1042-1T(A-3)(**a**) which prescribes that—

> *The election not to recognize the gain realized . . . under Section 1042(a) shall be made in a "statement of election" attached to the taxpayer's income tax return filed on or before the due date (including extensions of time) for the taxable year in which the sale occurs. If a taxpayer does not make a timely election . . . to obtain Section 1042(a) nonrecognition treatment . . ., it may not subsequently make an election on an amended return or otherwise. An election once made is irrevocable.*

There you have it! Either you expressly elect the nonrecognition treatment in a timely manner, or you forgo it entirely. Once the due date for your tax return is past, you cannot then elect the Section 1042(a) option. Nor can you wait to get replacement securities if the replacements are purchased after the due date of your return.

In Figure 10.2, we show how an "ordinary" Schedule D differs when seeking the tax deferment benefits of Section 1042.

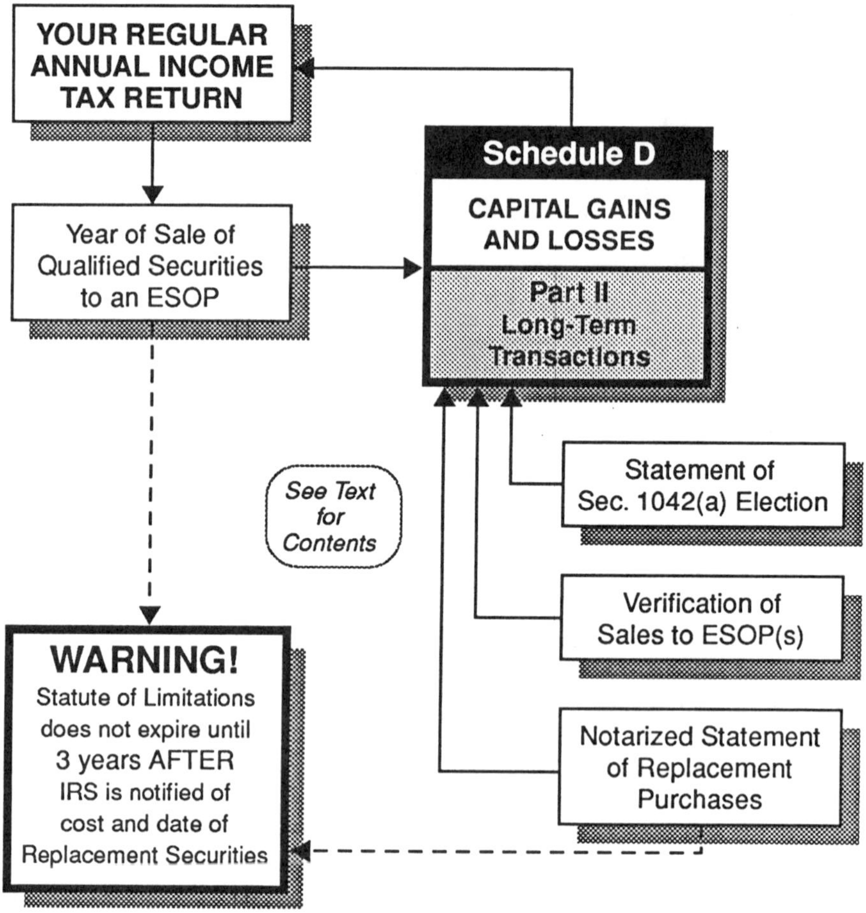

Fig. 10.2 - How Schedule D Differs With Section 1042 Election

Contents of Election Statement

The contents of the election statement are prescribed by Regulation § 1.1042-1T(A-3)(**b**). Beyond its preamble, we'll paraphrase the required contents in a manner that is more useful to busy taxpayers. The preamble reads—

The statement of election ***shall provide*** *that the taxpayer elects to treat the sale of* [employer] *securities as a sale of qualified securities under Section 1042(a), and* [the statement] *shall contain the following information:*

(1) *A description of the qualified securities, including number and type of shares;*
(2) *The date of the sale;*
(3) *The adjusted basis of the securities* [sold to an ESOP];
(4) *The amount realized upon the sale;*
(5) *The identity of the ESOP or eligible worker-owned cooperative to which . . . sold; and*
(6) *The names and Tax IDs of other taxpayers . . . under a prearranged* [multi-party] *agreement of . . . interrelated transactions involving other sales of qualified securities.*

Attach **verification** of the sale by the ESOP administrator, on the ESOP's letterhead. Then indicate whether qualified replacement securities were purchased in the previous year, in the same year, or will be purchased in the following year. Section 1042(c)(3) prescribes a replacement period which begins three months before and ends 12 months after the date of sale (to an ESOP). This is a 15-month window within which to acquire the replacement securities, once having elected the nonrecognition-of-gain provision.

Qualified Replacement Securities

What constitutes *qualified* replacement securities?

Answer: As prescribed by the 350-word Section 1042(c)(4): ***Qualified Replacement Property***. In substance, qualified replacement is a security issued by a domestic operating corporation *other than* the corporation that issued the employer securities that were sold to an ESOP. The idea here, of course, is to require the purchase of readily marketable securities that are "untainted" by ESOP-related transactions. Furthermore, the ESOP-unrelated corporation may not have passive investment income that exceeds 25 percent of the gross receipts of such corporation for its prior tax year. The term "passive investment income" means gross receipts derived from royalties, rents, dividends, interest, annuities, and sales or exchanges of stock or securities [Section 1362(d)(3)(C)].

A domestic *operating* corporation is generally defined as one of which *more than 50 percent of its assets* were used in the active conduct of a trade or business. This more-than-50-percent test applies at the time the replacement securities were purchased **or** before the close of the replacement period. Typically, an "operating corporation" is any corporation that, primarily, designs, manufactures, or sells products or services to the pubic at large. Certain financial institutions and insurance companies qualify as operating corporations [Section 1042(c)(4)(B)].

Notarized Statement of Purchase

Ordinarily, when one buys stock or securities of a corporation, no one needs to know about it except the purchaser and his broker. The IRS does not need to know — and does not care to know — until the stock is sold in a fully taxable transaction. Then the "sales price" is entered in column (d) of Schedule D: Capital Gains and Losses.

The situation is dramatically different when acquiring replacement securities for those sold to a qualified ESOP. Since no gain was tax recognized at the time of the sale, how is the IRS going to know whether or not qualified replacement securities were purchased? When you don't pay tax on a transaction, the IRS has the right to know why. Thus, here's a case where the traditional taxpayer honor system is disregarded. Be introduced now to IRS Regulation § 1.1042-1T(A-3)(b)(6) and (A-3)(c).

This regulation, with respect to the Section 1042(a) election, requires that—

> *The taxpayer **must attach** . . . to his income tax return a "notarized statement of purchase" describing the qualified replacement property, the date of the purchase, the cost of the property, and **declaring** such property to be the qualified replacement property with respect to the sale of qualified securities. Such statement of purchase must be notarized* [no later than] *thirty days after the purchase.*

The term "notarized statement" means that you prepare a declaratory statement in your own words, then go to a notary public to have it notarized. Your own stock broker may have a preprinted form especially for this purpose.

Basis of Replacement Securities

Ordinarily, when you purchase a security with after-tax proceeds, your basis in that security is its purchase cost plus the expense of purchase (if any). But, under Section 1042(d): ***Basis of Qualified Replacement Property***, we have a situation where the purchase was not made with after-tax proceeds. Consequently, the basis of the replacement securities is their purchase cost LESS the amount of capital gain not recognized by virtue of the Section 1042(a) election. We believe that you can appreciate better this "basis adjustment" with our depiction in Figure 10.3.

For example, suppose you purchased qualified replacement securities for $10,000. You did so in a timely manner after electing to exchange-defer $7,500 in realized gain on the sale of qualified securities to an ESOP (which initially cost you $2,500). Your basis in the replacement securities is $2,500 [$10,000 cost – $7,500 gain deferred]. This is the general rule: a simple "transfer of basis."

But suppose your sales price to an ESOP was $10,000 (with $7,500 of nonrecognized gain) and you bought $7,500 worth of replacement securities. Is your basis in those new securities zero?

Answer: In no way! You are not going to be able to reduce your replacement basis below that of your initial basis in those employer securities sold to an ESOP. When your replacement cost is less than your sales price, you pay tax on the difference. This is the message of Case (1) in Figure 10.3. Your replacement cost is expected to be equal to or greater than your sales price. If it is greater, your replacement basis is increased proportionately. This is the message of Case (2) in Figure 10.3.

If you sell the replacement securities in downstream time,

> *the gain (if any)* ***shall be recognized*** *to the extent of the gain which was not recognized under subsection (a)* [Section 1042(e)(1): ***Recapture of Gain on Disposition; General Rule***].

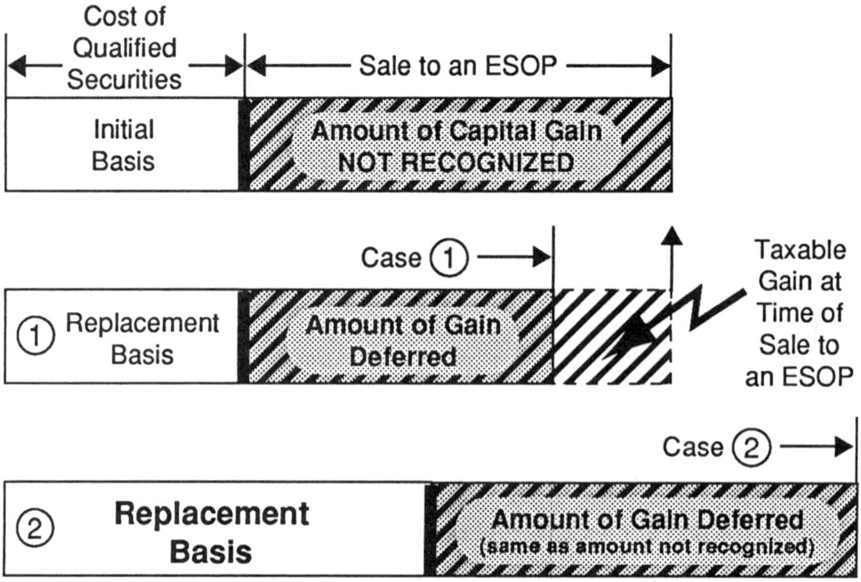

Cost of Replacement Securities

① Less than sales price to ESOP

② More than sales price to ESOP

Fig. 10.3 - Basis Adjustments when Replacement Securities Purchased

All of the above brings us back to the basic premise of all tax-deferred exchanges. If you elect nonrecognition of gain, when allowed, at some point in downstream time you have to tax account for that gain. Depending on your investment twists of fate, the net effect may indeed be a tax recognized capital loss instead of capital gain. Such is the significance of the "if any" clause above—

The gain (if any) shall be recognized . . .

11

STOCK FOR PROPERTY, ETC.

The Term "Property" Means Money, Property (Real, Tangible, Intangible), And/Or Services. It Has An Ascertainable Fair Market Value. In Contrast, Corporate Stock (And Its Many Variants) Is A Creation Of State Law . . . Out Of Thin Air. In And Of Itself, Stock Has No Inherent Market Value. It Is Only When Stock Has Been Exchanged For Property That It Acquires Value. At The Moment Of Exchange, There Is No Tax Consequence To The Corporation Inasmuch As No Gain Or Loss Is Presumed To Take Place. This Nonrecognition-Of-Gain Rule Is The Underpinning For All Corporate Formations, Reorganizations, Mergers, And Acquisitions.

The "Etc." in the heading of this chapter was purposely chosen. It was chosen as a warning signal re the complexities that arise in the stock swapping and bartering deals — characterized as tax-free exchanges — that take place among C corporations, corporate officers, sophisticated investors, and their entourages of prestigious attorneys, underwriters, and accountants. In the exclusivity of corporate high finance, stock and its variants (warrants, debentures, bonds, notes, certificates, options, futures, derivatives, etc.) — **all truly just pieces of paper** — have become a medium of exchange of their own. They are treated as after-tax money and property . . . which they clearly are **not**!

Needless to say, all we can hope to cover in this chapter are the highlights of "stock-for-property" and "stock-for-stock" exchanges authorized by Sections 1032 and 1036 of the Internal Revenue Code. The respective titles of these two sections are—

Sec. 1032 — ***Exchange of Stock for Property***
Sec. 1036 — ***Stock for Stock of Same Corporation***

Both start with the premise that: *No gain or loss shall be recognized* . . . etc. Both have almost exactly the same number of statutory words: about 85. As straightforward as these two sections appear, it is amazing how things can get complicated when there are corporate formations, reorganizations, mergers, acquisitions, distributions, and liquidations. All of these "maneuverings" rely on these two sections . . . which cross reference other sections of the tax code.

There are approximately 15 cross references mentioned in the regulations to Sections 1032 and 1036. Many of these cross references also say: "No gain or loss shall be recognized" . . . etc. For example, Sections 337, 354, and 361 use these exact words to introduce other exchange-type transactions involving C corporations. These three cross-referenced exchange rules are titled:

Sec. 337 — *Nonrecognition for Property Distributed to Parent in Complete Liquidation of Subsidiary*

Sec. 354 — *Exchanges of Stock and Securities in Certain Reorganizations*

Sec. 361 — *Nonrecognition of Gain or Loss to Corporation; Treatment of Distributions*

These and other exchange-like transactions are limited to C corporations only. As such, they are outside the scope of this book, as outlined in our Chapter 1.

The Simplest Rule: Section 1036

For ease of understanding, Section 1036 is clearcut and straightforward. Recall above that its title is: ***Stock for Stock of Same***

Corporation. Here, the term "stock" means both common stock and preferred stock only. It excludes all other forms of securities. In particular, "nonqualified preferred stock" (because of restrictions on its free transferability) is not treated as stock.

Section 1036(a): ***General Rule***, is a good example of how clarity in a tax law can be formulated. Its 40 words read precisely as follows—

> *No gain or loss shall be recognized if common stock in a corporation is exchanged* ***solely for*** *common stock in the* ***same corporation, or*** *if preferred stock in a corporation is exchanged* ***solely for*** *preferred stock in the* ***same corporation***. [Emphasis added.]

Note our emphasis on the term "solely for." There's not much wiggle room for variant or mischievous interpretation. Common stock for common stock; preferred stock for preferred stock . . . period! No exchange crossover from common to preferred or from preferred to common is allowed. However, Section 1036(a) applies even though voting stock is exchanged for nonvoting stock or nonvoting stock is exchanged for voting stock. Furthermore, the exchanging is not limited to that between two individual stockholders; it includes an exchange between a stockholder and the issuing corporation.

If there are several classes of common or preferred stock outstanding, exchanges of any class of common stock for a different class of common stock (such as class A for class B), or between different classes of preferred stock, come within the nonrecognition rule. The nonrecognition treatment may be lost if stock called common is not actually common stock, or if stock designated as preferred is not actually preferred stock. On these matters, the stock certificates themselves must be examined and compared.

Also note in the subsection (a) citation above, our emphasis on the term "same corporation." There is no express statutory or regulatory definition of this term. When there is legislative silence on a tax term, the everyday, ordinary dictionary definition prevails. The word "same," therefore, has to be interpreted as—

being the very one; identical; unchanged; not different.

Attempts to misconstrue the term "same corporation" occur when one management team controls a group of corporations. In such an arrangement, each corporation is a separate legal entity of its own. Hence, any stock crossovers from corporation X to corporation Y, or vice versa, are invalid for Section 1036 purposes, even though the same management controls both corporations.

Regulation § 1.1036-1(a); *Stock for stock of the same corporation*, makes the point clear that—

The provisions of Section 1036(a) do not apply if stock is exchanged for bonds, or . . . common stock in one corporation is exchanged for common stock in another corporation.

The exchanging of stock between corporations under the same management comes up frequently with mutual fund investment companies. A particular fund management team may oversee 10, 15, or more different mutual funds, each with different investment objectives. When a fund holder changes his investment objectives, he thinks in terms of rolling over from fund M to fund N, for example. He considers the "rollover" a nontaxable, non-tax-accounting event because he never physically took possession of the money involved. To the contrary: the withdrawal from fund M is a fully taxable event. The amount of capital gain or capital loss, if any, is tax recognized. Section 1036(a) does not apply.

Section 1031 for Boot and Basis

Section 1036(a) is a refined version of like-kind exchanges discussed in earlier chapters on Section 1031. That section, recall, is titled: ***Exchange of Property Held for . . . Investment.*** It addresses both like and nonlike properties exchanged in the same event. The use of nonlike property in an exchange transaction is often necessary to equalize the fair market values of like-kind properties being exchanged. In such case, the use of a nonlike item (money or property) is called "boot"; it is fully taxable. Tax deferment (via Section 1036(a)) applies only to the like-kind properties being exchanged.

Section 1036(a) contemplates that stock-for-stock exchanges may also include nonstock items. The nonstock items do not disqualify the exchange; they merely add a taxable component to it. The clearest indication of this contemplation is Section 1036(**b**). This subsection is titled: ***Nonqualified Preferred Stock not Treated as Stock***. For purposes of subsection (**a**), any item not treated as stock in a disposition event is taxable. This is automatic. Subsection (a), recall, carries the mandate that—

No gain or loss shall be recognized if—

The "if" relates solely to stock-for-stock (of like kind) in the same corporation.

The contemplation of "boot" being involved in a 1036 exchange is directly addressed by paragraph (1) of Section 1036(**c**): ***Cross References***. This paragraph reads—

(1) *For rules relating to* ***recognition*** *of gain or loss where an exchange is* ***not solely in kind****, see subsections (b) and (c) of Section 1031*. [Emphasis added.]

Although we covered in earlier chapters these two cross-referenced subsections, we repeat their titles here for refresher purposes. Accordingly,

Sec. 1031(b) — *Gain from Exchanges not Solely in Kind*
Sec. 1031(c) — *Loss from Exchanges not Solely in Kind*

No matter what exchange law is involved, there is always the requirement to redetermine one's basis in the exchange-acquired item. Paragraph (2) of Section 1036(c) contemplates this by expressly saying—

(2) *For rules relating to the basis of property acquired in an exchange described in subsection (a)* [of Section 1036], *see subsection (d) of Section 1031* [Basis].

The impact on the new stock received in a 1036 exchange depends on whether any boot was received. If no boot was received, the basis of the new stock takes the same basis as the old stock. If boot (money or property) was received, the basis transferred to the new stock is *decreased* by the amount of **money** received and *increased* by the amount of gain recognized due to the **property** received. When boot involves money, the money is treated as "return of capital" up to the amount of basis in the old stock. The return of capital is not taxed. By its reducing the basis in the new stock, there is the potential of greater capital gain when the new stock is ultimately sold.

We summarize in Figure 11.1 the significant features of Section 1036 exchanges. What makes Section 1036 particularly attractive is that any two or more shareholders in the same corporation can arrange for the exchanging of stock among themselves . . . if truly at arm's length. The corporation's approval is not required. However, whenever there is any change in the ownership of stock, the issuing corporation should be notified. All corporations are required to keep an updated ledger of their stockholders at all times.

Introduction to Section 1032

Although its title: ***Exchange of Stock for Property***, sounds straightforward enough, Section 1032 is much more complicated in practice than Section 1036. This is largely because the corporate entity itself is the taxpayer-exchanger. In its formation process, the corporation applies to its legal home office state for authorization to issue X numbers of shares of common stock at a hypothetical par value of, usually, 10 **cents** per share. Par value has no relationship to fair market value. It is simply a convenient reference amount for imposing a registration fee by the state of incorporation. It is when these shares are sold to the public at large that real money comes into the corporate treasury. In the process, money and other property are exchanged for stock, at which time no gain or loss is recognized to the corporation.

Section 1036 is also complicated by another reason: *officious entrepreneurs*. These are the founders, officers, executives, and elite participants who provide little or no money or property towards

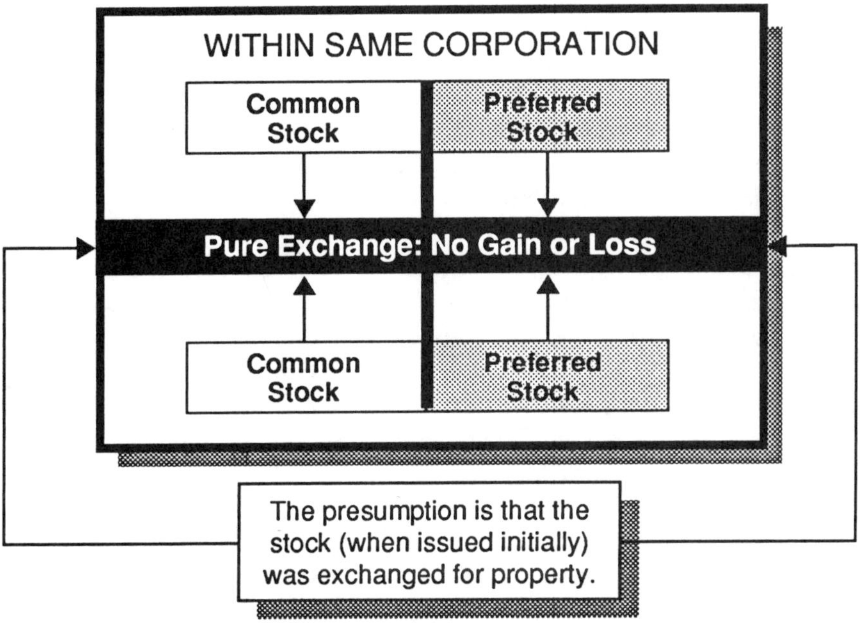

Fig. 11.1 - Gain/Loss Nonrecognition When Exchanging Stock-for-Stock

the enterprise. Yet, they want lavish stock grants, options, and loans . . . right off the top. Their offer in exchange for the stock is their name, influence, experience, reputation, and services. Tax-technically, stock in exchange for these intangibles is treated as compensation and is income taxed. In reality, very few of these officious elite pay any income tax on their stock grabs. If the stock rises significantly in the public marketplace, the elite are the first to sell and hide their wealth. Since there is no tax to the corporation, why should it care?

The basic principle of Section 1032 that invites its complexity (and abuse) is set forth in its subsection (a): ***Nonrecognition of Gain or Loss***. Its leadoff sentence reads precisely as—

> *No gain or loss shall be recognized* ***to a corporation*** *on the receipt of* ***money*** *or* ***other property*** *in exchange for stock (including treasury stock) of such corporation.* [Emphasis added.]

Can't you see the loophole here? It's that term "other property." Just what is "other property"?

It is whatever a clever and egregious person wants it to be. Congress has not defined the term even though it enacted Section 1032 as far back as 1954. IRS regulations do not define it either.

The legal definition of property is—

> *Every species of valuable right or interest that is subject to ownership has an exchangeable value or adds to one's wealth or estate. Property describes one's exclusive right to possess, use and dispose of a thing, as well as the object, benefit, or prerogative that constitutes the subject matter of that right.* [***Dictionary of Legal Terms***, Barron's Educational Series, Inc., Hauppauge, NY 11788.]

You take it from here. Our position is that property should have a readily determinable market value when offered, at arm's length, on an established market, and which, if desired, can be immediately converted into dollars. The term "at arm's length" means: a relatively equal bargaining position between contracting parties, in which the agreement reached is seen as free of one-sidedness, duress, unconscionability, or overreaching by either party.

Options, Futures, Warrants, & More

We are not through with Section 1032(a). It has a second sentence which we have yet to cite to you. It opens the door to other interpretations of property when a derivative of it is sold or exchanged, and there is gain or loss.

The second (and last) sentence of Section 1032(a) reads—

> *No gain or loss shall be recognized* ***by a corporation*** *with respect to any lapse or acquisition of an option or with respect to a securities futures contract (as defined in Section 1234B), to buy or sell its stock (including treasury stock).*

The target of concern here is a corporation that buys and sells its own issue of stock and securities. This rule is aimed at ending the practice of corporations taking inconsistent positions with respect to warrants they issue. (A "warrant" is the right or option to purchase a share of stock for a specified price within a specified time.)

The inconsistency aspect goes like this. A corporation issues a warrant for $2 and shortly thereafter buys it back for $1. Technically, the corporation made $1 of gain (per warrant). It sold an item for $2 which cost it only $1. The corporation argues, however, that this gain is not tax recognized by virtue of the first sentence in Section 1032(a). On the other hand, should the warrant buyback be for $3, there would be a loss of $1 (per warrant). That is, the corporation sold an item for $2 which cost it $3. That's a loss, isn't it? So the corporation argues for the loss which it can use to offset other positive sources of income from its regular trade or business. For its loss argument, the corporation ignores the first sentence of Section 1032(a). The second sentence of Section 1032(a), cited above, is designed to thwart the "cooking of books" by corporations dealing in their own securities.

When it comes to securities futures contracts, Section 1032(a), second sentence, leads to other involvements. Note the parenthetical clause cited in the tax law above: (*as defined by Section 1234B*). This cross-referenced section is titled: ***Gains or Losses from Securities Futures Contracts***. Section 1234B targets ordinary investors who seek legitimate capital gain or capital loss with real money on the line. A securities futures contract is treated as *property which has the same character as the property to which the contract relates*, as if said property had been acquired directly by the taxpayer. Said taxpayer is **other than** a corporation self dealing in its own securities.

Three Applicable Regulations

Section 1032(a) gets worse than we have already portrayed. This is because it is supported by three regulations totaling more than 3,000 words. The titles of each of these regulations are—

Reg. § 1.1032-**1**: ***Disposition by a corporation of its own capital stock.*** (Adopted in 1956.)

Reg. § 1.1032-**2**: ***Disposition by a corporation of stock of a controlling corporation in certain triangular reorganizations***. (Adopted in 1994.)

Reg. § 1.1032-**3**: ***Disposition of stock or stock options in certain transactions not qualifying under any other nonrecognition provisions***. (Adopted in 2000.)

For chronological reference purposes, we show the year in which each of these regulations was adopted by the IRS. We'll refer to these as Regulation **1**, Regulation **2**, and Regulation **3**, respectively. Note that all three start with the same word: ***Disposition*** . . . by a corporation of its own stock. Regulation **1** has been in effect for the longest time (nearly 50 years). It is the shortest and most straightforward of all three. A few selected excerpts from it should be informative.

The essence of Regulation **1**-(a) is that—

> *The disposition by a corporation of shares of its own stock . . . for money or other property does not give rise to taxable gain or deductible loss to the corporation regardless of the nature of the transaction or the facts and circumstances involved.* [This is so] *whether the subscription or issue price be equal to, in excess of, or less than, the par or stated value of such stock. . . . A transfer by a corporation of shares of its own stock . . . as compensation for services is considered, for purposes of Section 1032(a) as a disposition by the corporation of such shares for money or other property.*

This regulatory wording, we think, is clear and unequivocal. It exudes in simplistic terms the very essence of Section 1032(a). That essence, in case you haven't read between the lines, is that the value of stock (or any other corporate security) is created out of thin air. As a piece of paper or electronic account entry, stock has no inherent value of its own. For reality thinking purposes, we depict in Figure 11.2 the essence of the stock-for-property law.

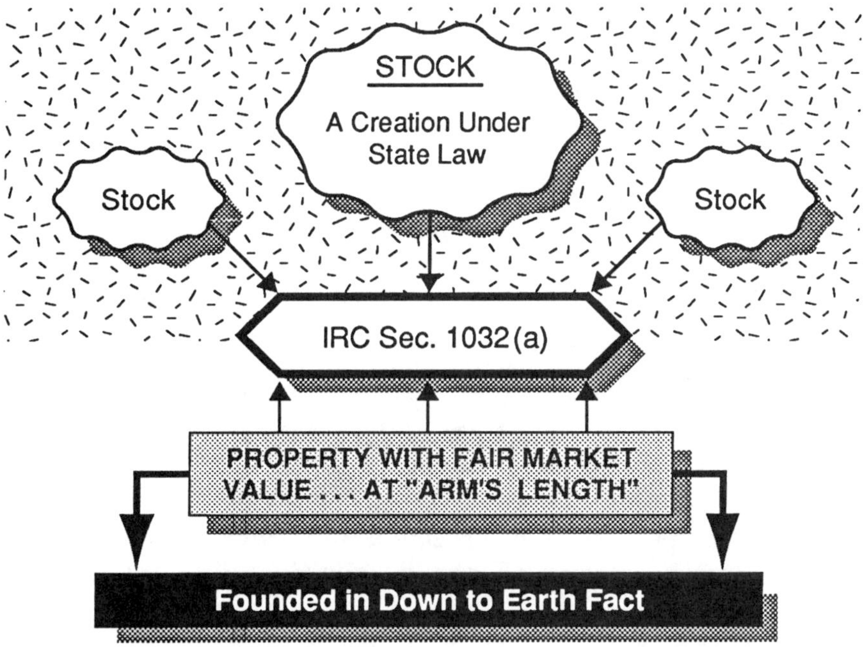

Fig. 11.2 - The Creation of Stock Value Out of "Thin Air"

Unfortunately, it is this value creativity out of thin air that leads to distortions, complexities, and — yes — abuses, of Section 1032.

The Tip of the Iceberg

Regulation 1-(**b**) makes it clear that—

> *Section 1032(a)* ***does not*** *relate to the tax treatment of the* ***recipient*** *of a corporation's stock.* [Emphasis added.]

This is the other side of the thin air coin. That is, a "recipient" (be he a buyer, borrower, or donee) of stock may make or lose money . . . also out of thin air. When considered together, Regulations 1-(a) and 1-(b) form a unique mystique to the financial underpinnings of every corporate entity. This mystique is the tip of the iceberg to corporate creative accounting.

Regulation 1-(**c**) reveals some of the subsurface refinements to Section 1032(a). This particular regulation reads—

> *Where a corporation acquires shares of its own stock in exchange for shares of its own stock . . . the transaction may qualify not only under Section 1032(a), but also under Section 305(a) . . . or Section 368(a)(1)(E).*

What is **this** all about?

The answer key is to recognize that the regulation addresses a corporation dealing in its own stock and all derivatives thereof. Obviously, we need to examine the substance of referenced Sections 305 and 368.

Section 305 is titled: ***Distributions of Stock and Stock Rights***. This section comprises slightly more than 1,000 statutory words, and is supported by more than 15,000 regulatory words. Its gist is its subsection (a): ***General Rule***, which reads—

> *Except as* [prescribed in subsection (b)], *gross income does not include the* ***amount of any distribution*** *of the stock of a corporation made by such corporation* **to its shareholders** *with respect to its stock.* [Emphasis added.]

The term "gross income" applies both to the corporation and to its shareholders. The term "with respect to its stock" means that of a like kind to that which a shareholder already has or had. Exceptions to subsection (a): noninclusion in gross income, occur where there are deviations from the like-kind-stock principle.

Subsection 305(b): ***Exception***, together with subsection 305(c): ***Certain Transactions***, describes six situations where distributions of stock are treated as distributions of *property* (instead of as stock). All property-type distributions are treated as dividends and taxable accordingly. In highly abbreviated form, the six property-like distributions are:

(1) Distributions in lieu of money;

(2) Disproportionate distributions to different shareholders;

(3) Mixed distributions **of** common and preferred stock;

(4) Distributions **on** preferred stock;

(5) Distributions of convertible preferred stock; and

(6) Premium dividends on the redemption of callable stock.

Regulation 1-(c) also makes reference to Section 368, its subsection (a)(1)(E) in particular. Section 368 is titled: ***Definitions Relating to Corporate Reorganizations***. Paragraph (1) of subsection (a) lists seven types of reorganizations: Type A through Type G. Type E, to which Regulation 1-(c) relates, is captioned: *Recapitalization.* The term "recapitalization" is the recasting of the capital structure of a corporation. If the recasting consists of a pure rearrangement of its existing securities via a well-thought-out plan, no gain or loss is recognized to the corporation.

Now to Regulation § 1.1032-2

So much for Regulation **1**; now on to Regulation **2** of Section 1032(a). Regulation 2 is about twice the word count of Regulation 1. It thrusts us into a more sophisticated form of stock rearrangement called: ***Triangular Reorganizations***. A triangular reorganization consists of three corporations: P, S, and T. Corporation P (for **p**arent) controls corporation S (for **s**ubsidiary) which is a subsidiary of P. Together, P and S target corporation T (for **t**akeover) in a three-way merger. This is all done under a **Plan of Reorganization** approved by the Boards of Directors of each of the three participating corporations. The "plan" must follow the rules and regulations of applicable subsections of Section 368.

The types of reorganization contemplated by Regulation 2 are:

Type A — Statutory merger or reorganization [Subsec. 368(a)(1)(A)].

Type B — Acquisition and exchange of all voting stock of the participants by the acquiring corporation [Subsec. 368(a)(1)(B)].

Type C — Acquisition and exchange of all voting stock **plus all properties** of the participants by the acquiring corporation [Subsec. 368(a)(1)(C)].

Type D — Transfer of substantially all of a corporation's assets to the acquiring corporation, immediately after which, shareholders in the acquiring corporation control more than 50% of all combined voting stock [Subsec. 368(a)(1)(D)].

Type E — Recapitalization [Subsec. 368(a)(1)(E)].

Regardless of the issue of control, all Section 368-type reorganizations seek to wind up with no taxable gain or loss to the participating corporations nor to their current shareholders. This is encouraged by Regulation 2-(**b**): ***General nonrecognition of gain or loss***. To accomplish this nonrecognition, it becomes a mixing and matching of the capitalization of all outstanding securities, both before and after the reorganization. Before the reorganization, each corporation will have its own mixture of stock and securities (of different classes, series, rights, etc.). The precondition is that no shareholder sell or buy any shares until after the reorganization is complete. The computational challenge to the reorganizers is to redetermine the tax basis in all different classes of shares in the final issuing corporation's stock. This is a **very** formidable task. Rather than trying to explain this *basis redetermination task* with numerical examples, we present our conceptual depiction of it in Figure 11.3.

Regulation § 1.1032-3: In Brief

Although we cited it earlier in this chapter, we'll repeat the full title of IRS Regulation § 1.1032-3 ("Regulation **3**") here for your convenience. Said title reads: ***Disposition of stock or stock options in certain transactions not qualifying under any other nonrecognition provision***. Read the term "Disposition of" as "Issuance of" stock in exchange for money or other property. What Regulation 3 attempts to do is to broaden the scope of corporate activities qualifying under Section 1032(a): ***Nonrecognition of Gain or Loss***.

In fact, paragraph (a) of Regulation 3 states forthrightly that—

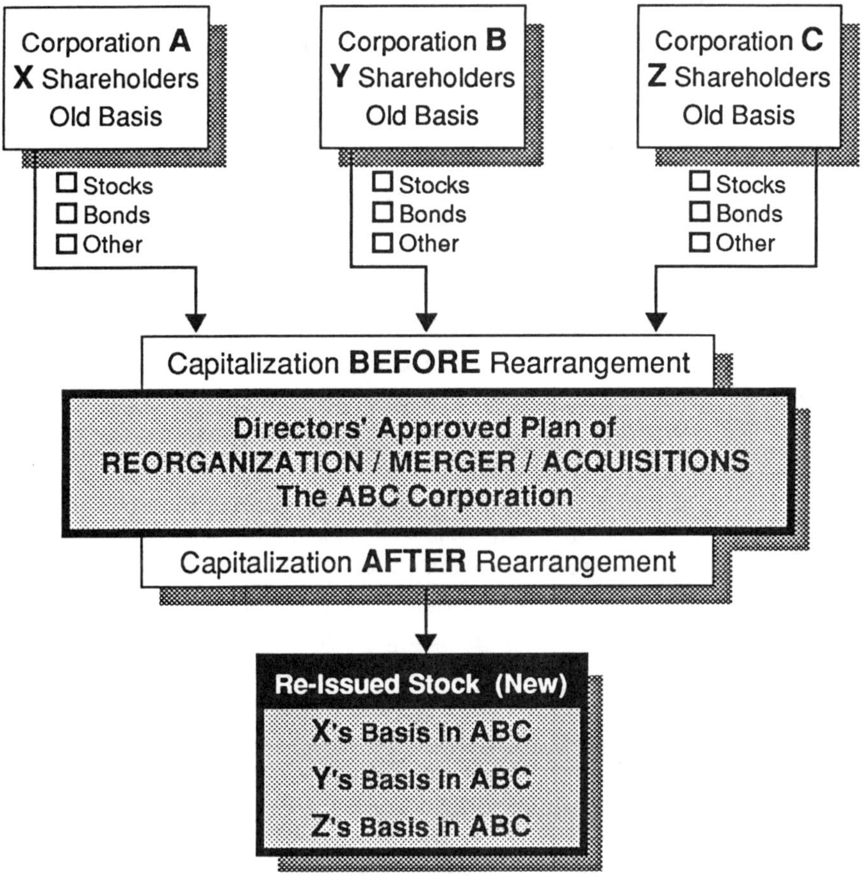

Fig. 11.3 - Establishing Tax Basis in Stock After Corporate Rearrangment

> *This* [regulation] *provides rules for* [those] *transactions in which a corporation* ***or a partnership*** [or an LLC] ***(the acquiring entity)*** *acquires money or other property* [or services] . . . *in exchange, in whole or part, for stock of a corporation* ***(the issuing corporation)****.* [Emphasis added.]

Then some 650 words of rules follow, which, in turn, are followed by some 2,150 words of numerical illustrations. There are 10 regulatory examples given. Their intent is to provide as much flexibility in interpreting Section 1032(a) as is reasonable and nonabusive. An underlying precondition is that there be a "Plan of

Acquisition of Assets" in place, showing the type of stock and stock options to be exchanged.

It appears that Regulation 3 focuses on the pure buyout of the entire assets of usually a smaller or startup business, after which that business disappears. The term "entire assets" means all monies, accounts receivable, depreciable assets, amortizable assets, accounts payable, capital interests, and all debts of the acquired entity. This is a classic case of the bigger fish gobbling up all of its surrounding smaller fish, thereby enhancing its market share (and simultaneously reducing its competition). Instead of using real money, the medium of exchange for all of this gobbling is the issuance of stock and stock options.

Determination of New Basis

Whenever an exchange involves the use of C corporation stock (and its variants), it is always necessary to determine the adjusted tax basis in the "new" stock. This is in the interest of both the issuing corporation and the participating shareholders. As we discussed in Chapter 2, tax basis is a measure of one's after-tax investment in a marketable asset. When said asset is ultimately sold, gain or loss is recognized at that time.

The problem with corporate reorganization is that basis adjustments to existing shareholders are messy and much delayed in time. We tried to depict this problem for you in Figure 11.3.

Generally, the controlling elite of a reorganized corporation are interested only in the new stock basis to the corporation itself and to themselves as privileged individuals. For "ordinary shareholders" a worksheet and a set of instructions are provided. The worksheet/ instructions explain (?) how each shareholder can compute his/her/its own basis in the reissued stock. These instructions are accompanied by the recommendation that—

> *If you have any questions* [don't contact us], *contact a tax professional of your own.*

12

SMALL BUSINESS STOCK

There Are Two Nonrecognition-Of-Gain Exchange Laws That Apply Only To Certain Businesses. One Type, An Investment Business, Is An SSBIC; The Other, A Productive Business, Is A QSB. Both Forms Of Stock Enjoy Rollover-Of-Gain And Exclusion-Of-Gain Benefits, But With Differences. SSBIC Stock Can Be Purchased Upon The Sale Of Any Publicly Traded Security, Whereas QSB Stock Must Be Purchased Directly As ORIGINAL ISSUE And Held More Than 6 Months Before Its Sale And Replacement. Multiple Rollovers Of QSB Stock, Aggregating More Than 5 Years' Holding, Can EXCLUDE Up To $10,000,000 From Capital Gains Tax.

In 1993 and again in 1997, Congress enacted two new nonrecognition-of-gain exchange laws that are favorably targeted at small businesses. These are Sections 1044 and 1045 of the Internal Revenue Code: the last two in the series of 14 common nontaxable exchanges introduced to you in Chapter 1. The respective titles of these two sections are—

Sec. 1044 — ***Rollover of Publicly Traded Securities Gain into Specialized Small Business Investment Companies*** [SSBIC]

Sec. 1045 — ***Rollover of Gain from Qualified Small Business Stock to Another Qualified Small Business Stock*** [QSBS]

Note three particular common words in these two tax code sections: **Rollover . . . Gain . . . Small Business**. The significant feature is that only capital gain on existing publicly traded stock and securities held by a taxpayer can be rolled over. The term "rollover" is a postponement-of-gain procedure, after which, when other conditions are met, a portion of the gain — up to 50% — can be excluded from tax altogether. This rollover-exclusion is a special inducement to small businesses only. The intent of Congress was to more level the playing field in the raising of capital for investment in new startup ventures when formulating an "active business" plan.

The term "small" is quantified differently in Sections 1044 and 1045. For Section 1044, "small" means up to $1,000,000 (*one million*) of excludable gain, whereas for Section 1045, "small" means up to $50,000,000 (*50 million*) of gross assets.

The exclusion part of the rollover gain is not found in either of these two sections. Both cross reference Section 1202: ***Partial Exclusion for Gain from Certain Small Business Stock***. Its statutory wording covers approximately 3,260 words. This contrasts sharply with the 300-word and 500-word counts for Sections 1044 and 1045. Much of the Section 1202 wording is to curb abuses by corporate executives who scheme to pay no capital gains tax on their interlocking rollovers. Obviously, we need to tell you more about all three of these rollover/exclusion sections.

General Rule: Section1044(a)

The title of Section 1044(a) is clear cut: ***Nonrecognition of Gain***. As with all such rules, the term "nonrecognition" (of tax) means: at the moment of exchange only. The implication is that, whatever tax accrues later, will be recognized at that time. Said amount, however, is recognized after the partial exclusion is elected and claimed.

Accordingly, the full text of Section 1044(a) is as follows:

> *In the case of the sale of* ***any*** *publicly traded security* [equity or debt] *with respect to which the taxpayer* ***elects*** *the application of this section, gain from such sale shall be recognized* ***only to the extent that*** *the amount realized on such sale* ***exceeds,—***

> *(1) **the cost of any common stock or partnership interest** in a specialized business investment company purchased by the taxpayer during the 60-day period beginning on the date of such sale, **reduced by***
>
> *(2) **any portion** of such sale previously taken into account under this section.*
>
> *This section shall **not apply to** any gain which is treated as **ordinary income*** [short term: one year or less] *for purposes of this subtitle* [Subtitle A — Income Taxes]. [Emphasis added.]

Any form of a previously-held publicly-traded security can be sold, so long as it derives from a C corporation. As such, all members of the same group of C corporations are treated as one corporation. Section 1044 does not apply to estates, trusts, nonpublicly-traded partnerships, or S corporations.

The repurchase-within-60-day rule applies only to common stock or partnership interest in an SSBIC. Many small business investment companies are in partnership form. This makes it easier to raise entrepreneurial capital, and gives a better tax writeoff in the event that the venture capital results in a loss rather than a gain. An "SSBIC" means any partnership or corporation licensed by the Small Business Administration under its rules in effect on May 13, 1993. This generally includes those investment companies that cater to the concerns of small businesses in their search for startup capital.

Limit on Rollover Amount

As you should expect, the amount of rollover gain allowed to a taxpayer/investor is not unlimited. There is both an annual and a lifetime limit, depending on whether the taxpayer is an individual or a C corporation. For *individuals*, the limitation on rollover gain is **the lesser of**—

(A) $50,000 per year, **or**

(B) $500,000 reduced by the amount of gain not recognized for all preceding taxable years.

For married individuals filing their returns separately, the limitations are $25,000 and $250,000, respectively. This permits a 10-year time span over which you can elect the rollover/exclusion-of-gain benefits. There appears to be no limit on the number of individuals who can participate.

For C corporations as taxpayers, the respective limitations are:

(A) $250,000 per year, **or**
(B) $1,000,000 reduced by the amount of gain not recognized for all preceding taxable years [Section 1044(**b**)(1), (2), and (3)].

In addition to the rollovers, any subsequent gain on the SSBIC stock may qualify for the 50-percent-exclusion-for-small-business stock under Section 1202 (previously mentioned). That is, if the purchase of the SSBIC stock also qualifies as small business stock under Section 1045. If the SSBIC stock does qualify, one's basis in said stock is **not** reduced for purposes of computing the gain eligible for the exclusion. This prevents the deferred gain from qualifying for the exclusion but makes it available for appreciation occurring after the SSBIC stock is acquired.

As to your tax basis in the SSBIC stock, Section 1044(**d**): ***Basis Adjustments***, says—

> *If gain from any sale is not recognized by reason of subsection (a), such gain shall be applied to reduce (in the order acquired) the basis for determining* ***gain or loss*** *of any common stock or partnership interest in any* [SSBIC] *which is purchased by the taxpayer during the 60-day period described in subsection (a). This subsection shall not apply for purposes of Section 1202.*

In other words, if you purchased $10,000 in publicly traded securities and you realized a gain of $6,500 which you rolled over into $16,500 worth of SSBIC stock, your new basis in that stock would be $3,500 [$10,000 cost less $6,500 deferred gain]. But if the SSBIC stock qualified for the 50% exclusion of gain under Section 1202, your basis remains at $10,000. Should you later sell the SSBIC stock for $26,500, you pay tax then on the $6,500 of deferred gain **plus** you *exclude* 50% of the additional gain of $10,000 [$26,500 – $6,500 deferred – $10,000 basis]. What a deal!

Time & Manner of Election

In order to claim the benefits of Section 1044 (as well as of Section 1045), you must expressly elect the application of subsection (a): Nonrecognition of Gain. How does one do this? Regulation § 1.1044(a)-1(b): ***Time and manner for making the election***, tells you how.

The regulation succinctly states that—

> *The election under Section 1044(a) must be made on or before the due date (including extensions) for the income tax return for the year in which the publicly traded securities are sold. The election is to be made by reporting the entire gain from the sale . . . on Schedule D of the income tax return, in accordance with instructions for Schedule D* [Capital Gains and Losses].

The Schedule D instructions tell you to report the gain and the rollover amount on two separate lines. On the first line, you report the gain as though it were all taxable in column (f): *Gain or <loss>*. On the line immediately below, you enter "Section 1044 election," followed by the amount of rollover allowed in column (f). Enter the rollover amount in brackets < > as a loss. As an individual, you would use Schedule D (Form 1040).

For example, if your realized gain was $6,500 and the amount eligible for the election was $5,000, you would show in column (f) as follows:

	Col. (f)
Description of sale, etc.	$6,500
Section 1044(a) election	<5,000>
Net taxable gain	$1,500

The regulation also tells you to attach a statement to Schedule D showing the following information:

(1) How the nonrecognized gain was calculated;
(2) The SSBIC in which common stock or a partnership interest was purchased;
(3) The date the SSBIC stock or partnership interest was purchased; and
(4) The basis of the SSBIC stock or partnership interest.

In way of summarizing the nonrecognition features of Section 1044 (and similarly for Section 1045), we present Figure 12.1 For instructive orderliness, we'll discuss the 50% exclusion feature separately below.

General Rule: Section 1045(a)

The title of Section 1045(**a**) is identical to that of Section 1044(**a**), namely: ***Nonrecognition of Gain***. The primary title of Section 1045, recall, is: *Rollover of Gain from Qualified Small Business Stock to Another Qualified Small Business Stock*: QSBS. In other words, Section 1045 addresses continuous rollovers of one QSBS for another QSBS for another . . . and so on.

Except for the distinctive qualifying clause (which we highlight below), the statutory wording of the two subsections (a) is very similar.

Accordingly, subsection (a) of Section 1045 reads in full as—

> *In the case of any sale of* ***qualified small business stock*** [QSBS] ***held by a taxpayer other than a corporation for more than 6 months****, and with respect to which, such taxpayer elects the application of this section, gain from such sale shall be recognized only to the extent that the amount realized on such sale exceeds—*
>
> *(1) the cost of any qualified small business stock purchased by the taxpayer during the 60-day period beginning on the date of such sale, reduced by*

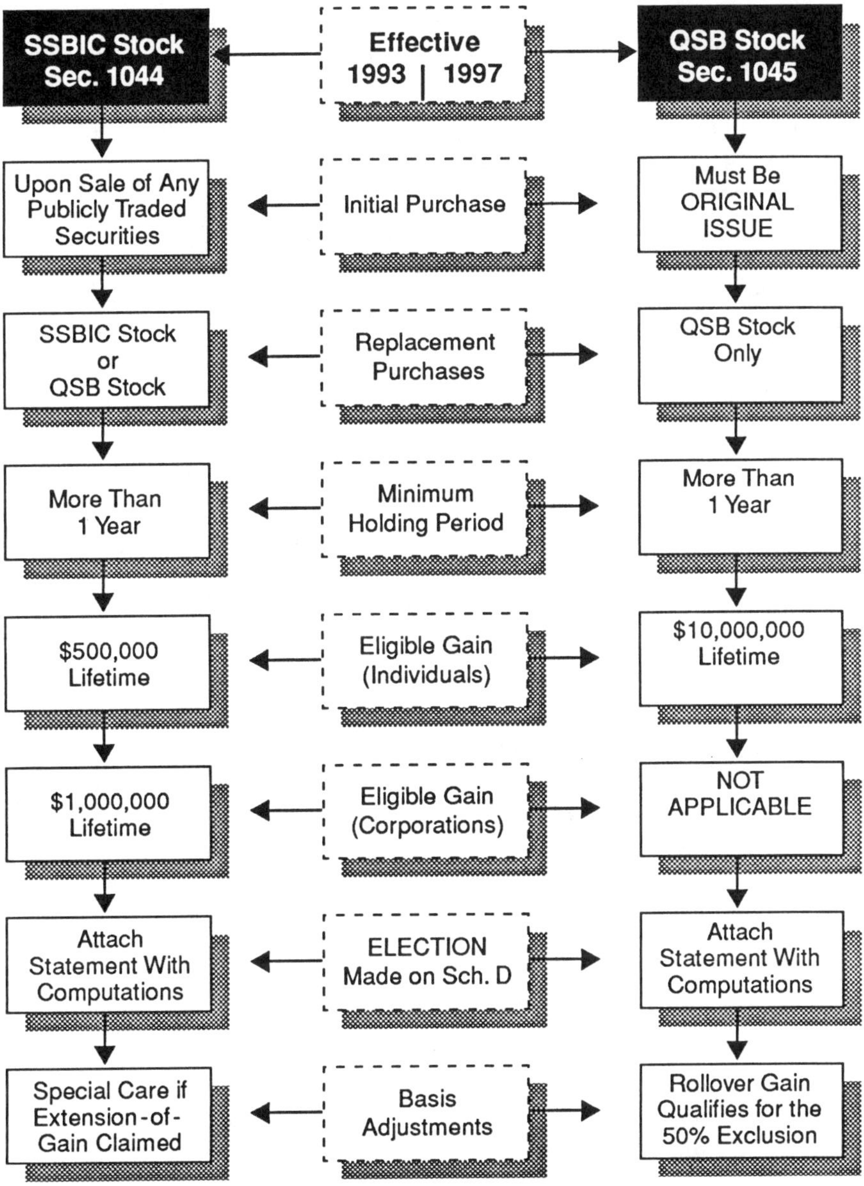

Fig. 12.1 - Comparative Features of Sections 1044 and 1045

(2) any portion of such cost previously taken into account under this section.

> *This section shall not apply to any gain which is treated as ordinary income* [when held one year or less].

The essence here is that you (any taxpayer other than a corporation) have to first purchase QSB stock, then hold it for more than six months. After this time period, you can sell your initially acquired QSB stock and roll over your eligible nonrecognition of gain into another QSB stock. To get the rollover benefit, however, you must hold the replacement stock for another more-than-six months. Your combined holding period then becomes more than one year, thus qualifying your QSB stock for long-term capital gain treatment on Schedule D.

The best definition of QSB stock is found in the official instructions to Schedule D. Excerpts from these instructions read—

> *To be **QSB stock**, the stock must meet **all** of the following tests:*
>
> *(1) It must be stock in a domestic C corporation (**not** that of an S corporation).*
>
> *(2) As of the date of its **original** issue, the total gross assets of the corporation must be $50,000,000 ($50 million) or less. Gross assets include those of any predecessor of the C corporation, and those members of the same parent-subsidiary controlled group.*
>
> *(3) You must have acquired the stock at its original issue, either in exchange for money, or other property, or as pay for services.*
>
> *(4) During substantially all of the time you held the stock, at least 80% of the value of the corporation's assets were used in the active conduct of one or more qualified businesses.*

As per Section 1045's underlying legislation: ***The Taxpayer Relief Act of 1997*** (P.L. 105-34), the corporation's working capital must be expended within five years in order to be treated as used in the active conduct of a trade or business.

The "Active Business" Requirement

Although Section 1045 does not say so directly, there is an active business requirement that must be met for the QSB stock to be considered "qualified." Said test is cross-referenced in Section 1045(b) to subsections (c) and (e) of Section 1202: ***Active Business Requirement.*** The title of Section 1202, recall, is: Partial Exclusion for Gain from Certain Small Business Stock. Here, the term "certain" means the active business test.

The best explanation of said test is found in the instructions to Schedule D (Form 1040), with respect to QSB stock. There, the IRS instructions say—

> *A **qualified business** is any business **other than a**—*
>
> 1. *Business involving services performed in the fields of health, law, engineering, architecture, accounting, actuarial science, performing arts, consulting, athletics, financial services, or brokerage services.*
>
> 2. *Business whose principal asset is the reputation or skill of one or more employees.*
>
> 3. *Banking, insurance, financing, leasing, investing, or similar business.*
>
> 4. *Farming business (including the raising or harvesting of trees).*
>
> 5. *Business involving the production of products for which percentage depletion can be claimed* [oil and gas, geothermal, minerals, gravel, etc.].
>
> 6. *Business of operating a hotel, motel, restaurant, or similar business.*

As mentioned above, at least 80% (by value) of the QSB's assets (including intangible assets) must be used in the active conduct of a qualified business. If in connection with any future business, the QSB uses its assets in certain start-up activities, research and development, or in-house research, the corporation is treated as using its assets in a qualified business. In any said active business, the corporation cannot own (i) real property the value of which exceeds 10% of its total assets, or (ii) portfolio stock or securities the value of which exceeds 10% of its total assets in excess of liabilities. The general idea here is to encourage productive effort at creating new products and new technology.

Basis Adjustments & Holding Periods

As with all nonrecognition-of-gain exchange laws, when all or part of the gain is deferred, the basis in the replacement QSB stock has to be adjusted. This is done by reducing the cost of the replacement stock by the amount of eligible gain not recognized. This is done by election on Schedule D for Section 1045(a), exactly as done for Section 1044(a). The election for QSB rollovers applies only to those sales occurring after August 5, 1997.

There appears to be no limitation on the number of QSB stock rollovers that a taxpayer can make. You may make three consecutive rollovers . . . or 10 . . . or more. The only requirement is that the initial purchase of stock and all replacement stock **each** be held for more than six months. During each more-than-6-month period, each business must separately qualify as pursuing the active conduct of a trade or business. Thus, if you timed your rollovers judiciously, you could buy initial QSB stock and roll it over nine times, giving you a total of 10 holding periods of more than six months each. At the end of this time, you would have held your QSB stock for more than five years (10 x 6 months = 60 months = 5 years).

QSB stock enjoys one very special benefit, called: the *tack-on* of holding periods [Section 1045(b)(4): Holding Period]. That is, the 6-month holding period for one batch of QSB stock is tacked on to the next batch of stock, and so on . . . until its final sale. As you'll see in a moment, the aggregate of five years of holding opens up the very gratuitous 50% exclusion-of-gain feature in Section 1202. Our depiction of this tack-on concept is presented in Figure 12.2.

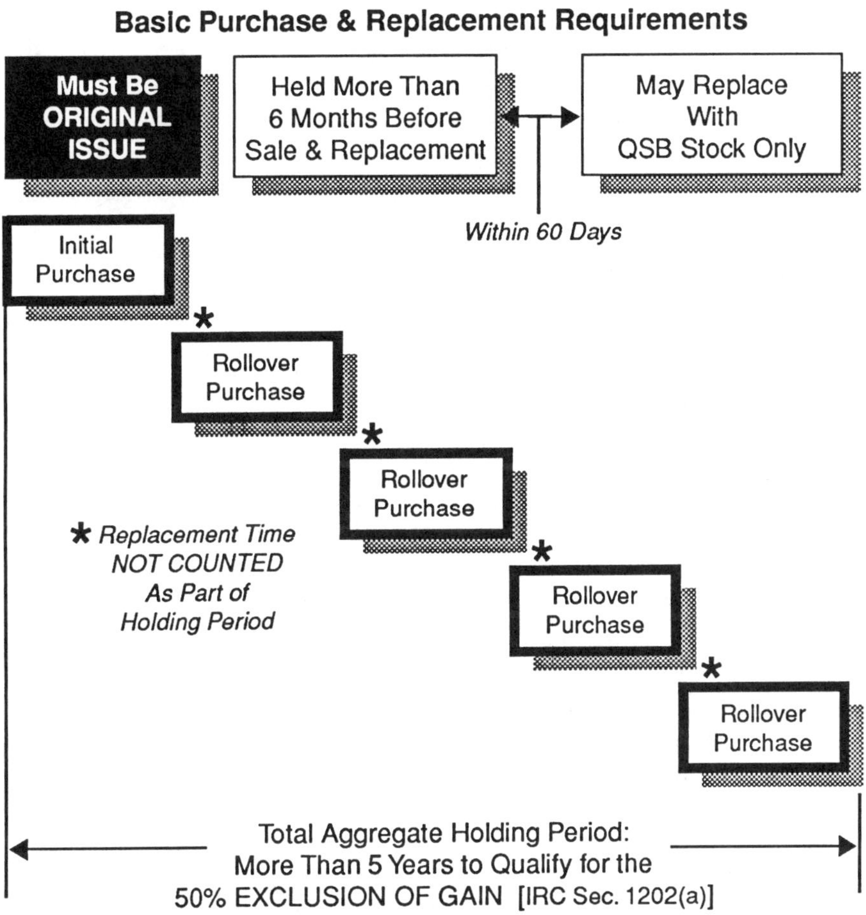

Fig. 12.2 - The Holding Period "Tack-Ons" With QSB Stock Rollovers

As to our Figure 12.2 point, IRS Revenue Procedure 98-48 (paragraph 3.03) says—

If a person has more than one sale of QSB stock in a taxable year that qualifies for the Section 1045 election, that person may make a Section 1045 election for any one or more of those sales.

General Rule: Section 1202(a)

We come now to the most exciting — and potentially the most abusive part — of QSB stock sales. We are referring, of course, to subsection (a): ***Exclusion; In General***, of Section 1202: ***Partial Exclusion of Gain from Certain Small Business Stock.***

Paragraph (1) of this subsection reads precisely as—

> *In the case of a taxpayer other than a corporation, gross income shall not include 50 percent of* ***any gain*** *from the sale* ***or exchange*** *of qualified small business stock held for more than 5 years.* [36 words]

This is about as clear and succinct as anyone could make concerning a tax law. The 50 percent exclusion of gain applies to any taxpayer *other than a corporation*. This means individuals, estates, trusts, partnerships, LLCs (limited liability companies), and S-corporation shareholders. Corporations — both C and S types — are ineligible as participating taxpayers in order to avoid a corporation self dealing in its own shares.

On this point is subsection (c)(3): ***Certain purchases by corporations of its own stock.*** The essence of this 200-word subsection is that any redemptions (within a 2-year period) by a person related to the corporation, or redemptions through the use of related corporations, and all redemptions *exceeding 5 percent of the aggregate value* of the corporation's stock . . . ***shall not be treated as QSB stock***! This is called the "anti-evasion" rule of Section 1202. Its legislative purpose is to prevent evasion of the requirement that the QSB stock be **newly issued** when purchased by an eligible taxpayer. Purchases by persons related to the issuing corporation (officers, directors, executives, etc.) are treated as purchases by the issuing corporation.

Paragraph (2) of subsection (a) increases the amount of exclusion to 60 percent for: ***Empowerment Zone Businesses.*** These are businesses located in economically depressed areas. Currently, there are 40 empowerment zones and 40 renewal communities where Congress has authorized special tax credits, deductions, and exclusions for revitalizing said areas.

The Genie in the Bottle

To sharpen your focus on a key point at hand, may we suggest that you reread again the 36-word paragraph (1) cited above. After doing so, particularly note the two terms: *any gain* and *or exchange* that we emphasized in bold print. Do you have any idea what these terms are intended to mean?

You know that the word *any* means "without limit," and that the word *gain* means "capital gain" (long term: more than one year). You also know that the word *or* means "an alternative" and that the word *exchange* means "to trade equivalently." Putting these words all together, it seems quite clear, therefore, that the 50 percent exclusion from gross income applies to ALL CUMULATIVE rollover/deferred gain, including the tack-on of any current gain. This is our spotting of the "genie in the bottle" buried in Section 1202(a)(1). When casually reading paragraph (1), the genie benefit does not shout out at you. This is why we suggest that you do reread paragraph (1).

In other words, in a series of consecutive QSB stock-holding-period tack-ons (as depicted in Figure 12.2) lasting more than five years, all of the cumulative untaxed gain is eligible for the 50 percent exclusion rule. This is the profound consequence of the express wording in the tax law itself. As a reminder of this profoundness, said law says—

> *Gross income* ***shall not include*** *50 percent of* ***any gain*** *from the sale* ***or exchange*** *of . . .* [QSB] *stock held for more than 5 years.*

Is there any catch to this genie profoundness that we allege? Yes; there is one catch.

A portion of the excluded gain (about one-half) is treated as a preference item for purposes of the alternative minimum tax (AMT). For most taxpayers, the AMT is computed on IRS Form 6251: ***Alternative Minimum Tax — Individuals***. The maximum AMT rate is 28 percent, compared to the maximum capital gains rate of 20 percent.

For Section 1202 AMT purposes, there is a special entry line on Form 6251 captioned: *Qualified Small Business Stock: Section 1202 exclusion.* The instructions to this line say—

> *If you claimed the exclusion under Section 1202 for gain on QSB stock held more than 5 years, multiply the excluded gain (as shown on Schedule D, Form 1040) by 42 percent (0.42).*

Let us illustrate how the 20 percent capital gains rate and the 28 percent AMT rate work out. Suppose your cumulative total capital gain was $150,000. Of this, you exclude $75,000 and pay tax at 20 percent on $75,000 (which is $15,000). Of the $75,000 excluded portion, 42 percent is subject to AMT tax at 28 percent. Thus, your AMT tax is—

[$75,000 x 0.42] x 0.28 = $8,820

Of note is that the effective AMT rate is 11.76 percent [0.42 x 0.28].

Altogether, your total tax (capital gain plus AMT) comes to $23,820 ($15,000 + $8,820). This is an effective tax rate of *only* 15.88 percent [$23,820 ÷ $150,000]. This puts a high-income shareholder on a par with a low-income individual paying the bottom rate of 15 percent. Now you know why there is entrepreneurial excitement over the Section 1202(a)(1) genie.

$10,000,000 of Eligible Exclusion

We are not yet through with the excitement of Section 1202. There's a bigger genie in its subsection (b)(1): ***Per-Issuer Limitation on Taxpayer's Eligible Gain***. The term "eligible gain" means: any gain from the sale or exchange of QSB stock held for more than five years. Correspondingly, the term "eligible exclusion" means 50 percent or one-half of the eligible gain. So, we ask ourselves: What is the limitation, if any, on the amount of eligible exclusion that a taxpayer can claim?

The short, sound-bite answer is: ***The greater of***—

(A) $10,000,000 ($10 million) **or**

(B) 10-times-basis of all QSB stock

The more correct answer is Section 1202(b)(1) itself. It reads—

> *If a taxpayer has eligible gain . . . from one or more dispositions of QSB stock issued by any corporation, **the aggregate amount of such gain** from dispositions . . . which may be taken into account under subsection (a)* [re the 50 percent exclusion] *for the taxable year, shall not exceed the greater of—*
>
> > *(A) $10,000,000* [10 million] ***reduced by** the aggregate amount of eligible gain taken into account by the taxpayer under subsection (a) for prior taxable years . . ., or*
> >
> > *(B) 10 times the aggregate adjusted basis of QSB stock issued by such corporation and disposed of by the taxpayer during the taxable year. The adjusted basis of any QSB stock shall be determined **without regard** to any addition to basis after the date on which such stock was originally issued.* [Emphasis added.]

Although there is some ambiguity in subsection (b)(1), it seems reasonably clear that the $10,000,000 (or so) allowable exclusion of gain is a *per-issuer, per taxpayer* limitation. This being the case, the implication is that you (as a taxpayer other than a corporation) could purchase QSB stock in more than one qualified small business.

We depict this limitation concept for you in Figure 12.3. Where we show "any taxpayer," we mean any taxpayer other than a corporation. Note that we show the maximum gross assets of any one issuer to be $50,000,000 (50 million) at time of original issue.

If you owned the stock of five QSB corporations, for example, conceivably you could fully exclude from the capital gains tax $50,000,000 (50 *million*). At the effective AMT rate of about 12 percent [0.42 x 0.28 = 0.1176, as above], you'd pay only $6,000,000 of AMT tax on $50,000,000 of excludable gain! From our perspective, this is an overgenerous tax-free gift of $44,000,000 by Congress to high-flying entrepreneurial risk takers. This kind of

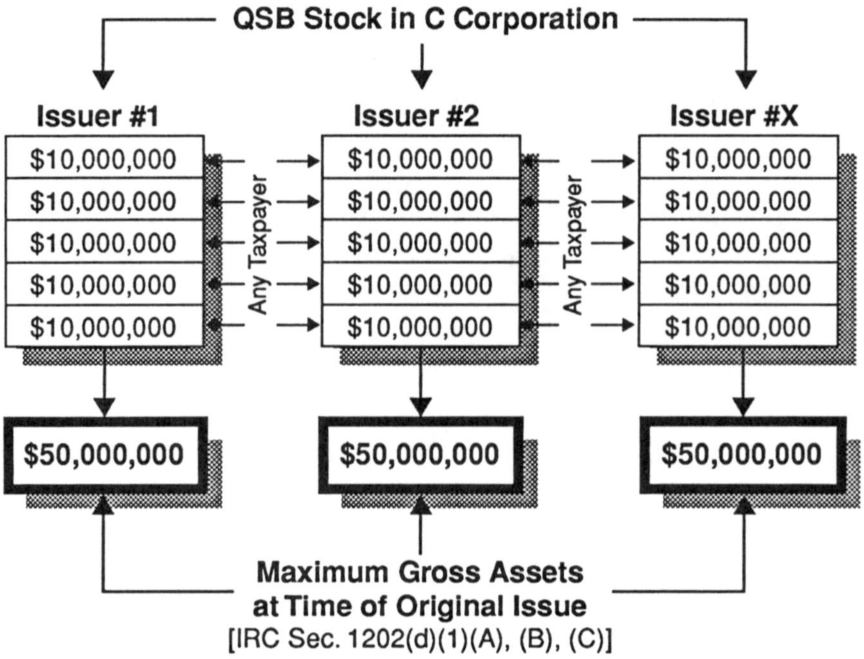

Fig. 12.3 - The "Per-Issuer, Per-Taxpayer" Limitation on Excludable Gain

Congressional largesse can lead — and has led — to widespread abuses of the U.S. tax system.

Illustrative of Congress's premonition that widespread abuse of Section 1202 could occur, we cite in full subsection (k): ***Regulations***—

> *The* {IRS} *shall prescribe such regulations as may be appropriate to carry out the purposes of this section* [1202], *including regulations* ***to prevent the avoidance of the purposes of this section*** *through* [corporate] *split-ups, shell corporations,* [QSB] *partnerships, or otherwise* [tax shelters and tax havens].

No wonder in the high-tech go-go years of 1993 to 2002, there has been so much media focus on executive greed, corporate malfeasance, stock fraud, and in-your-face secret accounts in off-shore tax havens. Congress and the IRS have much more to do in thwarting these kinds of abuses.

ABOUT THE AUTHOR

Holmes F. Crouch

Born on a small farm in southern Maryland, Holmes was graduated from the U.S. Coast Guard Academy with a Bachelor's Degree in Marine Engineering. While serving on active duty, he wrote many technical articles on maritime matters. After attaining the rank of Lieutenant Commander, he resigned to pursue a career as a nuclear engineer.

Continuing his education, he earned a Master's Degree in Nuclear Engineering from the University of California. He also authored two books on nuclear propulsion. As a result of the tax write-offs associated with writing these books, the IRS audited his returns. The IRS's handling of the audit procedure so annoyed Holmes that he undertook to become as knowledgeable as possible regarding tax procedures. He became a licensed private Tax Practitioner by passing an examination administered by the IRS. Having attained this credential, he started his own tax preparation and counseling business in 1972.

In the early years of his tax practice, he was a regular talk-show guest on San Francisco's KGO Radio responding to hundreds of phone-in tax questions from listeners. He was a much sought-after guest speaker at many business seminars and taxpayer meetings. He also provided counseling on special tax problems, such as divorce matters, property exchanges, timber harvesting, mining ventures, animal breeding, independent contractors, selling businesses, and offices-at-home. Over the past 25 years, he has prepared well over 10,000 tax returns for individuals, estates, trusts, and small businesses (in partnership and corporate form).

During the tax season of January through April, he prepares returns in a unique manner. During a single meeting, he completes the return . . . *on the spot!* The client leaves with his return signed, sealed, and in a stamped envelope. His unique approach to preparing returns and his personal interest in his clients' tax affairs have honed his professional proficiency. His expertise extends through itemized deductions, computer-matching of income sources, capital gains and losses, business expenses and cost of goods, residential rental expenses, limited and general partnership activities, closely-held corporations, to family farms and ranches.

He remembers spending 12 straight hours completing a doctor's complex return. The next year, the doctor, having moved away, utilized a large accounting firm to prepare his return. Their accountant was so impressed by the manner in which the prior return was prepared that he recommended the doctor travel the 500 miles each year to have Holmes continue doing it.

He recalls preparing a return for an unemployed welder, for which he charged no fee. Two years later the welder came back and had his return prepared. He paid the regular fee . . . and then added a $300 tip.

During the off season, he represents clients at IRS audits and appeals. In one case a shoe salesman's audit was scheduled to last three hours. However, after examining Holmes' documentation it was concluded in 15 minutes with "no change" to his return. In another instance he went to an audit of a custom jeweler that the IRS dragged out for more than six hours. But, supported by Holmes' documentation, the client's return was accepted by the IRS with "no change."

Then there was the audit of a language translator that lasted two full days. The auditor scrutinized more than $1.25 million in gross receipts, all direct costs, and operating expenses. Even though all expensed items were documented and verified, the auditor decided that more than $23,000 of expenses ought to be listed as capital items for depreciation instead. If this had been enforced it would have resulted in a significant additional amount of tax. Holmes strongly disagreed and after many hours of explanation got the amount reduced by more than 60% on behalf of his client.

He has dealt extensively with gift, death and trust tax returns. These preparations have involved him in the tax aspects of wills, estate planning, trustee duties, probate, marital and charitable bequests, gift and death exemptions, and property titling.

Although not an attorney, he prepares Petitions to the U.S. Tax Court for clients. He details the IRS errors and taxpayer facts by citing pertinent sections of tax law and regulations. In a recent case involving an attorney's ex-spouse, the IRS asserted a tax deficiency of $155,000. On behalf of his client, he petitioned the Tax Court and within six months the IRS conceded the case.

Over the years, Holmes has observed that the IRS is not the industrious, impartial, and competent federal agency that its official public imaging would have us believe.

He found that, at times, under the slightest pretext, the IRS has interpreted against a taxpayer in order to assess maximum penalties, and may even delay pending matters so as to increase interest due on additional taxes. He has confronted the IRS in his own behalf on five separate occasions, going before the U.S. Claims Court, U.S. District Court, and U.S. Tax Court. These were court actions that tested specific sections of the Internal Revenue Code which he found ambiguous, inequitable, and abusively interpreted by the IRS.

Disturbed by the conduct of the IRS and by the general lack of tax knowledge by most individuals, he began an innovative series of taxpayer-oriented Federal tax guides. To fulfill this need, he undertook the writing of a series of guidebooks that provide in-depth knowledge on one tax subject at a time. He focuses on subjects that plague taxpayers all throughout the year. Hence, his formulation of the "Allyear" Tax Guide series.

The author is indebted to his wife, Irma Jean, and daughter, Barbara MacRae, for the word processing and computer graphics that turn his experiences into the reality of these publications. Holmes welcomes comments, questions, and suggestions from his readers. He can be contacted in California at (408) 867-2628, or by writing to the publisher's address.